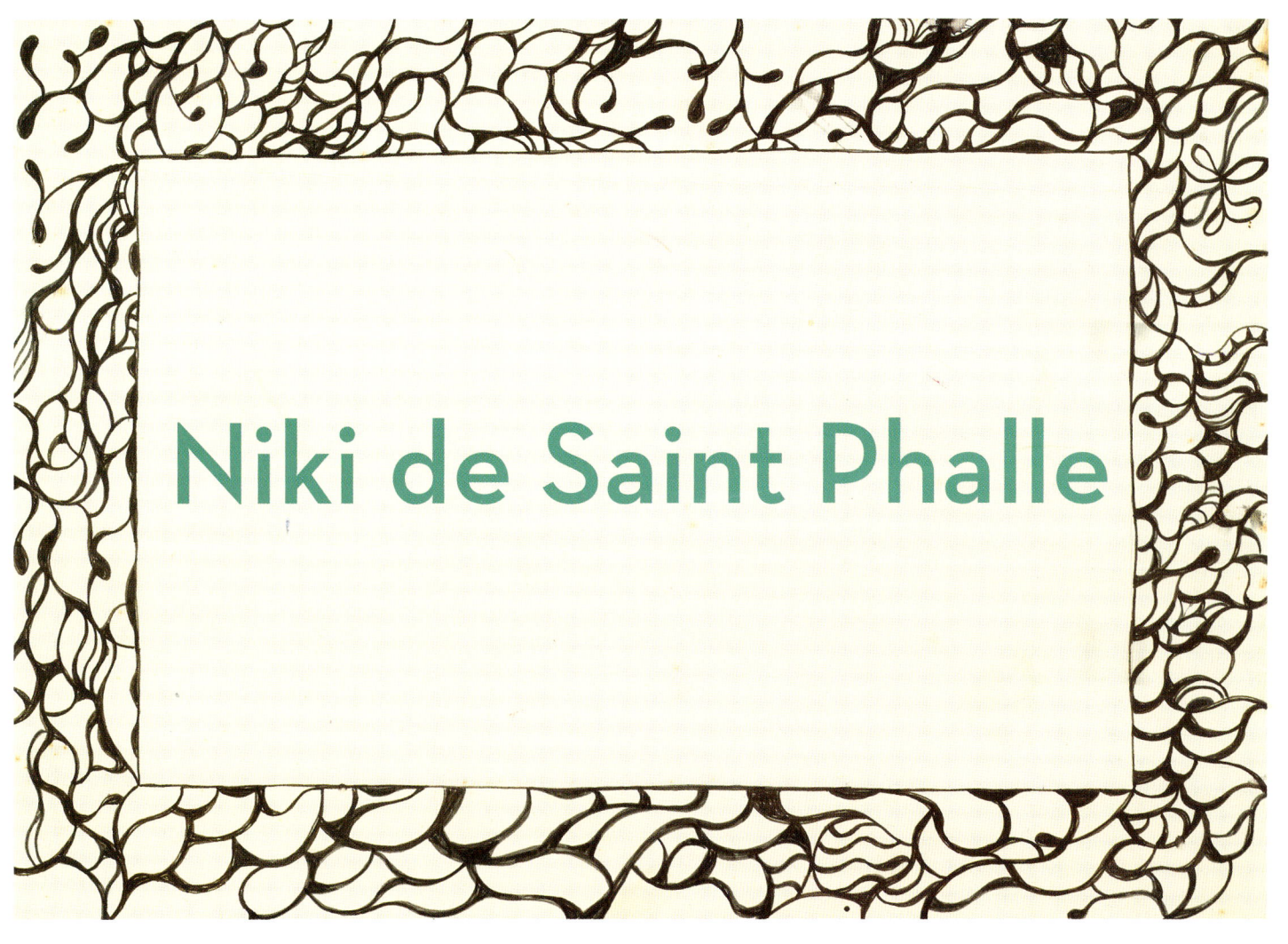

Niki de Saint Phalle

Niki de Saint Phalle

THE SKETCHBOOKS

Edited by Larry Warsh

Essay by Kyla McDonald

Published by
Princeton University Press
in association with
No More Rulers

Published by Princeton University Press
throughout the world, excluding China
41 William Street, Princeton, New Jersey, 08540
99 Banbury Road, Oxford OX2 6JX
press.princeton.edu

In association with No More Rulers
nomorerulers.com 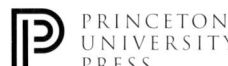 @nomorerulers

GPSR Authorized Representative: Easy Access System Europe–Mustamäe
tee 50, 10621 Tallinn, Estonia, gpsr.requests@easproject.com

Design by Hannah Alderfer, HHA design

All image photography by Aaron Serafino

Front Cover
Nana sans bras (Nana without Arms), n.d.
Black felt-tip pen on paper (spiral bound book)
11 x 9 $\frac{1}{16}$ inches (28 x 23 cm)

Back Cover
Azteca Nana Vase, 1999–2000
Aquarelle, marker, and colored crayon
11 x 8 $\frac{1}{2}$ inches (28 x 21.6 cm)

Title page
Border design, 1980s
Black marker on paper carton
11 $\frac{11}{16}$ x 16 $\frac{1}{2}$ inches (29.7 x 41.9 cm)

This book has been composed in Neutra Text

Printed on acid-free paper

Printed in China

10 9 8 7 6 5 4 3 2 1

Contents

Introduction

"Everything starts with drawing for me," Niki de Saint Phalle wrote on one of her sketches. To me, that says a lot. After all, Saint Phalle's creative output included not only paintings, prints, and books but films, children's playgrounds, and architectural-sized sculptures. And almost all of those projects began with sketches and drawings, including some of the works in this book.

When I think of Saint Phalle, I see a fire child. There's a fierceness in her vibrant colors and whimsical creatures that speaks of an inner intensity. Her personal life, with its pleasures, crises, and challenges, was the fuel for her art, and as an artist she burned brightly—a force of nature. She unleashed her mind in free-flowing kaleidoscopes of shapes, colors, and ideas. In a way, her work on paper is like the ultimate doodle. Drawing set her imagination loose, letting it run wild.

Saint Phalle was also a gifted storyteller. Her pictorial narratives can be avant-garde to the max. The pair of text-filled heads on pages 112 and 113, the meditations on anxiety on pages 104 and 105, and the wry letter to a friend on page 60 reveal an innate fluidity of thought and a rare a unity of word and image. In all her drawings, Saint Phalle's consciousness, her inner world, comes through clearly.

Over a long career Saint Phalle collaborated with many artists—Jasper Johns, Robert Rauschenberg, Larry Rivers, among others—but none more than her life partner, Swiss sculptor Jean Tinguely, another master of the universe. He worked closely with Saint Phalle to realize some of her most ambitious projects. And she inspired others to join her. Visionary works like *The Tarot Garden* and her final project, *Queen Califia's Magical Circle*, relied on many craftspeople, artisans, and volunteers for their successful completion.

In her insightful essay in this volume, Kyla McDonald talks about Saint Phalle's exuberant *Nana* sculptures as emblems of "radical femininity, maternity, strength, and ultimately liberation." That's a brilliant description of Saint Phalle herself, who explored femininity at the highest creative level, always with liberation in mind.

Niki de Saint Phalle: The Sketchbooks invites us to immerse ourselves in Saint Phalle's exuberant, sensual, highly personal visual language. That in itself is one of the most important goals of the No More Rulers Sketchbook series. Spotlighting innovative and influential artists, the series puts their original sketches, drawings, and notes directly into the hands of readers. With *Niki de Saint Phalle: The Sketchbooks*, as with all No More Rulers Sketchbooks, the idea is to open us to visual thinking, to capture creativity, and inspire the inner artist in us all.

Larry Warsh

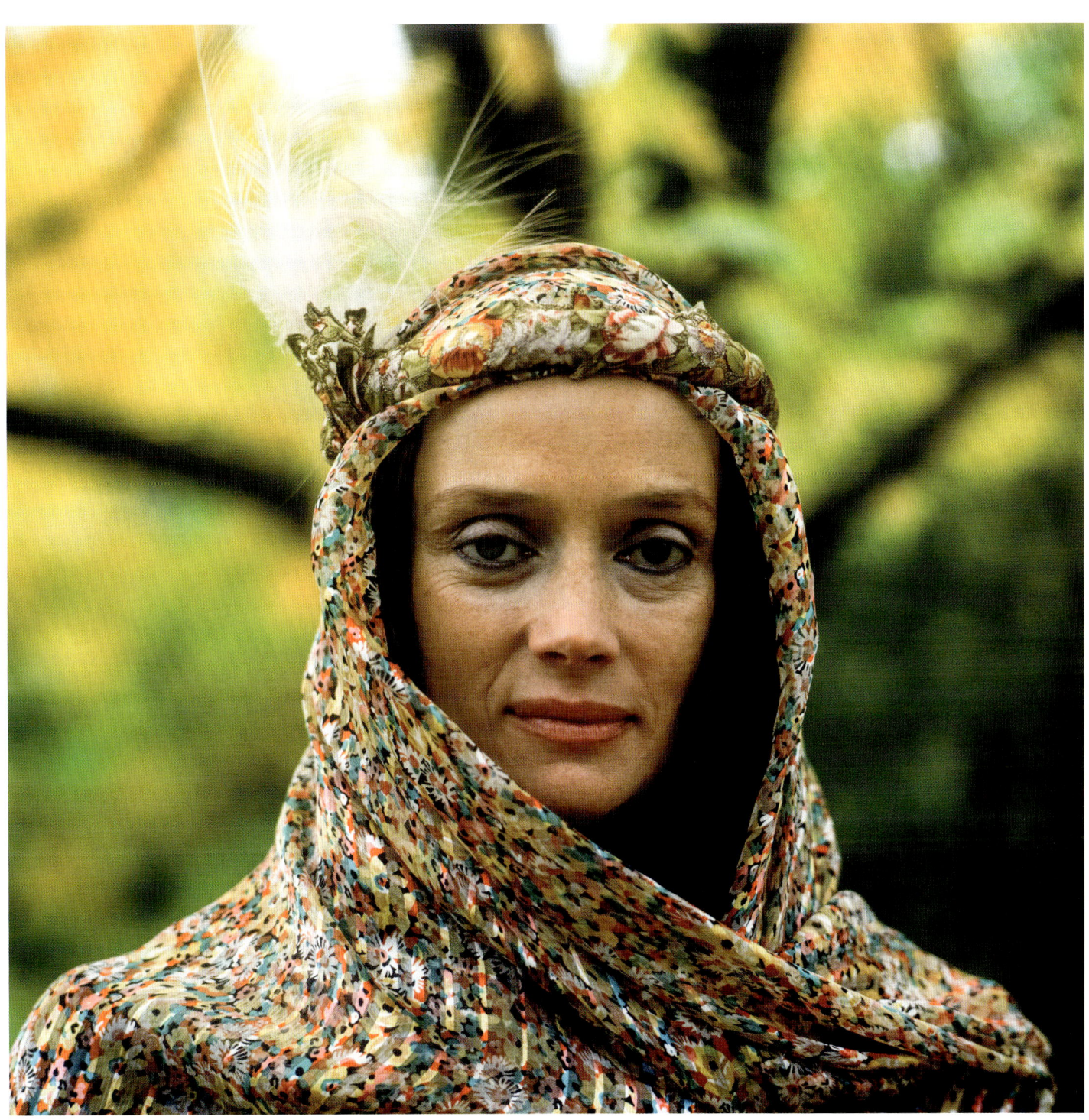

Niki de Saint Phalle. Portrait © Michael Schuijt

Niki de Saint Phalle: Matter Without Edges

"My imagined better is boundless," feminist writer and critic Rose Higham-Stainton writes in her 2024 article "Baroque as Being." Embracing Martinican philosopher Édouard Glissant's 1987 essay "Baroque as a World Philosophy,"[1] Higham-Stainton claims the Baroque not as an art movement or style, but as a way of thinking through the rigid structures that govern us—a positive and radical approach to "being-in-the-world."[2] Upending the Baroque's pejorative reputation to champion its revolutionary nature, Higham-Stainton proposes it as a means of working through crisis, where its notable characteristics—excess, opacity, emotional depth, and hybridity—become forms of resistance, of breaking free from control, offering opportunities for endless and necessary change.

I think of Higham-Stainton's text as I look through Niki de Saint Phalle's drawings and sketches. I think of how Saint Phalle is an artist who has in many ways exemplified a kind of excess, through the scale of her art and the works' bright, kaleidoscopic colors and decorative patterns—from the larger-than-life *Nana* sculptures of women to her expansive sculpture park *The Tarot Garden*. I reflect on the raw, confessional approach Saint Phalle employed in sharing her personal experiences, crises, and resultant emotions in her numerous autobiographical writings, allowing messy complexity to shine through. I think of how those choices set her apart from the prevailing movements and artists of her day, as she actively pushed against all forms of convention. I also see correspondences with the limitless potential that the page (or art more generally) seemed to hold for her.

Like Higham-Stainton, Saint Phalle used much of her work to imagine a hopeful, better way of being in the world. Proceeding from her desire for personal freedom from the patriarchal constraints imposed by her mother and a strict Catholic upbringing, Saint Phalle's vision quickly matured into something more universal, touching upon not only gender politics but a wide range of sociopolitical issues to emerge as a collective idea of living together better. Of her positive nature, the artist once remarked, "To an optimist nothing seems impossible."[3] She transformed this position into an artistic process that allowed her boundless imagination to run free, often actualized through sheer determination. Her vision for a better world remained grounded in an acute understanding of the complexity of the human condition, particularly the condition of women. Saint Phalle was not afraid to explore emotion, nor to express difficulties or contradictions, developing a style that could speak to serious issues through naive and saccharine forms.[4] This hybridity is typical of the artist—an approach that may not have won her critical acclaim but garnered mass appeal.

While Saint Phalle may be well-known for producing art on a grand scale, as a modest space to work in, paper was a constant companion. Catherine Francblin, the artist's biographer, has stated that Saint Phalle was constantly drawing, not stopping even while talking to visitors.[5] In that space, she worked instinctually and unreservedly, pouring out ideas, designs, and notes for art works, along with letters and text that voiced her deepest emotions. Long before she had the means to begin working on public sculpture, for example, she was sketching out plans for future architectural projects on small scraps of paper.[6] Sketching, it seems, provided an early and enduring means for her to exercise her bold creative potential. Francblin notes that drawing was where instinct and imagination merged for Saint Phalle, enabling them to flourish "at the moment of 'making' or producing works."[7]

Saint Phalle's draftsmanship is distinctive: simple lines drawn with black felt-tip pen, occasionally embellished with color or decorative patterning—flamboyant doodling, looping lines, and interconnected, irregular shapes. This mode is present throughout, seen in the *Nana* sketches but also in the drawings that encompass trees, dragons, animals, and thought-clouds spurting from heads. What is striking is how Saint Phalle maintains this primitive approach. There is no sense of practicing or reworking to improve technique. Writing about Jean Dubuffet's influence on Saint Phalle, art historian Ulrich Krempel has proposed that "the spontaneity of Dubuffet's language and the freedom of his lines were so much more to her than a style: they provided a model."[8] Compositionally, the images appear to float upon the page; they are rendered two-dimensionally, despite several of them having corresponding sculptural forms. Art historian Lea Kamecke has argued that Saint Phalle sought "an autonomous composition of known motifs and objects." This can be seen clearly in *Niki de Saint Phalle: The Sketchbooks*, as the motifs that make up her well-known repertoire recur throughout. Her compositional choices deliberately heighten that impact. The idea on the page, and its thematic association, are the primary concern.[9]

Similarly, any paring down of form does not simplify the intentions or meanings of the work. These sketches address many of the complex and political subjects Saint Phalle tackled. The buoyant *Nanas*, depicted here in their myriad expressive shapes, were her reaction against patriarchal constructs. Emblematic of radical femininity, maternity, strength, and ultimately liberation, the *Nanas* embody a new matriarchal society. They have foundations in pagan goddess worship and ancient matriarchal societies, and they anticipate that subject's wider engagement by many artist-women in the 1970s feminist arts movement, including Judy Chicago and Mary Beth Edelson.

Supportive of the civil rights movement, Saint Phalle's vision of matriarchal society was inclusive of all women, and as such she created white, black, and multicolored versions, including works in this volume such as *Sitting Nana* (n.d.), *Bathing Beauty* (1960s), and *Nana + Handbag* (n.d.). As curators Jill Dawsey and Ruba Katrib have stressed, however, Saint Phalle often conflated racial and gender oppression and could be accused of speaking to experiences with which she herself had no familiarity—a criticism levelled more broadly against second-wave feminism in general.[10] While this is a valid assessment, Saint Phalle was still progressive in her calls for inclusivity and equality. Likewise, she was ahead of her time in her discussion of climate change. She spoke out in favor of abortion, and during the global AIDS crisis (see the 1986–1988 drawing *AIDS is...* in this volume), she was among the first to use her art-world platform to bring attention to the epidemic and destigmatize it.[11]

Throughout Saint Phalle's lifetime she produced books, scripts, letters, drawings, and prints that reflected her preoccupation with existential themes of love, life, death, anxiety, and fear. In many respects these can be read as proto-autofiction, where autobiography was used performatively[12] and therapeutically.[13] An artist's writings are often considered as complimentary material to their practice, a means to think *through* the work. This collection of sketches, however, highlights how, for Saint Phalle, texts are often treated in the same manner as images. They are ideas, and an essential part of her creative outpouring. As she explained, "Every thought every emotion I feel and think is made visible and becomes a color a texture a subject a form."[14] Image and text are often made to play off one another. This is seen most clearly in her letters, where text elucidates image. In *Design Block* (n.d.), we see preliminary ideas, for example, for her print *My love what are you doing?* (1968). That work belongs to a larger series of pictorial-letter prints, in which Saint Phalle asks questions of an unnamed lover. This letter reflects her fondness for storytelling and narrative arc, in which she fuses fantasy with autobiographical details. This can be seen to great effect in her play *ICH* (1968) and feature-length films *Daddy* (1973) and *Un rêve plus long que la nuit* (A dream longer than the night, 1976).

Saint Phalle's biographer Catherine Francblin has always stressed the importance of joy in the artist's oeuvre—that her ultimate goal was to elicit joy and transform people's lives through their encounters with her work.[15] Undeniably, one of the Saint Phalle's most striking and pioneering qualities was her anti-elitist attitude. She stated, "My dream is for my things to be in the street, for everyone, so kids can play with them. They are for everyone."[16] Her lifelong practice of making public artworks (playgrounds, sculpture parks, fountains) was integral to that ambition. There is a visual immediacy to the work, apparent both in these sketches and in their sculptural counterparts. While their bright, decorative, naive forms often hide deeper complexities, as Francblin has maintained, they "substantiate the hypothesis of the democratization of art," enabling people unfamiliar with art to engage with the work and—in particular through her public works—to share in a collective experience of art with others.[17] Ruba Katrib has said of Saint Phalle that "she didn't consider herself to be someone who could change society through activism; instead, she aimed to model a way of being in the world with her art."[18]

In her ode to the Baroque, Rose Higham-Stainton asserts her idea for something better: "[It] is matter without edges, water for water's sake rather than water as limits in channels and ways; is a stateless state; a being beyond measure and beyond the dualism of formed and unformed, known and unknown, possessed and dispossessed, dressed and undressed."[19] I see an affinity here with Niki de Saint Phalle's own idea of an imagined better—one where thinking without boundaries is of critical importance, where excess is a model, and where imagining matter without edges is a way of life.

Kyla McDonald

Endnotes

1 Édouard Glissant, "Baroque as a World Philosophy," *UNESCO Courier: A Window on to the World*, September 1987, 18.

2 Rose Higham-Stainton, "Baroque as Being," *Flash Art*, June 3, 2024, https://flash---art.com/article/critic-dispatch/.

3 Cited in Niki de Saint Phalle, "Letter to Pontus," in *Niki de Saint Phalle*, ed. Pontus Hultén, exh. catalogue (Bonn: Verlag Gerd Hatje, 1992–1993), 148.

4 Lanka Tattersall, "On Tenderness," in *Niki de Saint Phalle: Structures for Life*, ed. Ruba Katrib (New York: MoMA PS1, 2021), 47–48.

5 Catherine Francblin in "Baroque Joy: Catherine Francblin Talks with Alison M. Gingeras & Fabienne Stephan," in *Niki de Saint Phalle: The Joy Revolution Reader* (New York: Salon 94, 2021), 11.

6 See "Letter to Jean," in *Niki de Saint Phalle*, ed. Pontus Hultén, 153, in which she describes showing Jean Tinguely her drawings early in her career.

7 Catherine Francblin in "Baroque Joy," 11.

8 Ulrich Krempel, "From Niki Matthews to Niki de Saint Phalle," in *Niki de Saint Phalle 1930–2002*, ed. Camille Morineau (Bilbao: La Fábrica, and FMGB Guggenheim Bilbao, 2015), 43.

9 Lea Kamecke, "Art Communication: Letter-Drawings from Niki de Saint Phalle and Jean Tinguely," in *Niki & Jean: L'art et L'amour* (Munich: Prestel, 2005), 254–58.

10 See both Ruba Katrib, "Niki de Saint Phalle: Building for the Future," in *Niki de Saint Phalle: Structures for Life*, 22–24; and Jill Dawsey, "The First Free Woman: Niki de Saint Phalle's *Nanas*," in *Niki de Saint Phalle in the 1960s*, ed. Jill Dawsey and Michelle White (Houston, Texas and La Jolla, California: The Menil Collection and Museum of Contemporary Art San Diego, 2022), 106-8.

11 Saint Phalle published the book *AIDS: You Can't Catch It Holding Hands* in 1987 to bring awareness to the disease.

12 I write about Saint Phalle's writing having a connection to authors such as Chris Kraus and their confessional style in "Niki de Saint Phalle: Here Everything Is Possible," in *Niki de Saint Phalle: Here Everything Is Possible*, ed. Kyla McDonald (Ghent: Snoeck, 2018). See also Rainer von Hessen, "At Last I Found the Treasure: Working with Niki," in *At Last I Found the Treasure: Niki de Saint Phalle and the Theatre*, ed. Beate Kemfert, exh. catalogue, Kunst– und Kulturstiftung Opelvillen Rüsselsheim (Heidelberg and Berlin: Kehrer, 2016); and Katrib, "Niki de Saint Phalle: Building for the Future," 13–14.

13 Written as an incredibly powerful and brave open letter to her daughter Laura, Saint Phalle's book *Mon Secret* (1994), for example, recounts that her father sexually abused her as an adolescent. She wrote: "I wrote this book primarily for myself, as an attempt to finally free myself from the drama which has played such a decisive role in my life. I'm someone who has escaped death. I needed to let the little girl inside of me speak at last. My text is her cry of desperation." Niki de Saint Phalle, "My Secret," republished in *Niki de Saint Phalle: Outside-In*, exh. catalogue (Heerlen: SCHUNCK, 2011), 147.

14 Niki de Saint Phalle, *The Wounded Animals* (London: Gimpel Fils; New York: Gimpel Weitzenhoffer, 1988), n.p.

15 See Catherine Francblin, "Niki de Saint Phalle: The Joy Factory," in *Niki de Saint Phalle: Here Everything Is Possible*.

16 In *Niki de Saint Phalle: Un rêve d'architecte* [Niki de Saint Phalle: An architect's dream], directed by Anne Julien and Louise Faure, written by Louise Faure (2014).

17 Francblin, "Baroque Joy," 10.

18 Katrib, "Niki de Saint Phalle: Building for the Future," 13.

19 Higham-Stainton, "Baroque as Being."

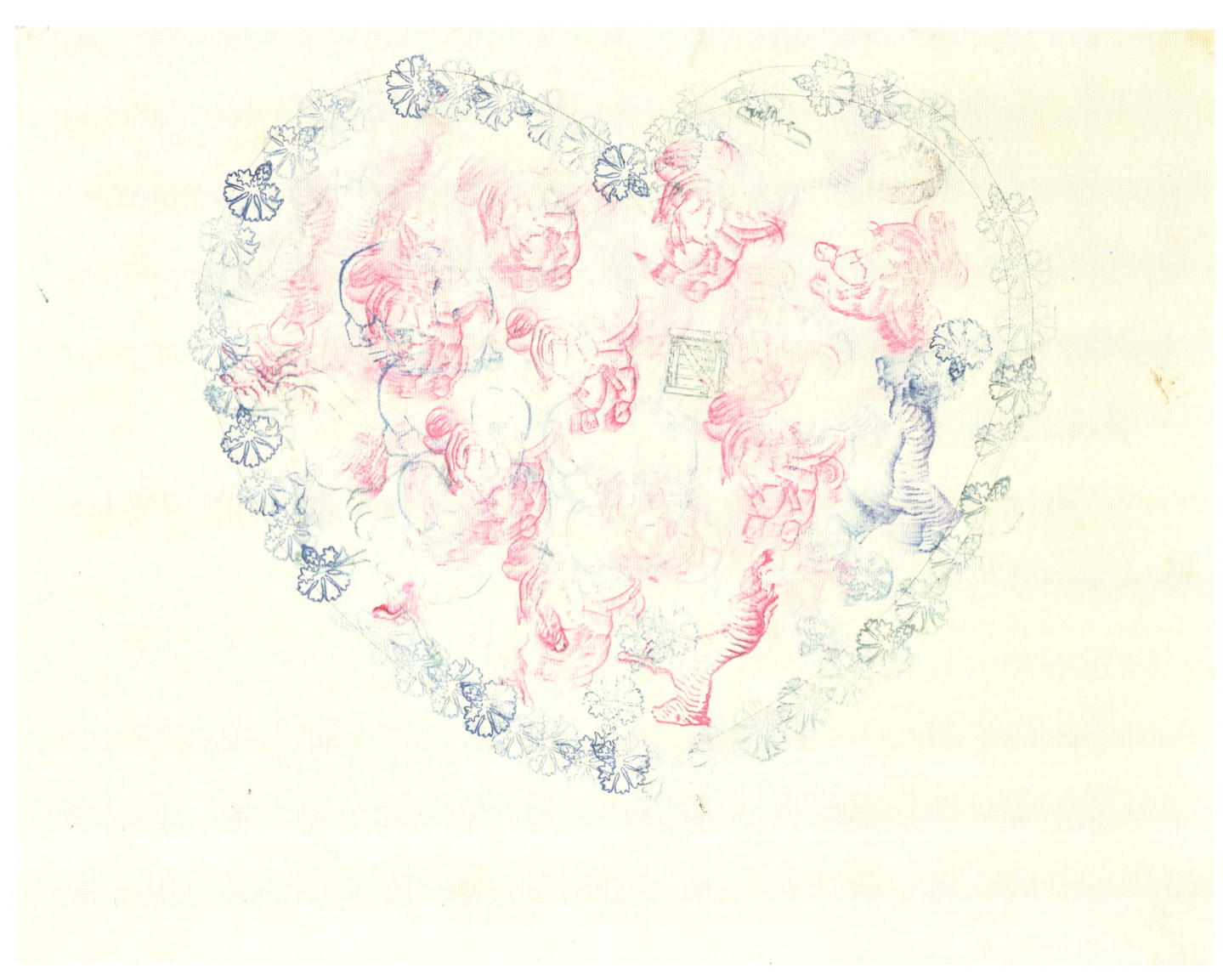

Coeur (Heart), 1962–1963
Stamps on drawing paper
11 $^1/_8$ x 14 inches (28.2 x 35.6 cm)

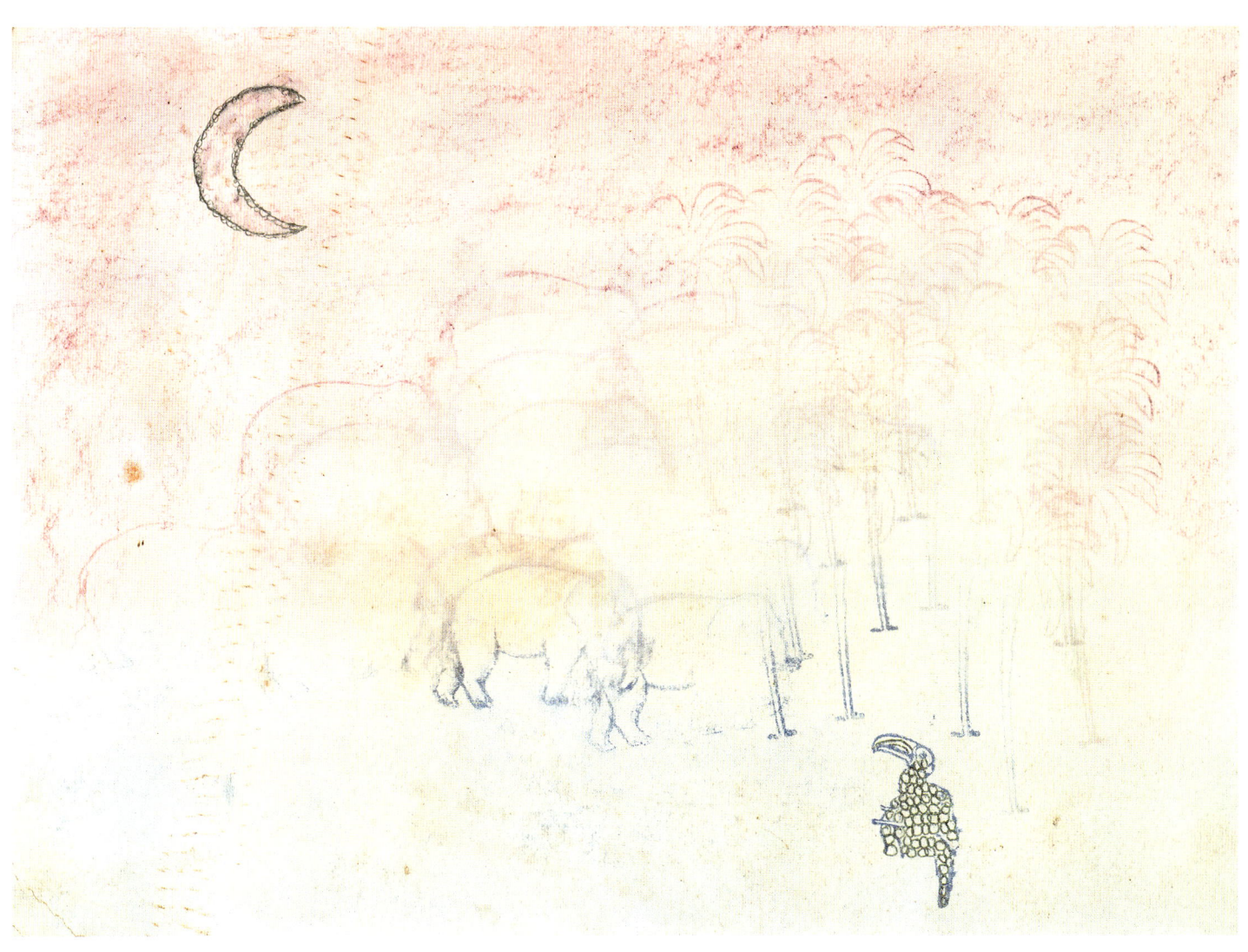

Eléphants, palmiers (Elephants, Palm Trees), n.d.
Stamps, ink, and colored pencil on cardboard
9 $\frac{1}{2}$ x 13 inches (24.1 x 33 cm)

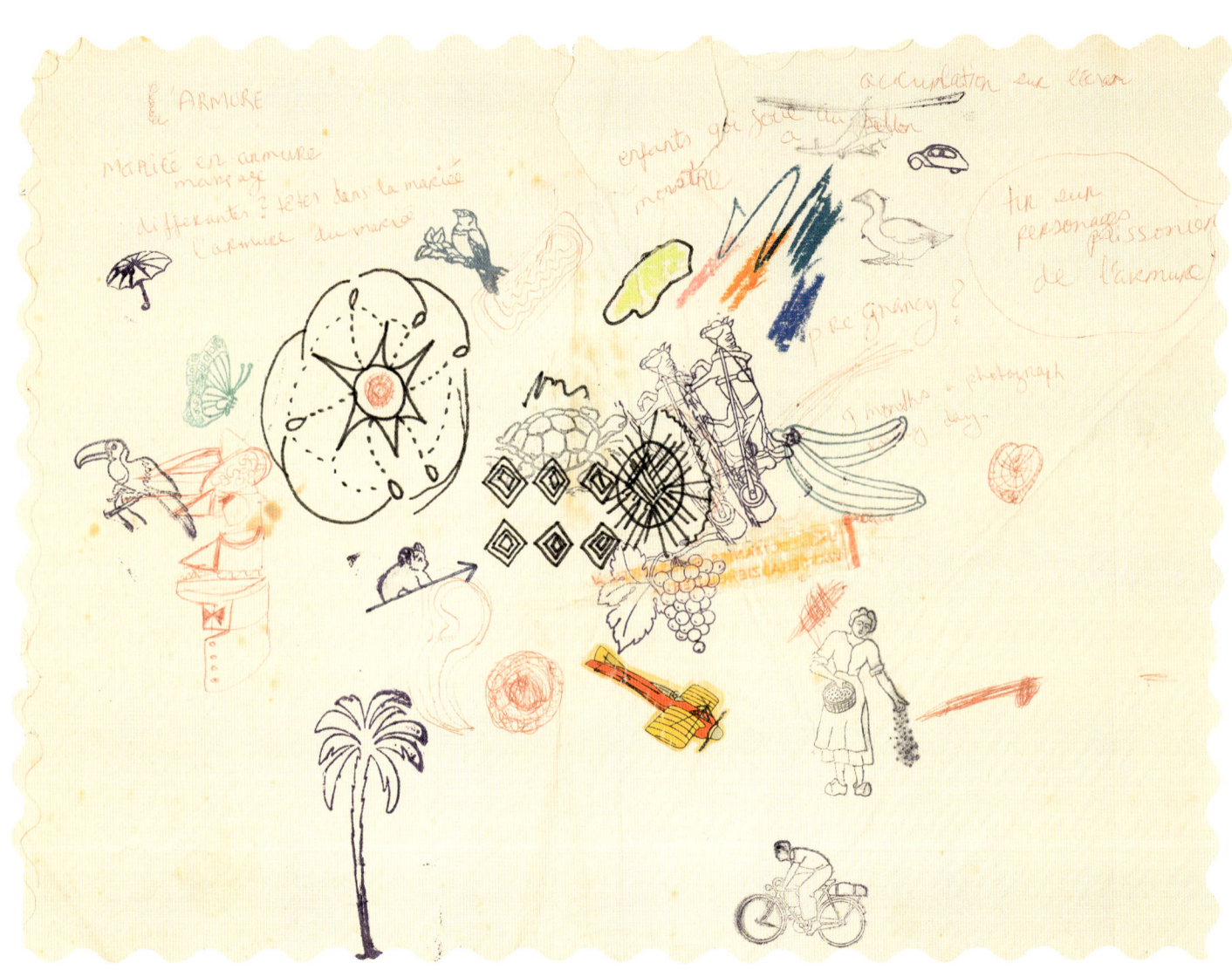

L'amore... (Love...), n.d.
Ballpoint pen, felt-tip pen, stamps, tape, pastel on paper placemat
11 $^{11}/_{16}$ x 15 $^{5}/_{8}$ inches (29.7 x 39.7 cm)

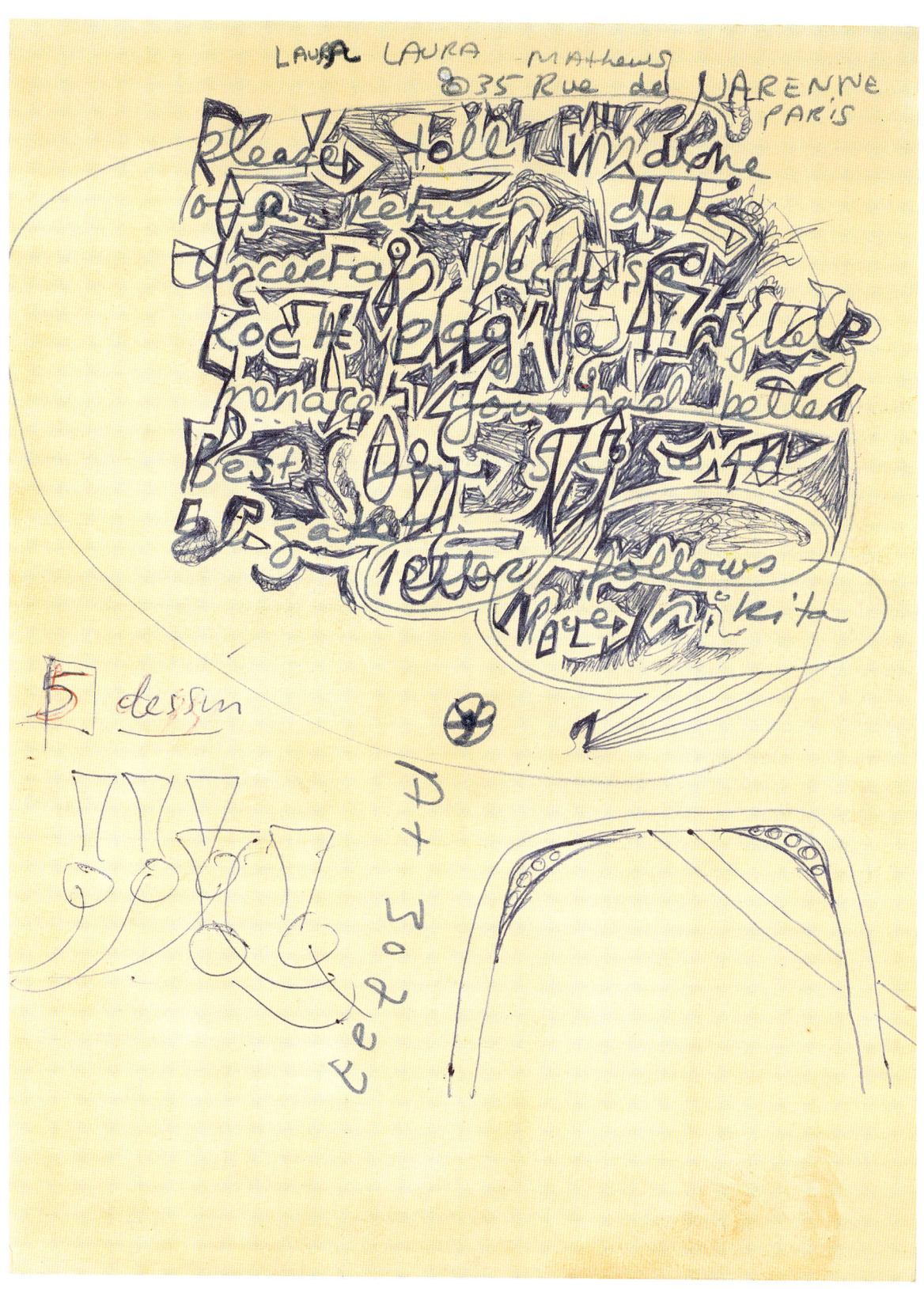

Sketchbook page, 1960s
Felt-tip pen and ballpoint pen on paper (spiral bound book)
11 x 9 $^{1}/_{16}$ inches (28 x 23 cm)

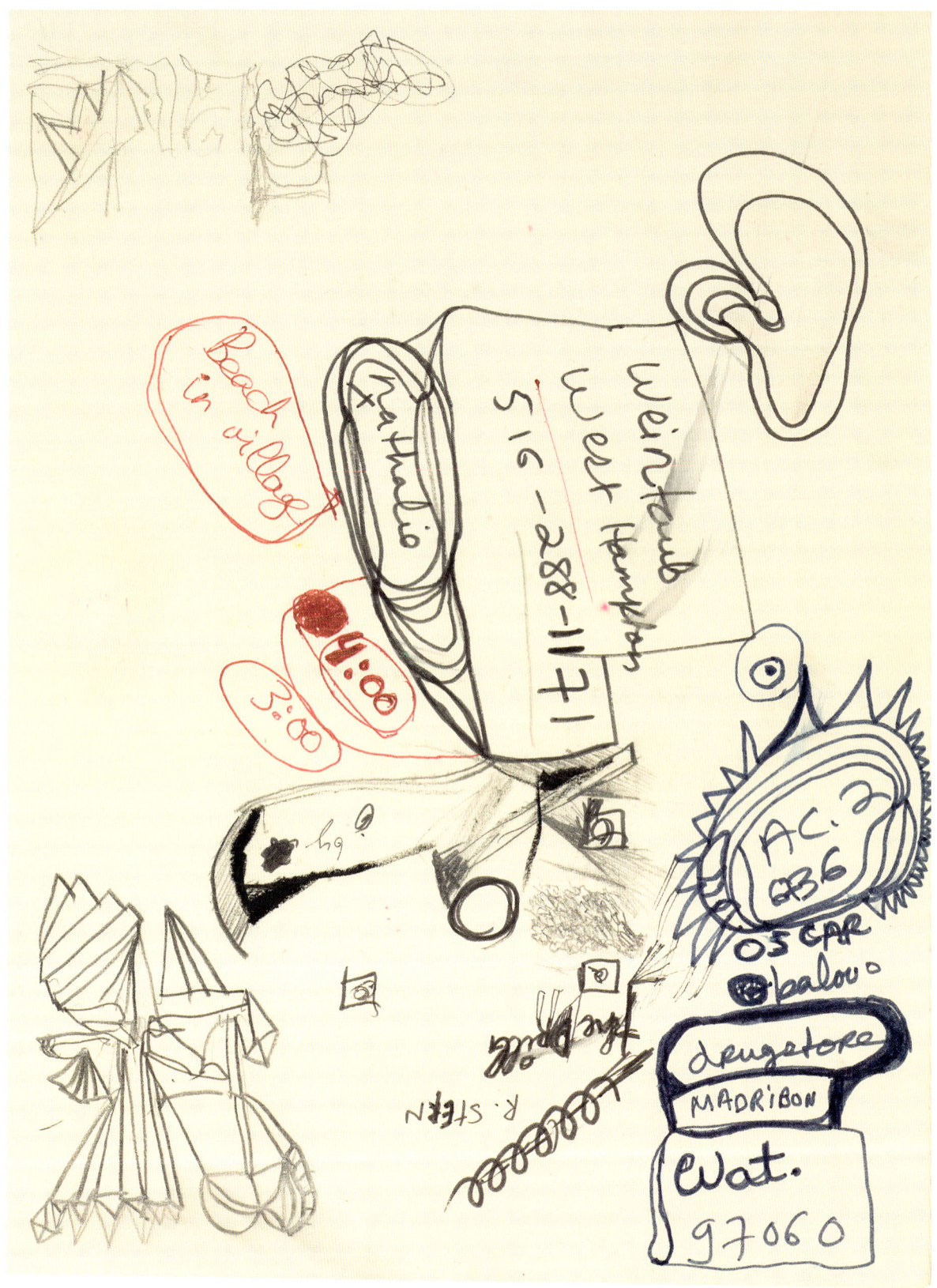

Beach in Village, 1960s
Black pencil, ballpoint pen, and felt-tip pen on paper (spiral bound book)
11 x 9 ¹/₁₆ inches (28 x 23 cm)

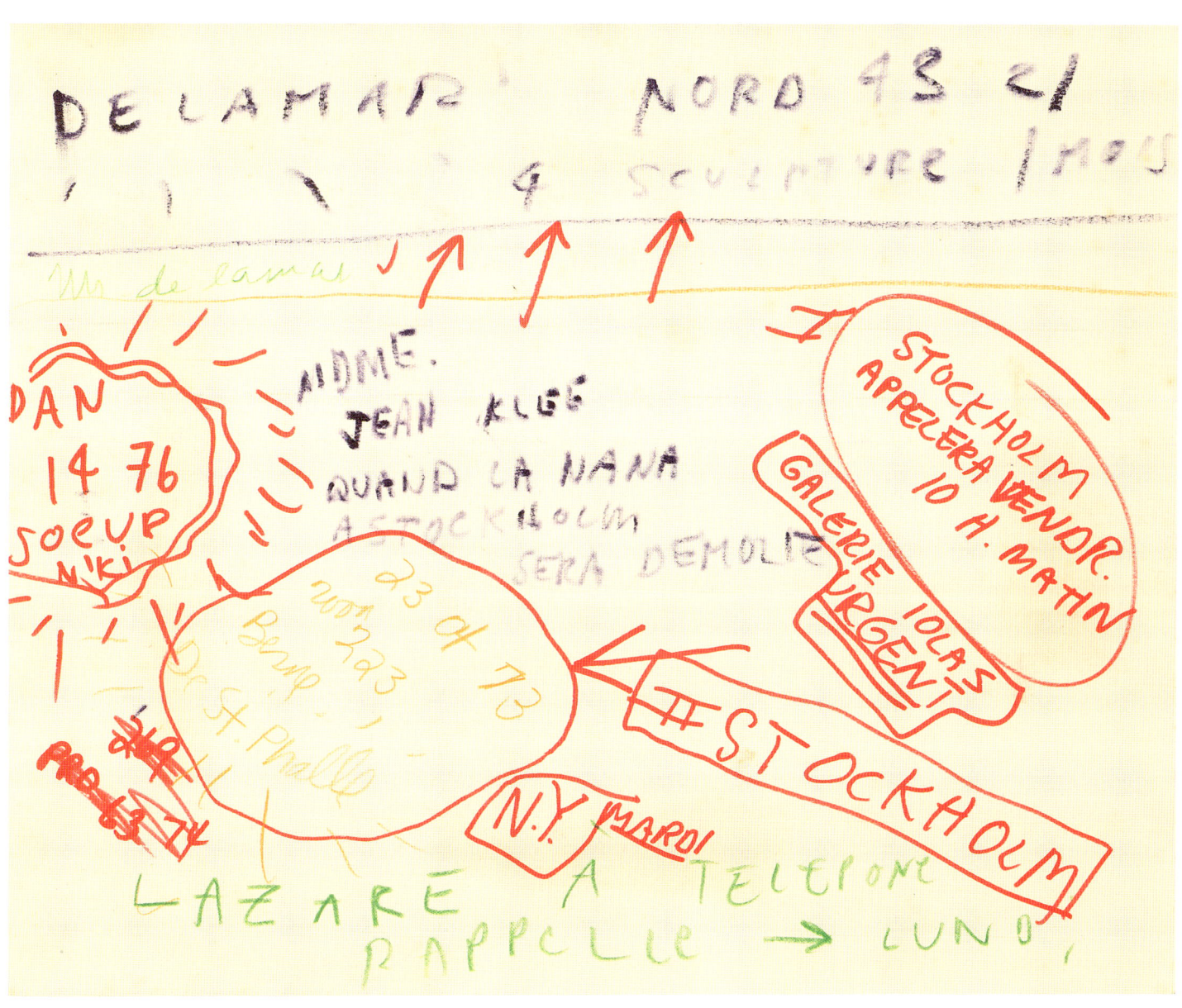

Lavis Aquarelle sketchbook page, 1965
Felt-tip pen and colored pencil on paper
12 1/2 x14 1/2 inches (31.8 x 36.8 cm)

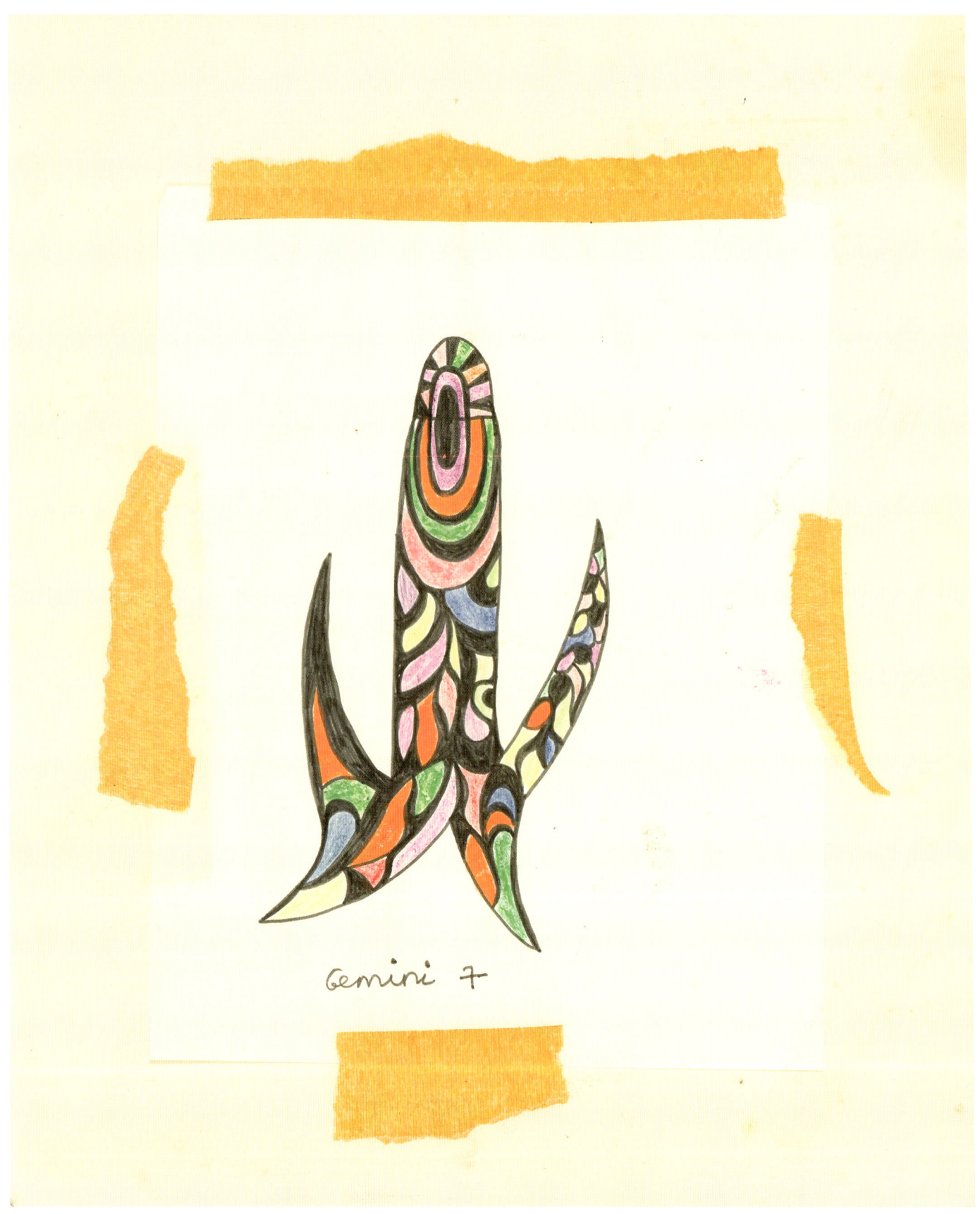

Gemini 7, 1965
Colored pencil, black felt-tip pen on paper taped into Lavis Aquarelle sketchbook
14 $\frac{1}{2}$ x 12 $\frac{1}{2}$ inches (36.8 x 31.8 cm)

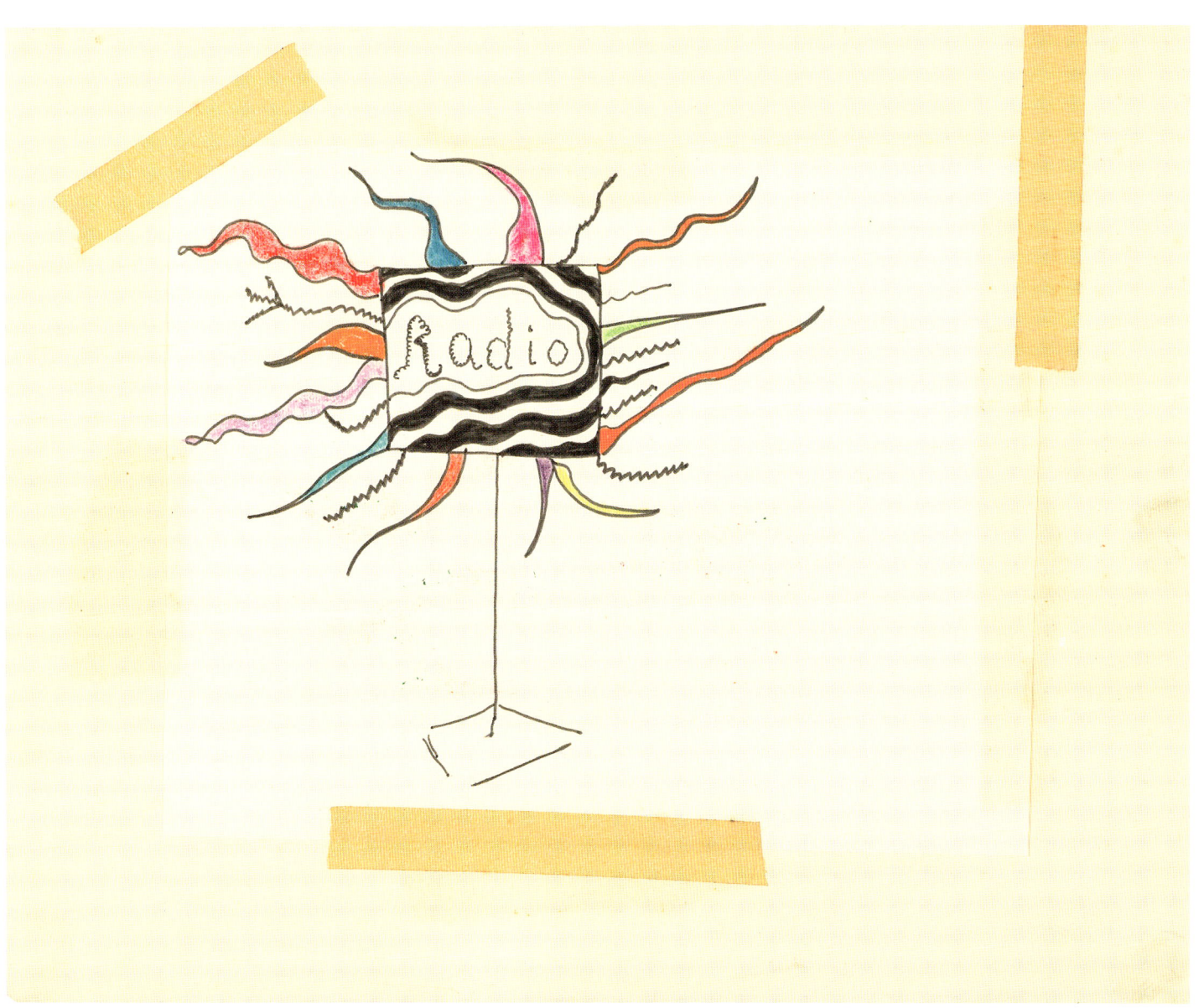

Radio, 1965
Colored pencil, black felt-tip pen on paper taped into Lavis Aquarelle sketchbook
2 $\frac{1}{2}$ x 14 $\frac{1}{2}$ inches (31.8 x 36.8 cm)

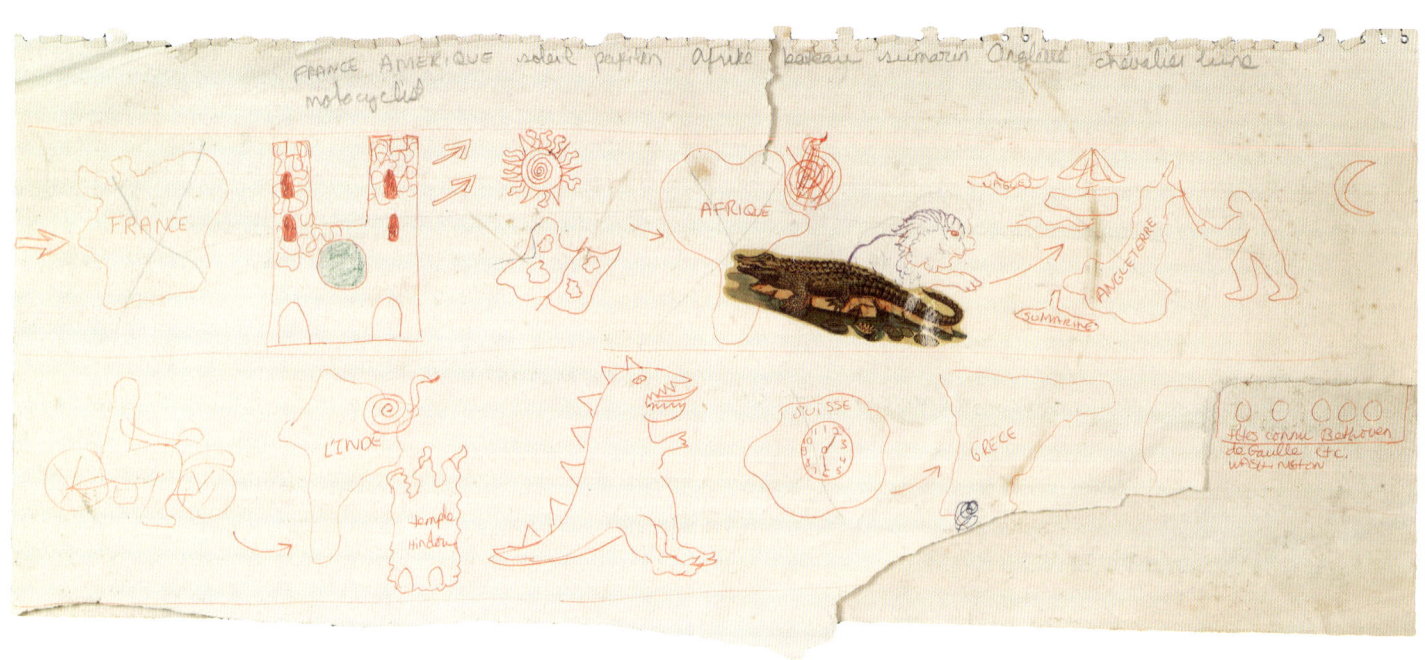

Etude avec pays (Study with Countries), c. 1963
Ballpoint pen, stamps, decals, black pencil, and colored pencils on paper
16 ¹⁵/₁₆ x 21 ¹/₄ inches (43 x 54 cm)

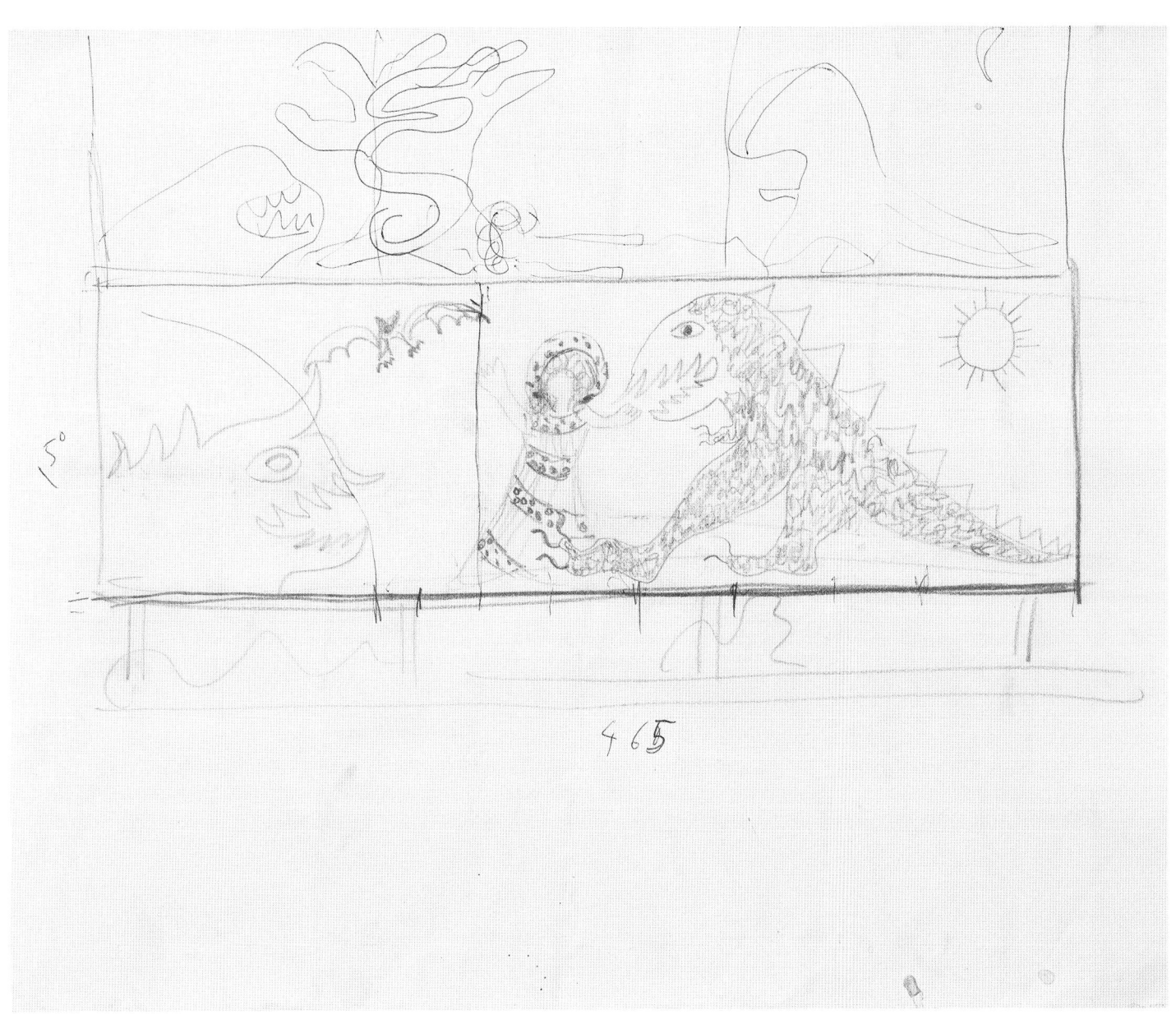

Dragons, c. 1963
Black pencil and ballpoint pen on drawing pad page
14 x 16 ³/₄ inches (35.5 x 42.5 cm)

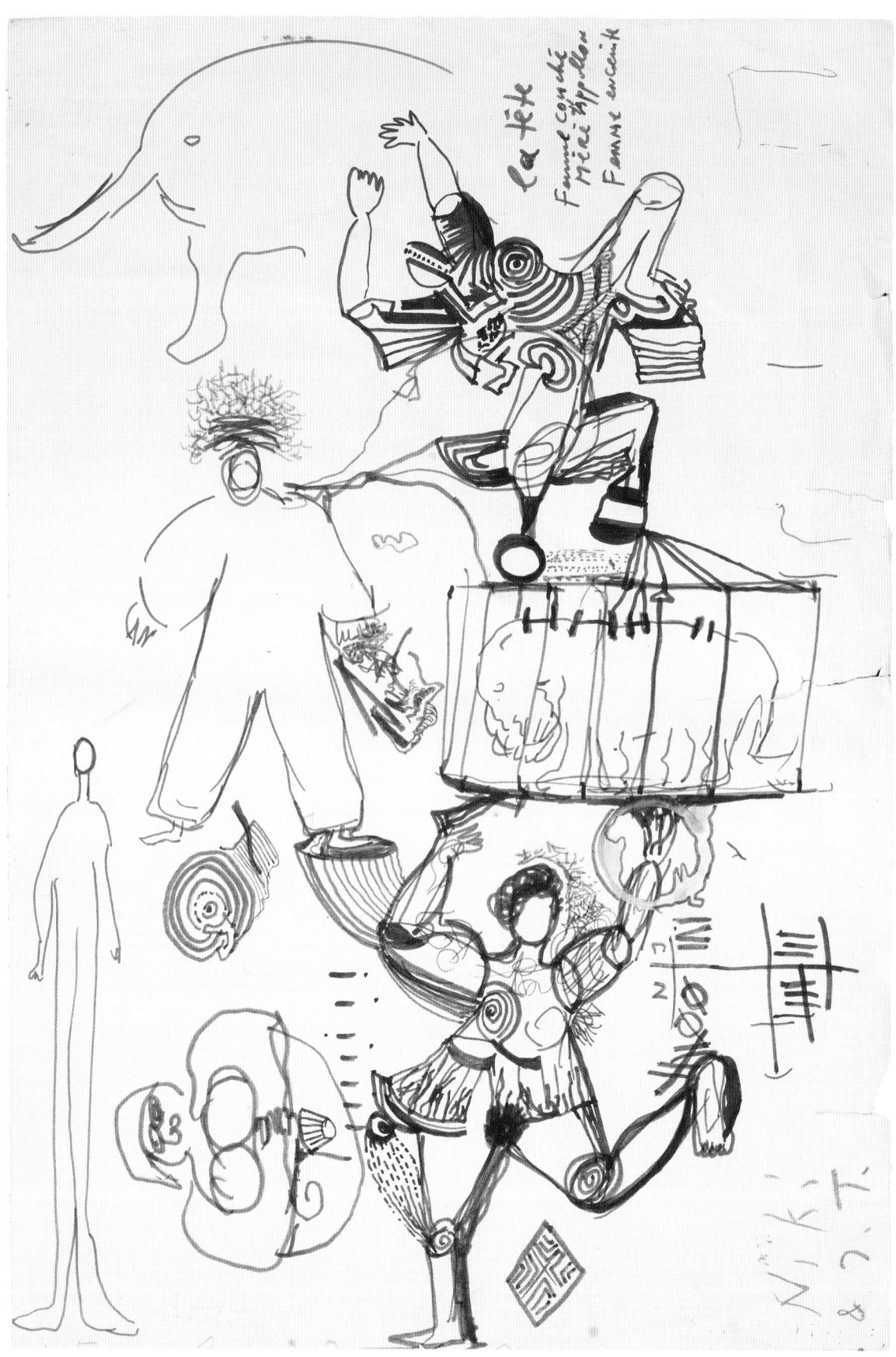

Collaboration with Jean Tinguely (*Femmes...*), n.d.
Black felt-tip pen on drawing pad page
17 ¹⁵/₁₆ x 12 inches (45.5 x 30.5 cm)

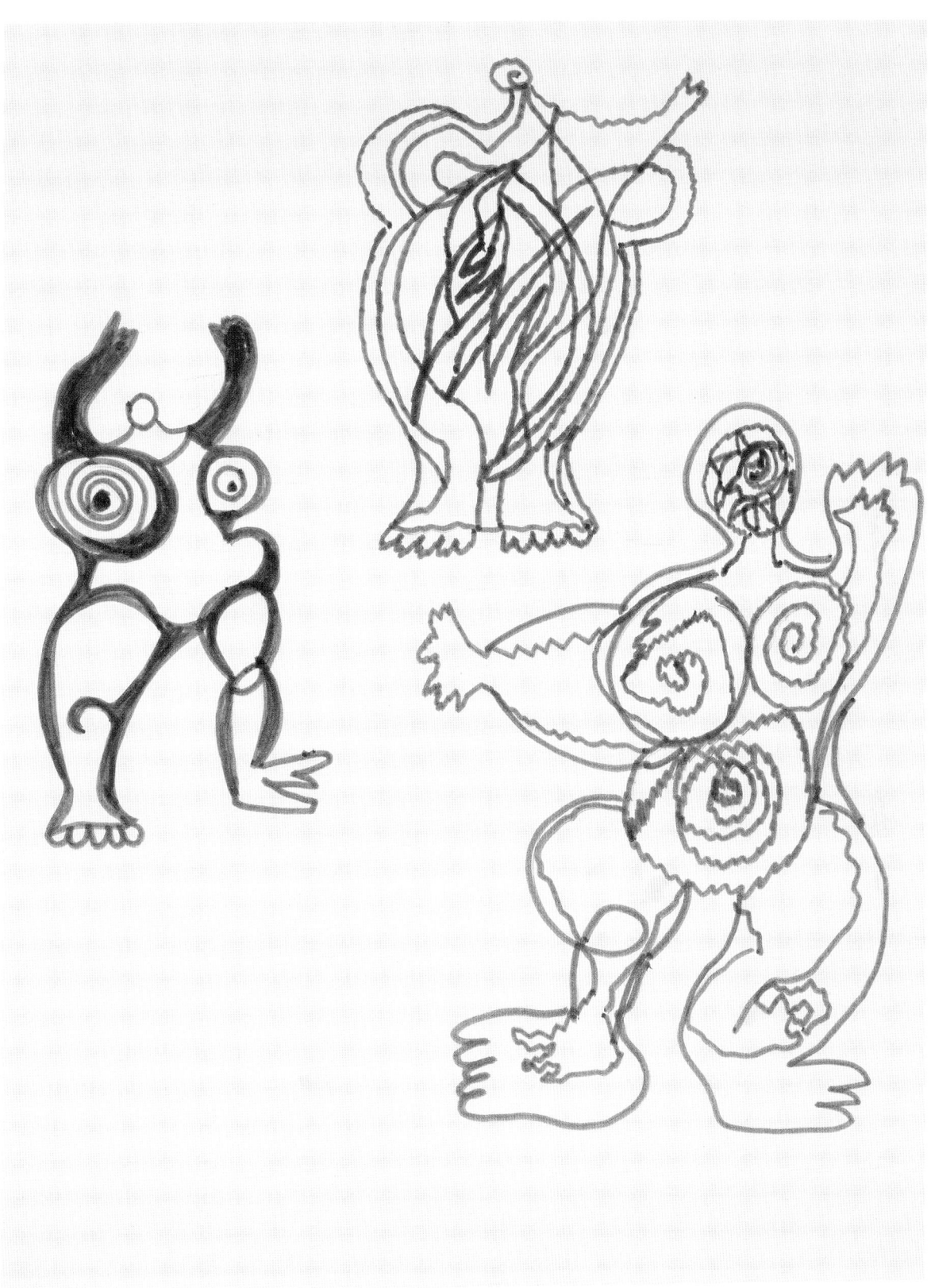

Nana tremblante (Trembling Nana), n.d.
Black felt-tip pen on paper (spiral bound book)
10 $^{15}/_{16}$ x 8 $^{7}/_{16}$ inches (27.8 x 21.4 cm)

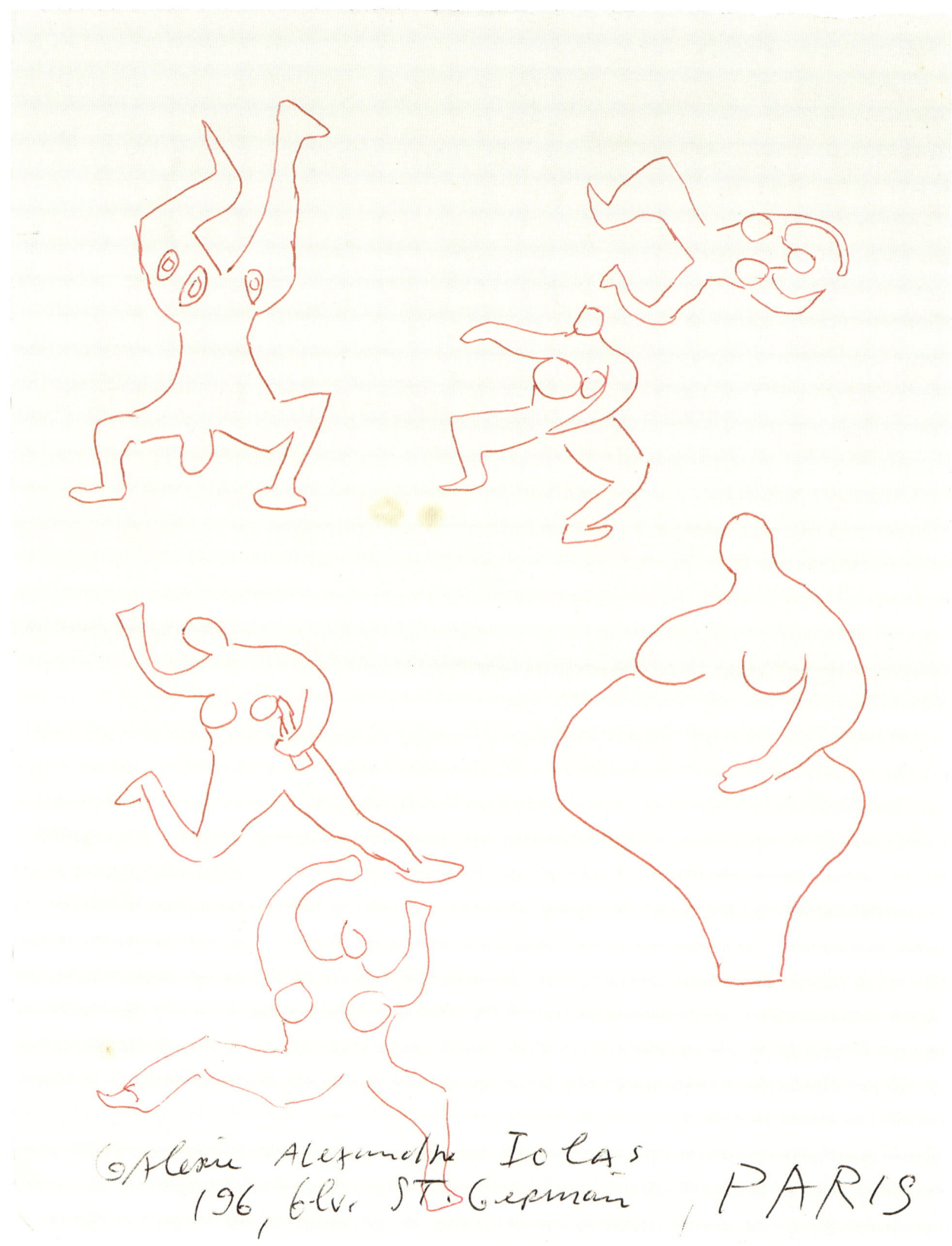

Galerie Alexandre Iolas, c. 1965
Red and black ballpoint pen on paper
10 $^5/_8$ x 8 $^3/_{16}$ inches (27 x 20.8 cm)

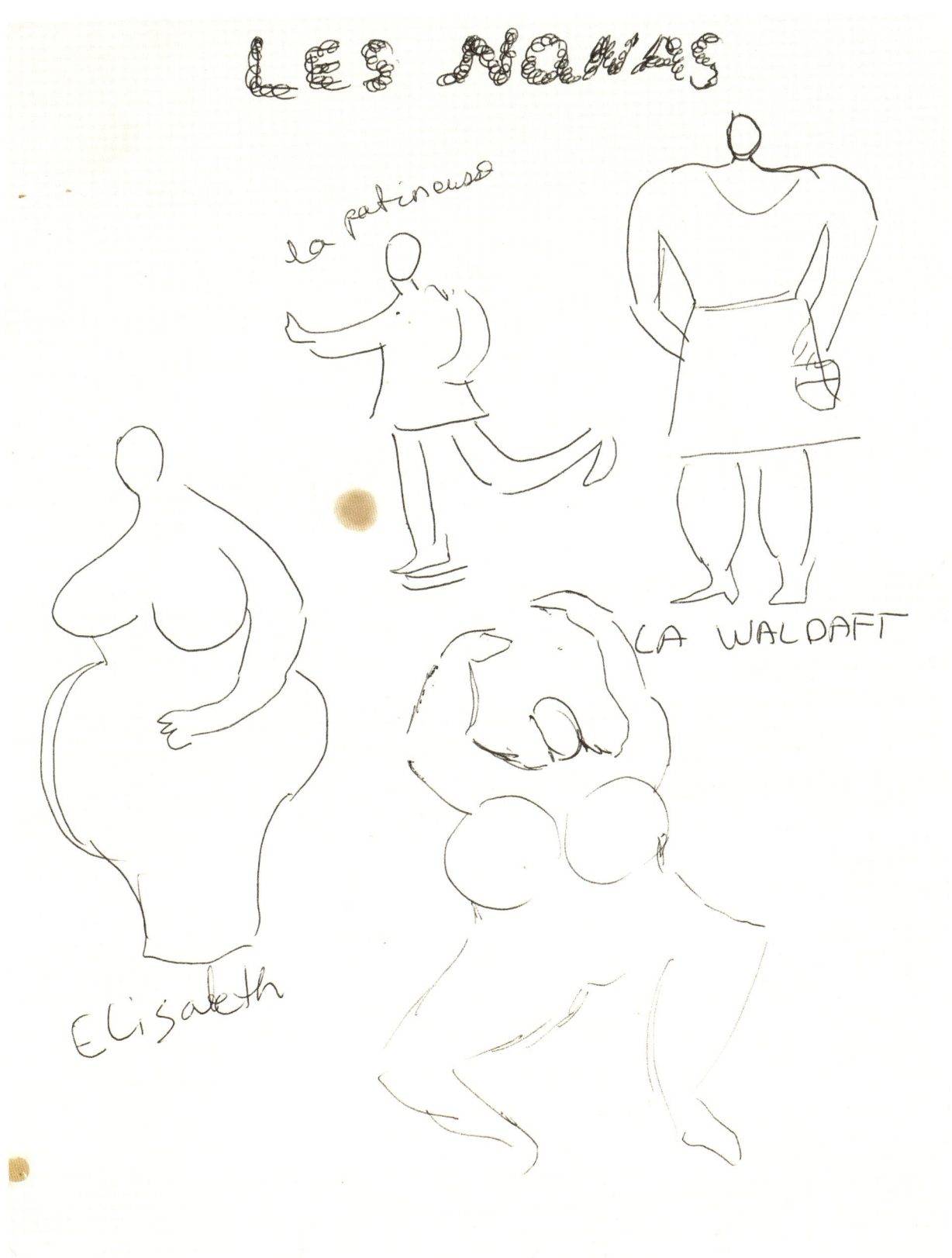

Les nanas, c. 1965
Black ballpoint pen on paper
10 $^5/_8$ x 8 $^3/_{16}$ inches (27 x 20.8 cm)

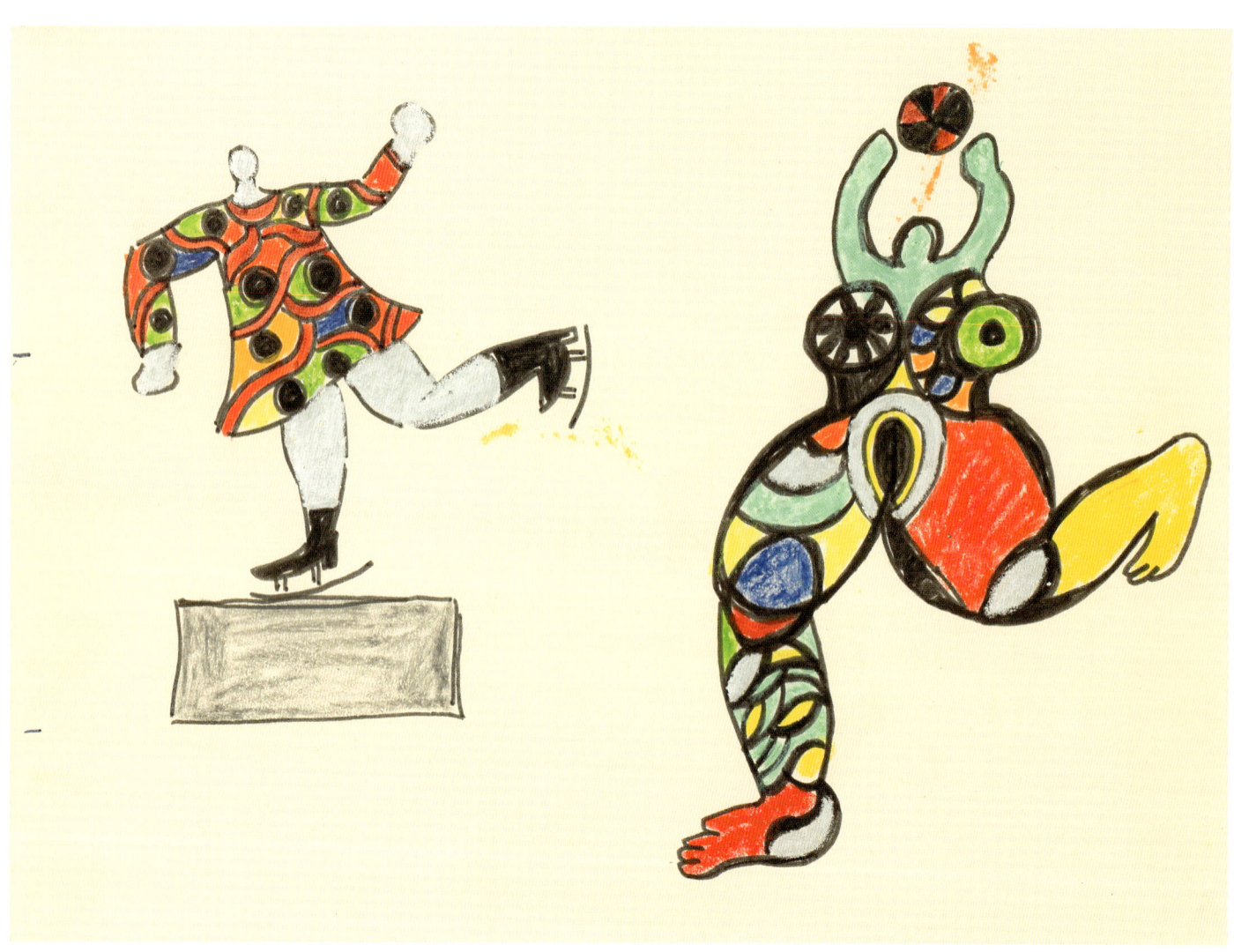

Patineuse et nana avec ballon (Skater and Nana with Ball), n.d.
Pastel and felt-tip pen on paper (spiral bound book)
8 7/16 x 10 15/16 inches (21.4 x 27.8 cm)

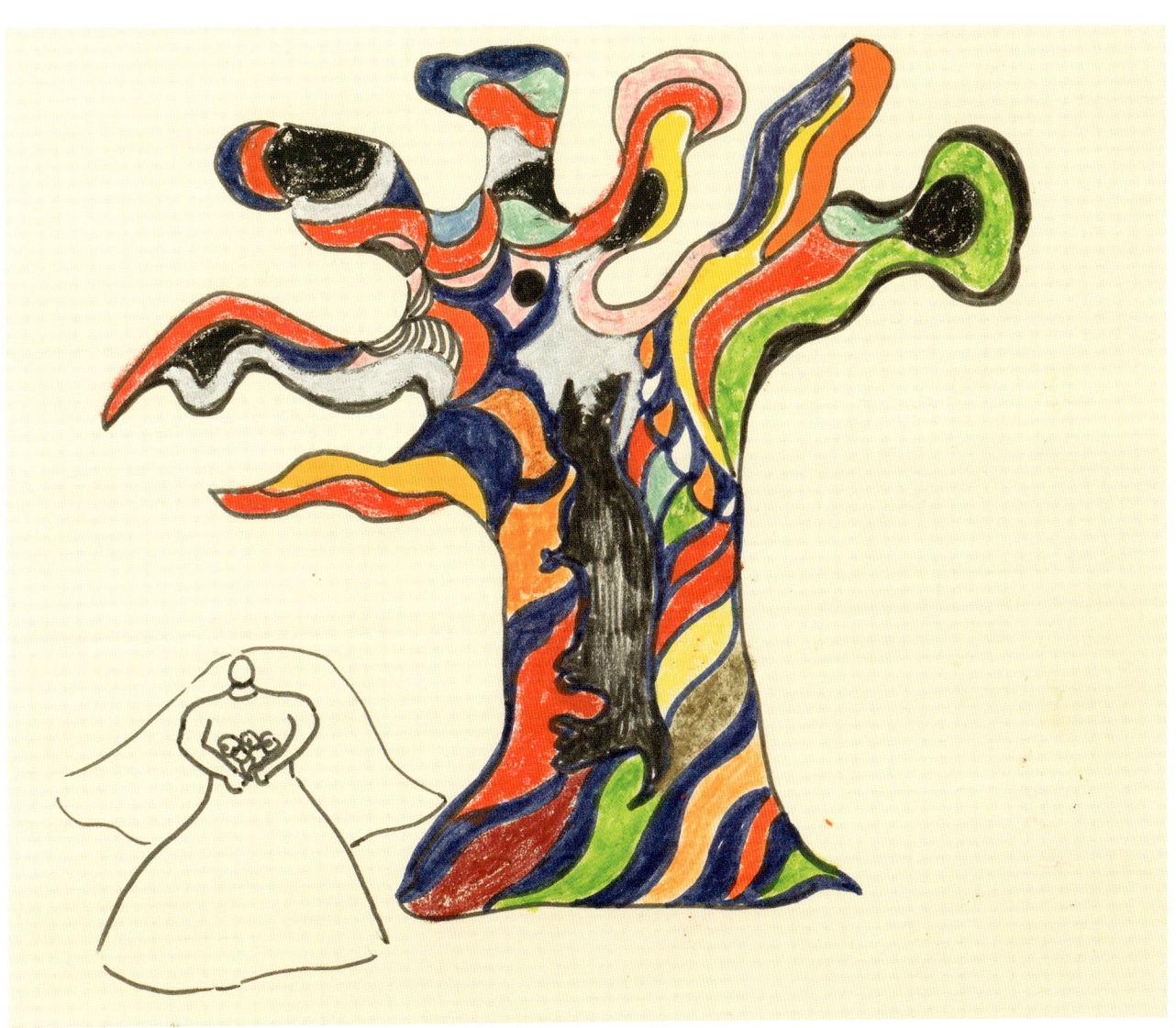

Arbre et mariée (Tree and Bride), n.d.
Pastel and felt-tip pen on paper (spiral bound book)
8 $^{7}/_{16}$ x 10 $^{15}/_{16}$ inches (21.4 x 27.8 cm)

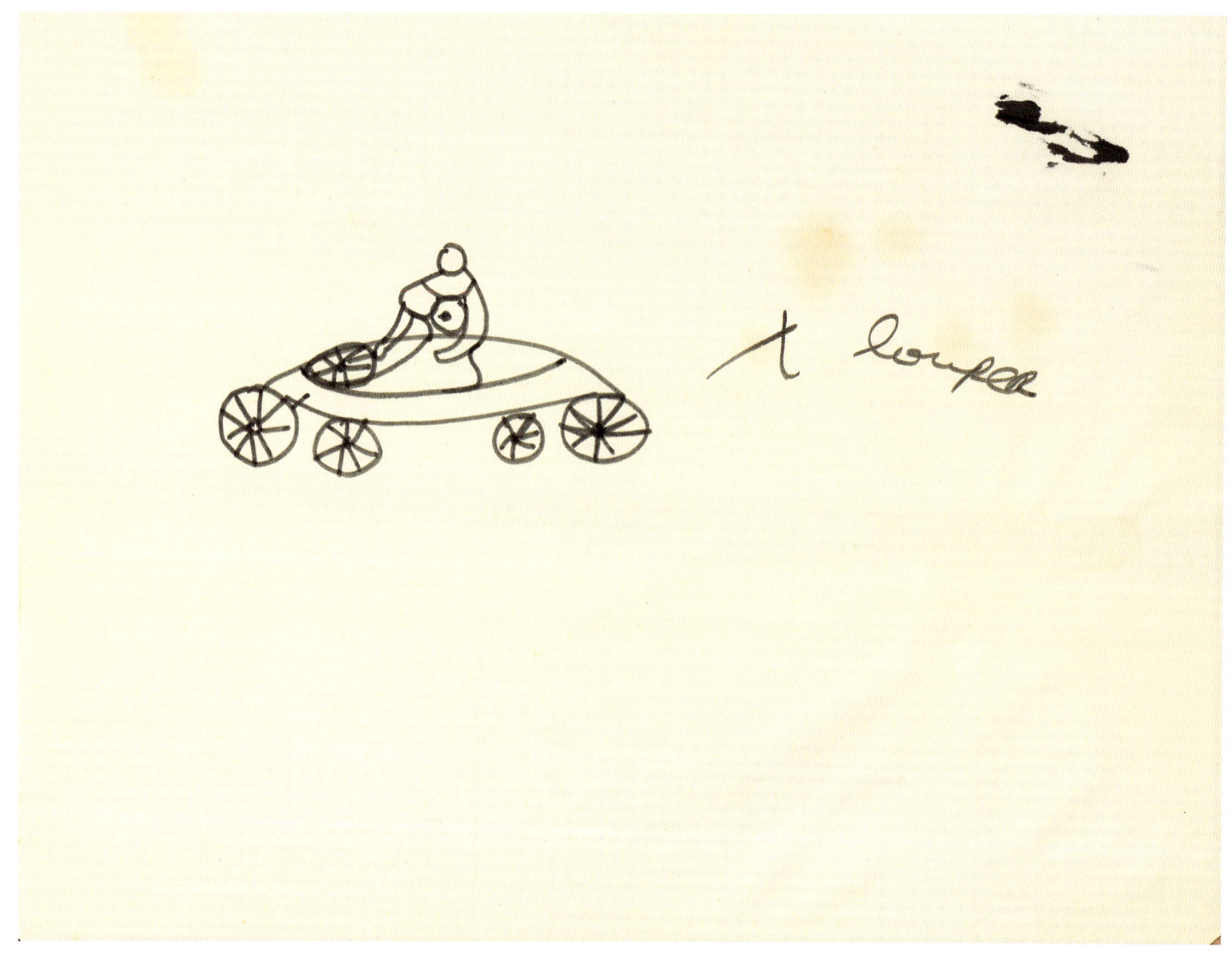

Femme et voiture (Woman and Car), n.d. 1967
Marker on paper (spiral bound book)
8 $^1/_4$ x 10 $^5/_8$ inches (21 x 27 cm)

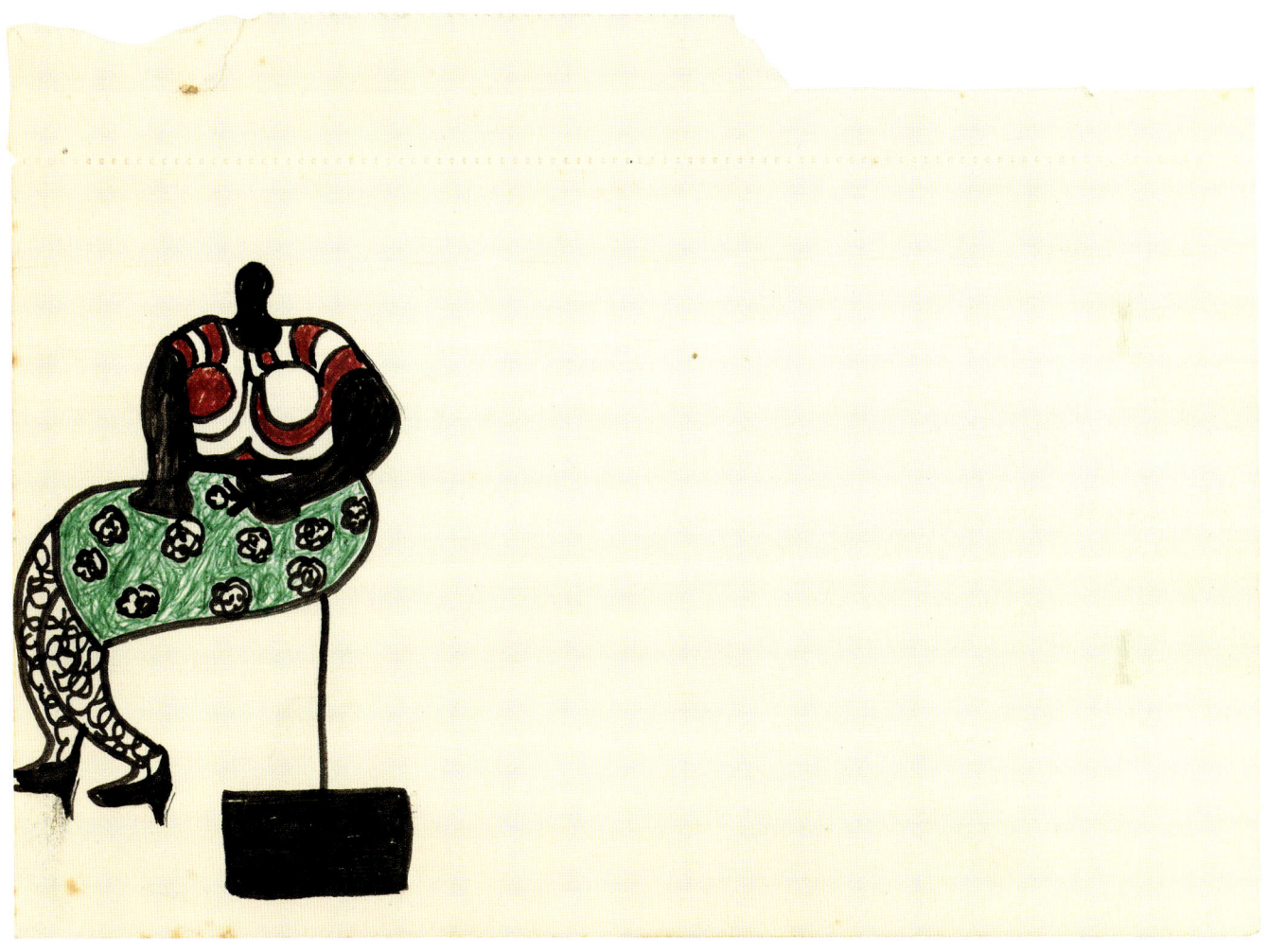

Nana assise (Sitting Nana), n.d.
Black felt-tip pen, red and green ballpoint pen on paper
5 $^3/_{16}$ x 7 $^3/_{16}$ inches (13.2 x 18.2 cm)

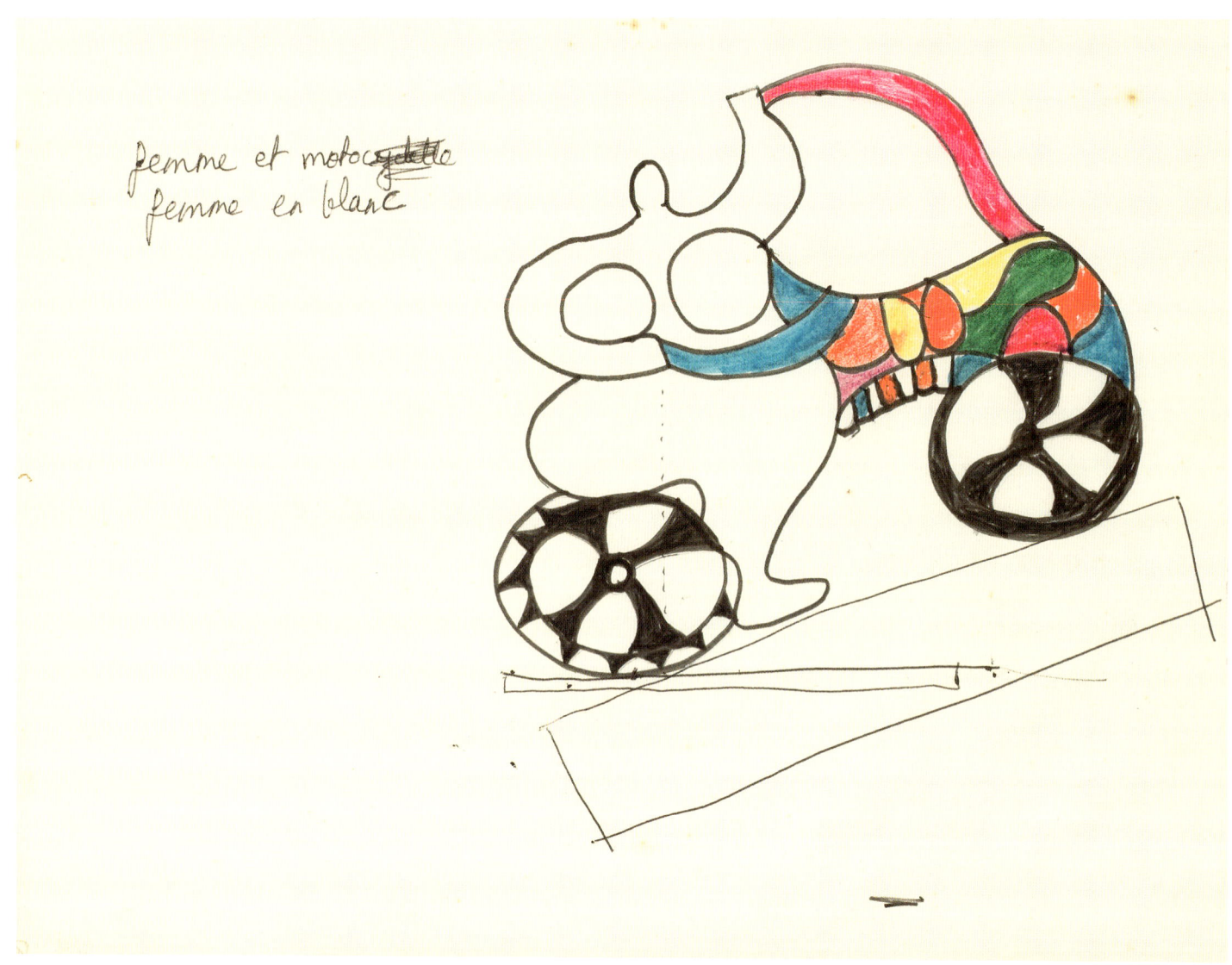

femme et motocyclette
femme en blanc

Femme et moto (Woman and Motorcycle), 1967
Colored pencil, pencil, and marker on paper (spiral bound book)
8 $^1/_4$ x 10 $^5/_8$ inches (21 x 27 cm)

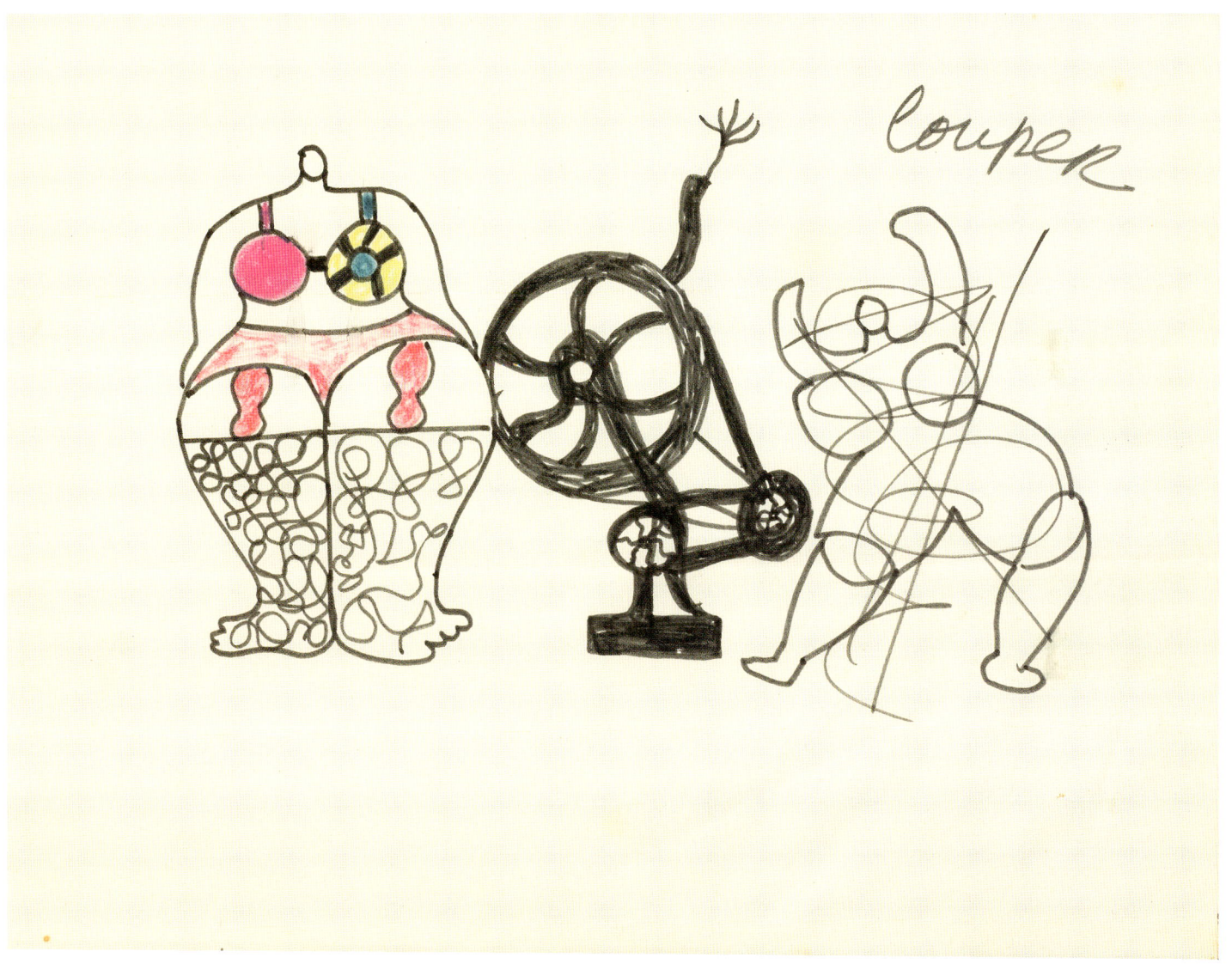

Femme et roues (Woman and Wheels), 1967
Marker on paper (spiral bound book)
8 $\frac{1}{4}$ x 10 $\frac{5}{8}$ inches (21 x 27 cm)

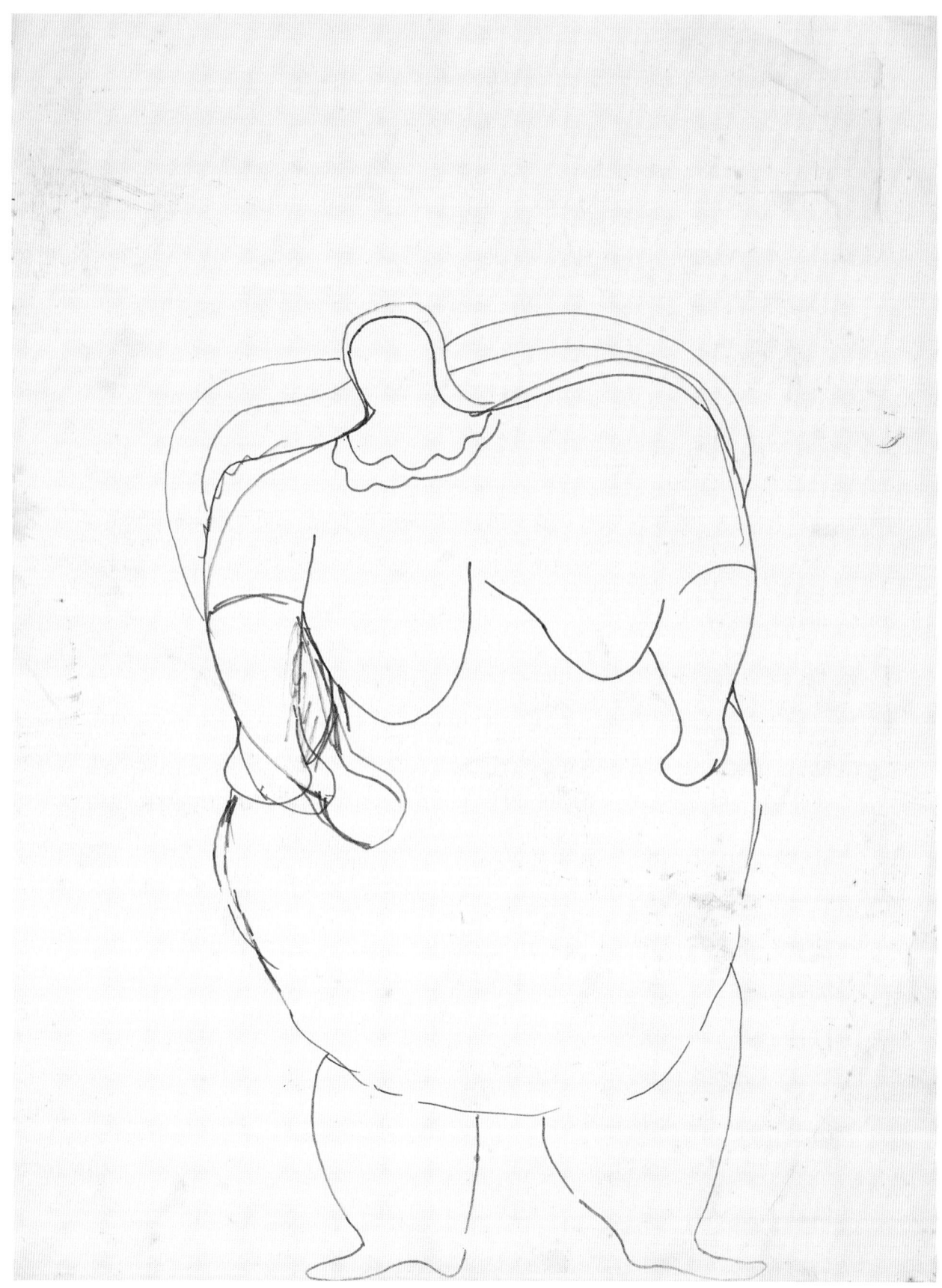

Femme (Woman), 1960s
Black felt-tip pen on paper
15 $^7/_8$ x 11 $^{13}/_{16}$ inches (40.4 x 30 cm)

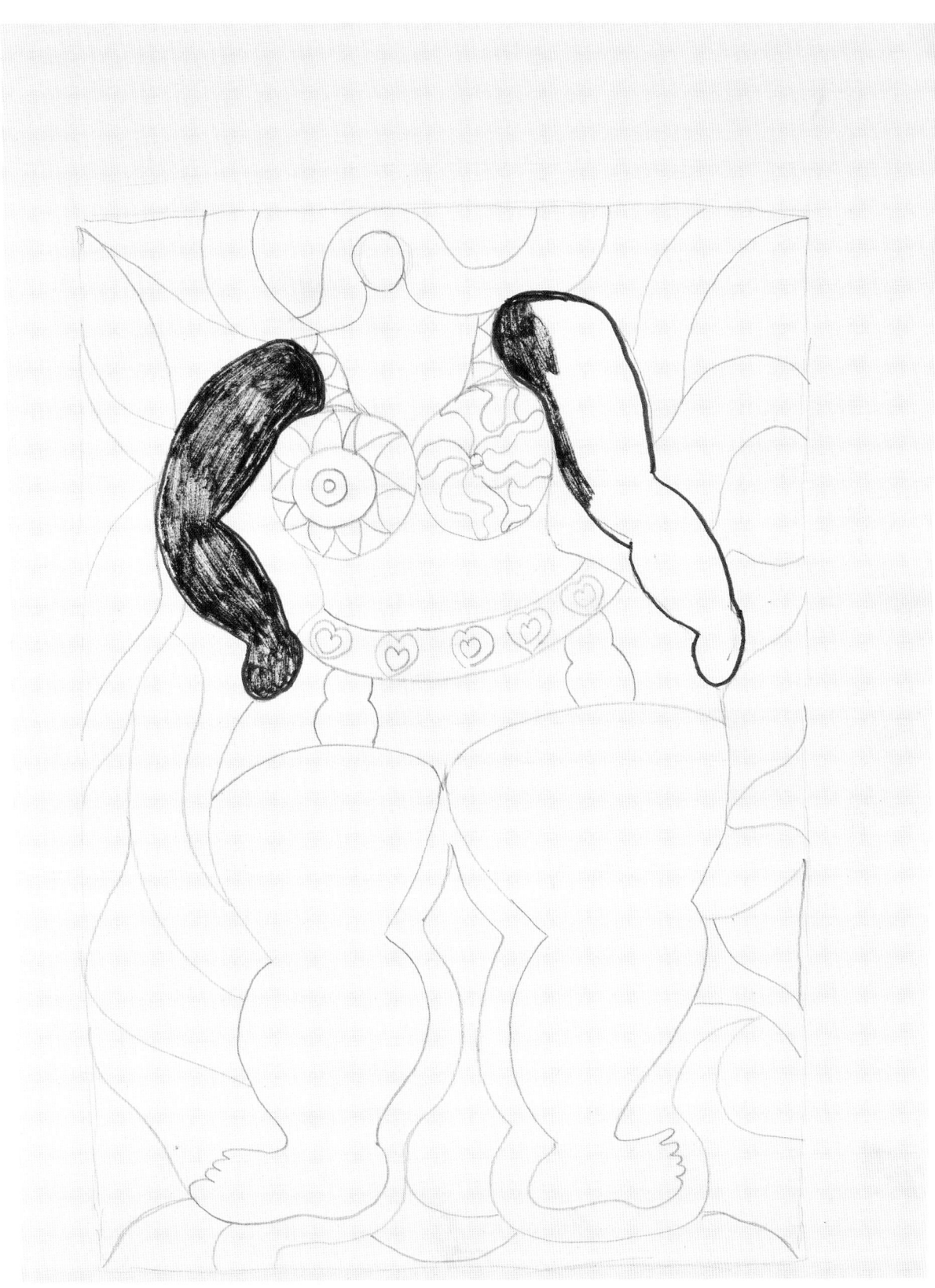

Nana couchée (Nana Lying Down), n.d.
Black felt-tip pen, black pastel on paper (spiral bound book)
10 $^{15}/_{16}$ x 8 $^{7}/_{16}$ inches (27.8 x 21.4 cm)

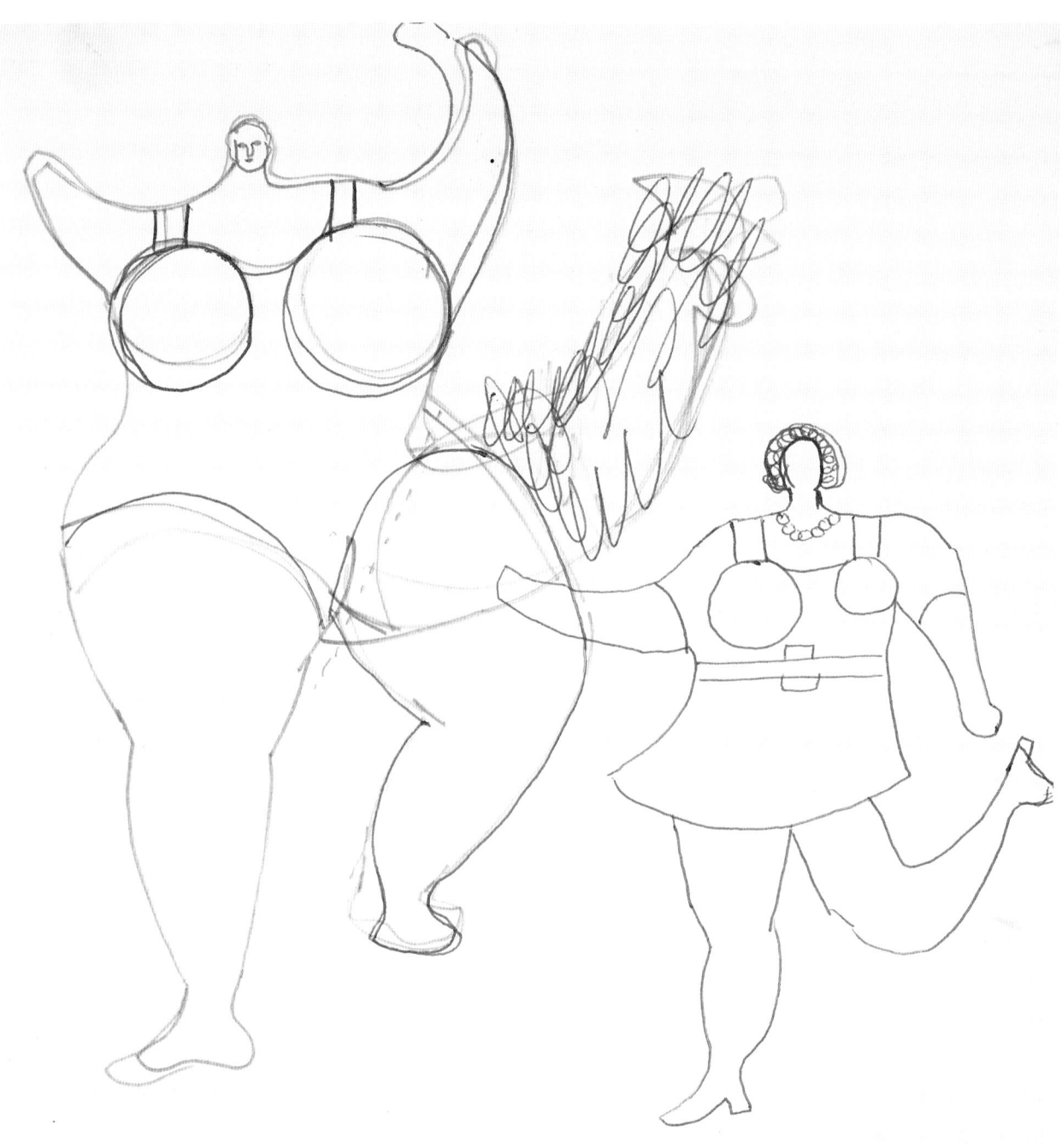

Sketchbook page, n.d.
Marker, pencil, and crayon on paper (spiral bound book)
10 $^{13}/_{16}$ x 8 $^{1}/_{4}$ inches (27.5 x 21 cm)

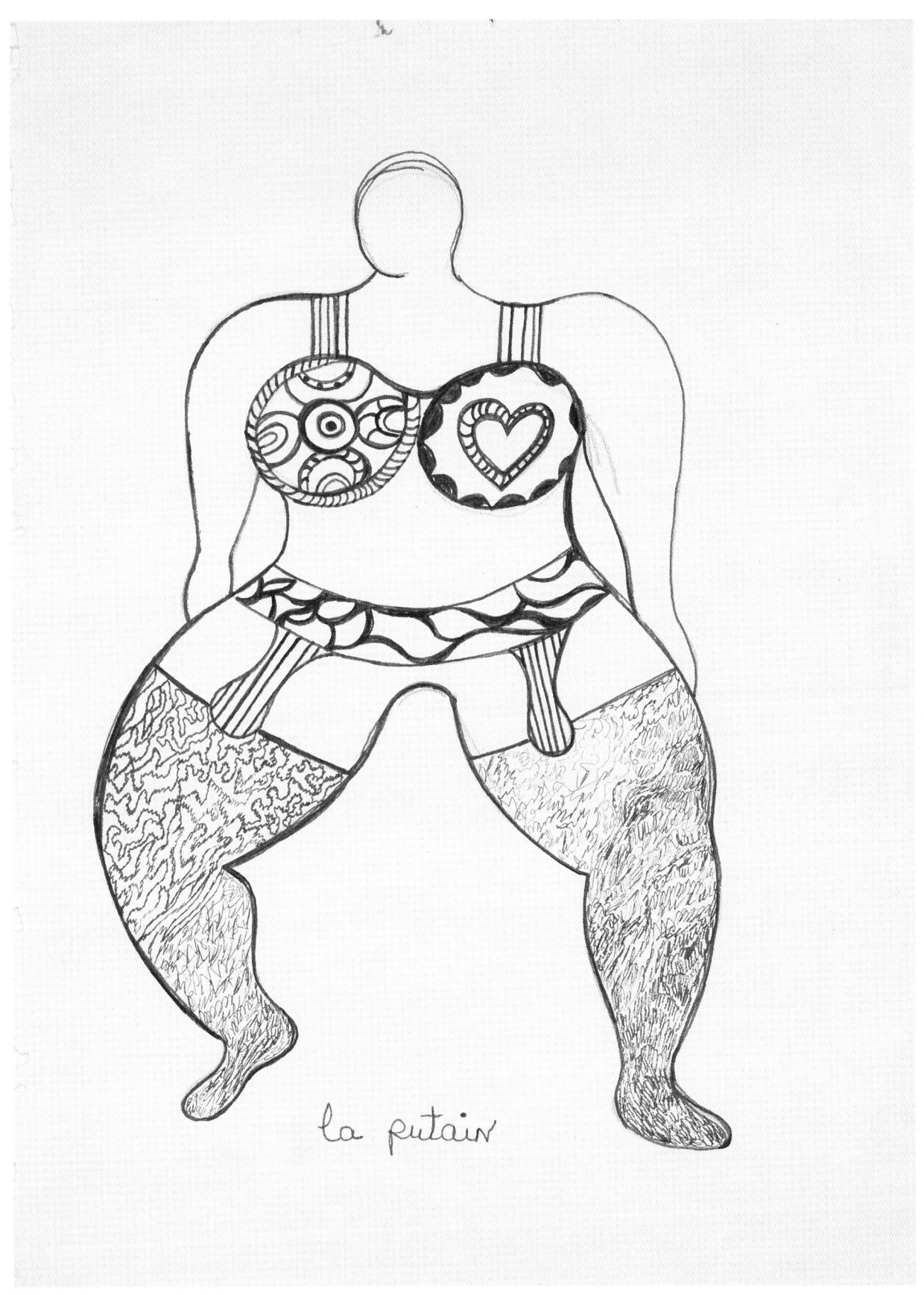

La putain (The Whore), 1960s
Felt-tip pen and black pencil on paper
12 $^{7}/_{16}$ x 8 $^{13}/_{16}$ inches (31.6 x 22.4 cm)

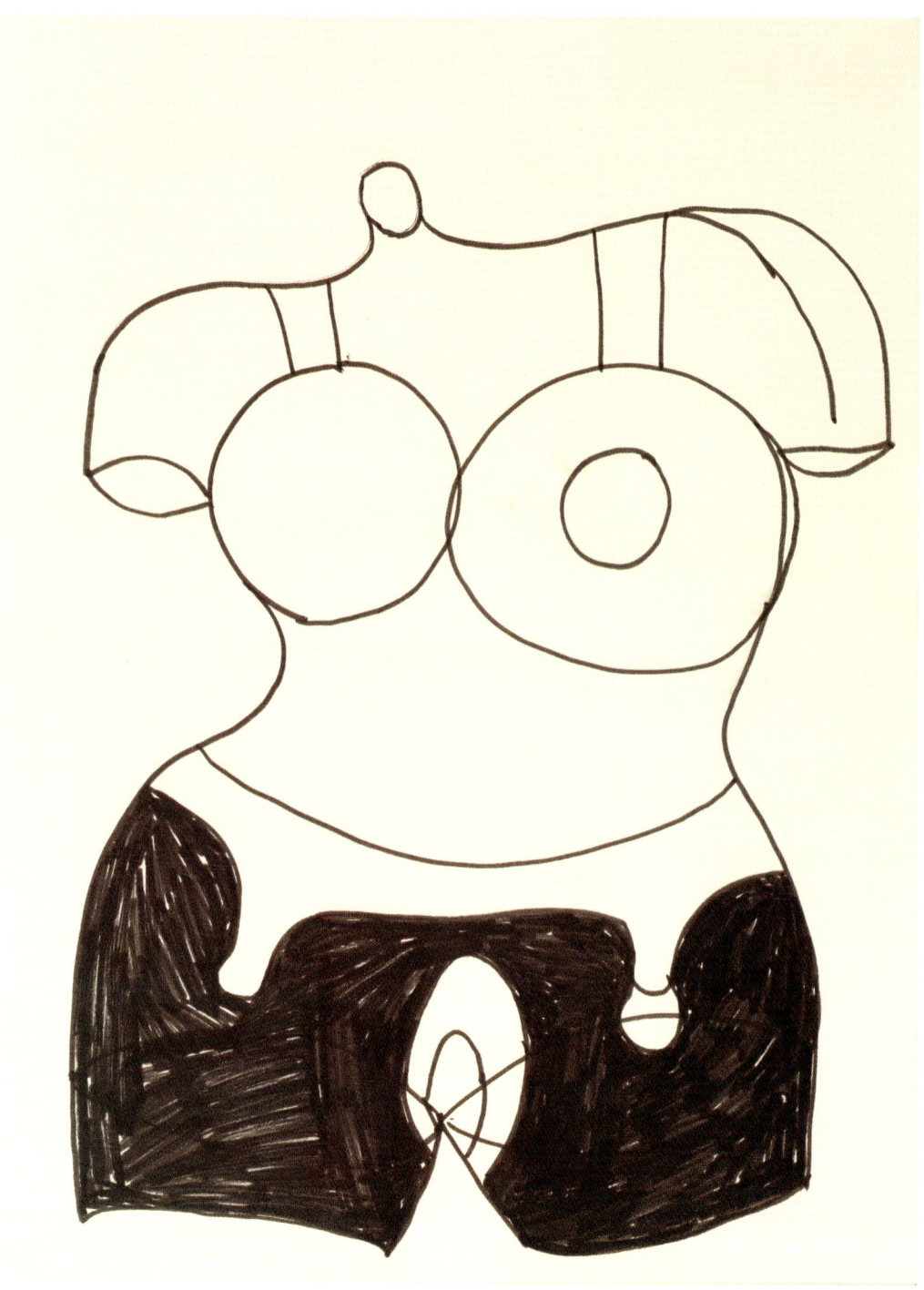

Nana sans bras (Nana without Arms), n.d.
Black felt-tip pen on paper (spiral bound book)
11 x 9 $\frac{1}{16}$ inches (28 x 23 cm)

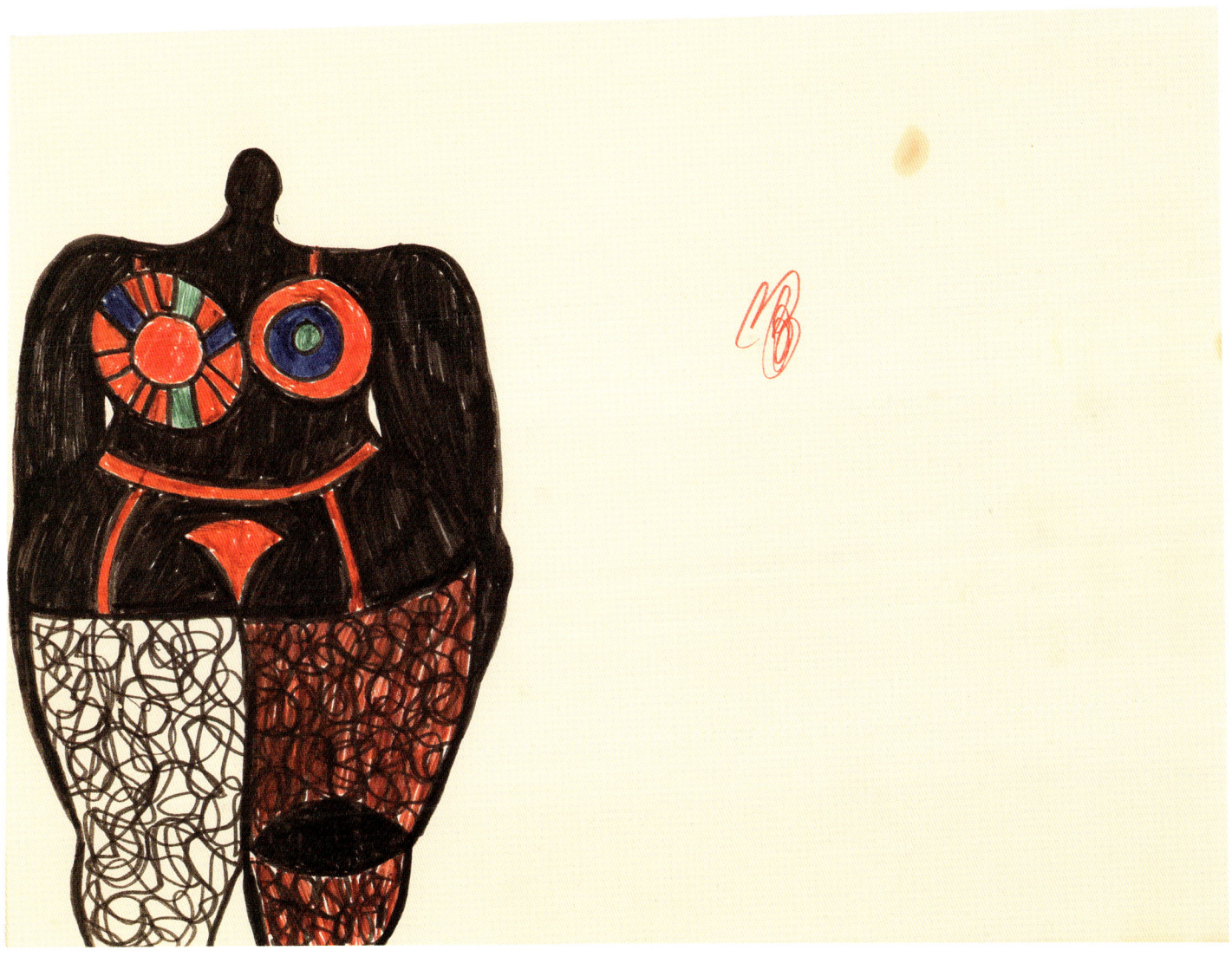

Nana, n.d.
Felt-tip pen on paper (spiral bound book)
8 $^7/_{16}$ x 10 $^{15}/_{16}$ inches (21.4 x 27.8 cm)

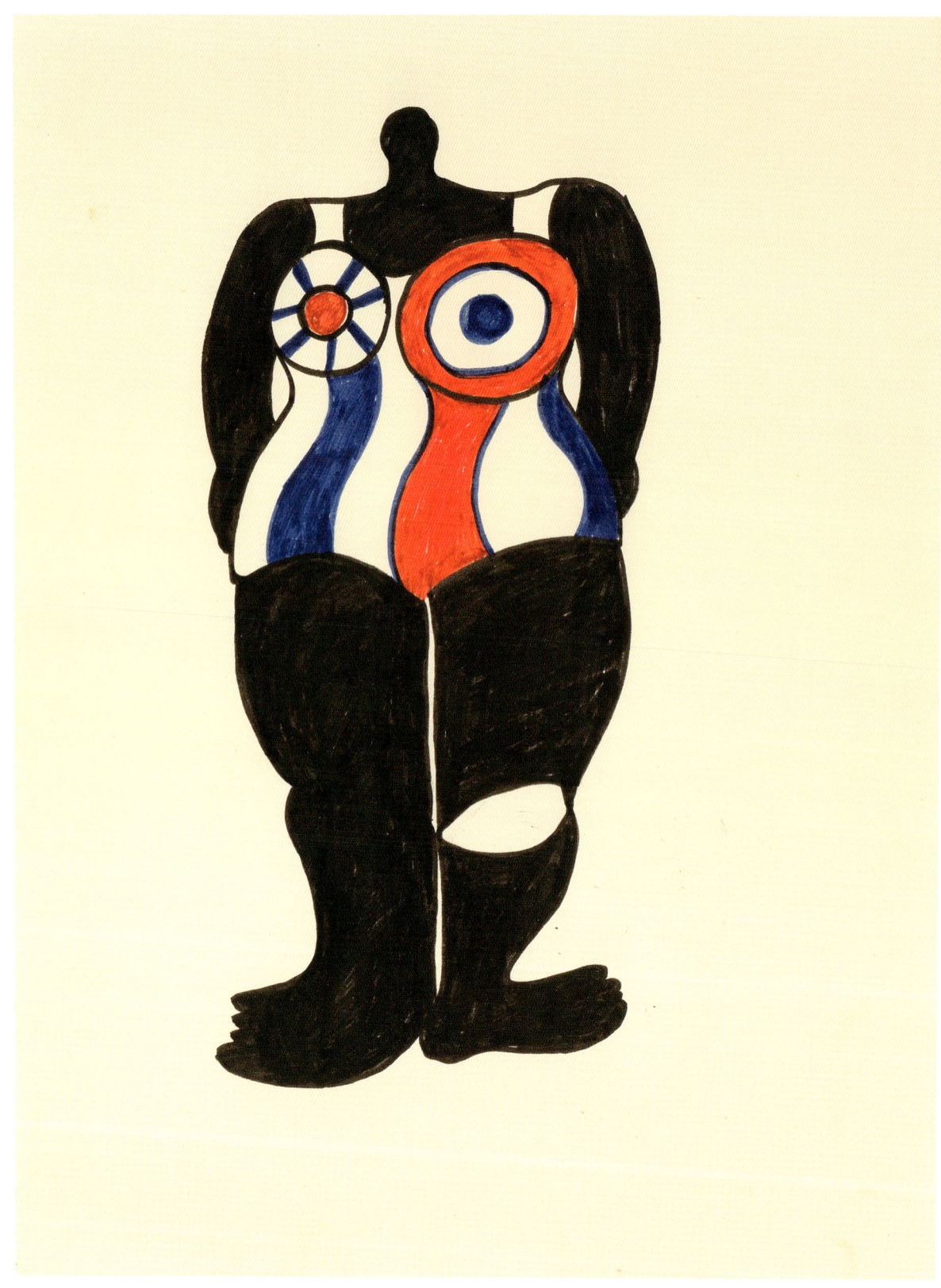

Bathing Beauty, 1960s
Felt-tip pen on paper (spiral bound book)
11 x 9 $\frac{1}{16}$ inches (28 x 23 cm)

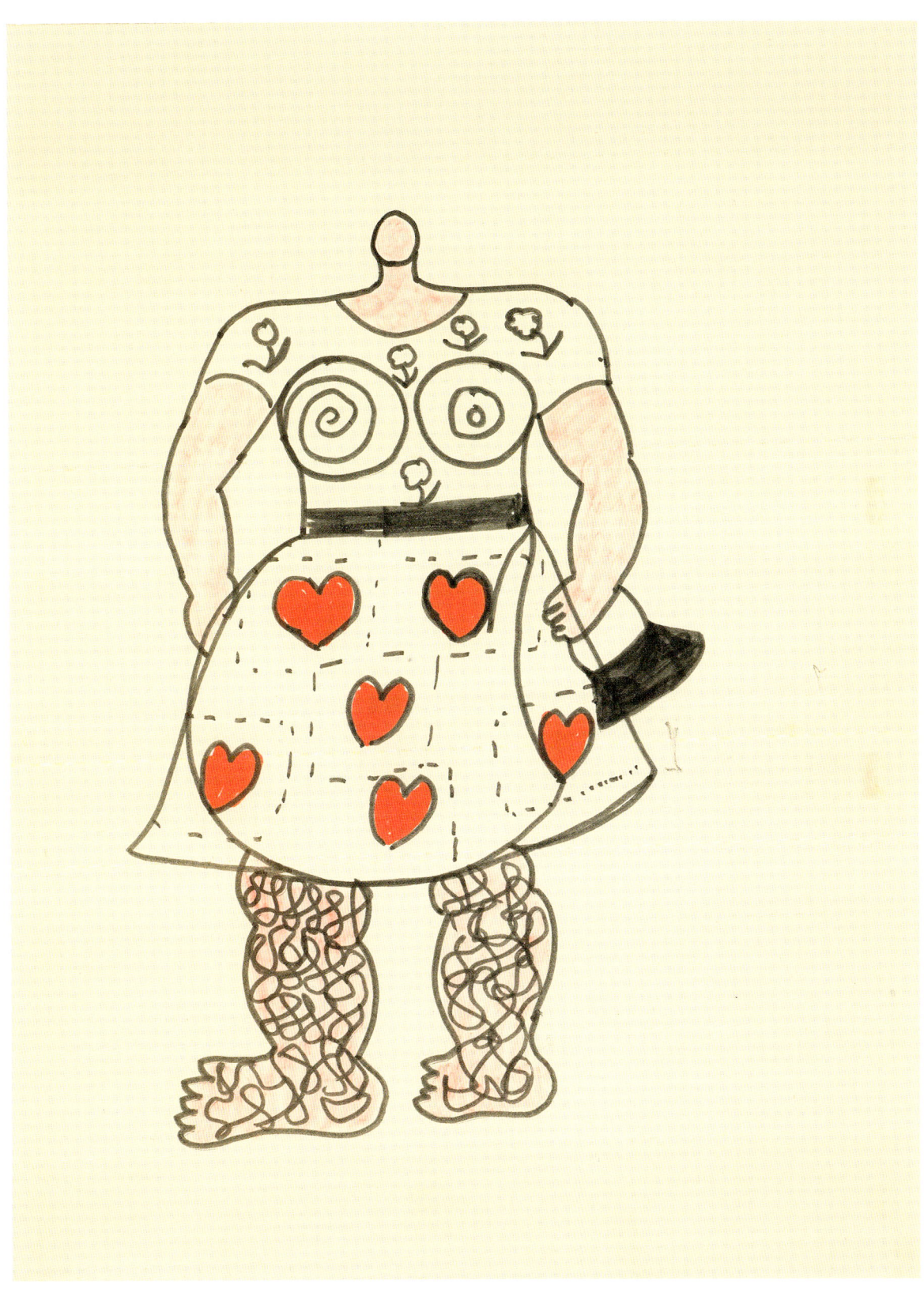

Nana & sac, jupe coeurs rouges (Nana & Purse, Red Hearts Skirt), 1960s
Felt-tip pen on paper (spiral bound book)
11 x 9 ¹/₁₆ inches (28 x 23 cm)

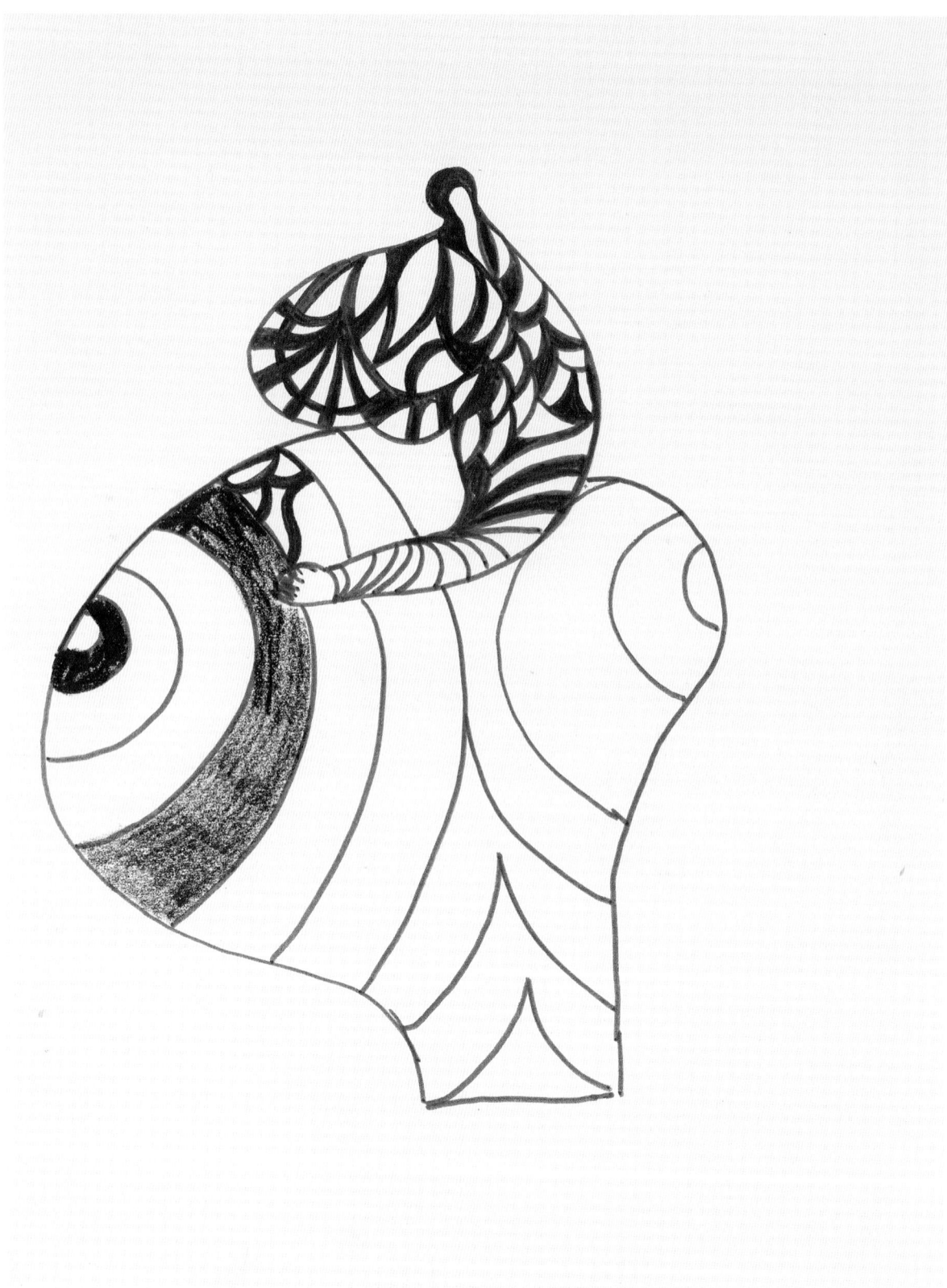

Nana enceinte (Pregnant Nana), n.d.
Pastel and felt-tip pen on paper (spiral bound book)
10 ¹⁵/₁₆ x 8 ⁷/₁₆ inches (27.8 x 21.4 cm)

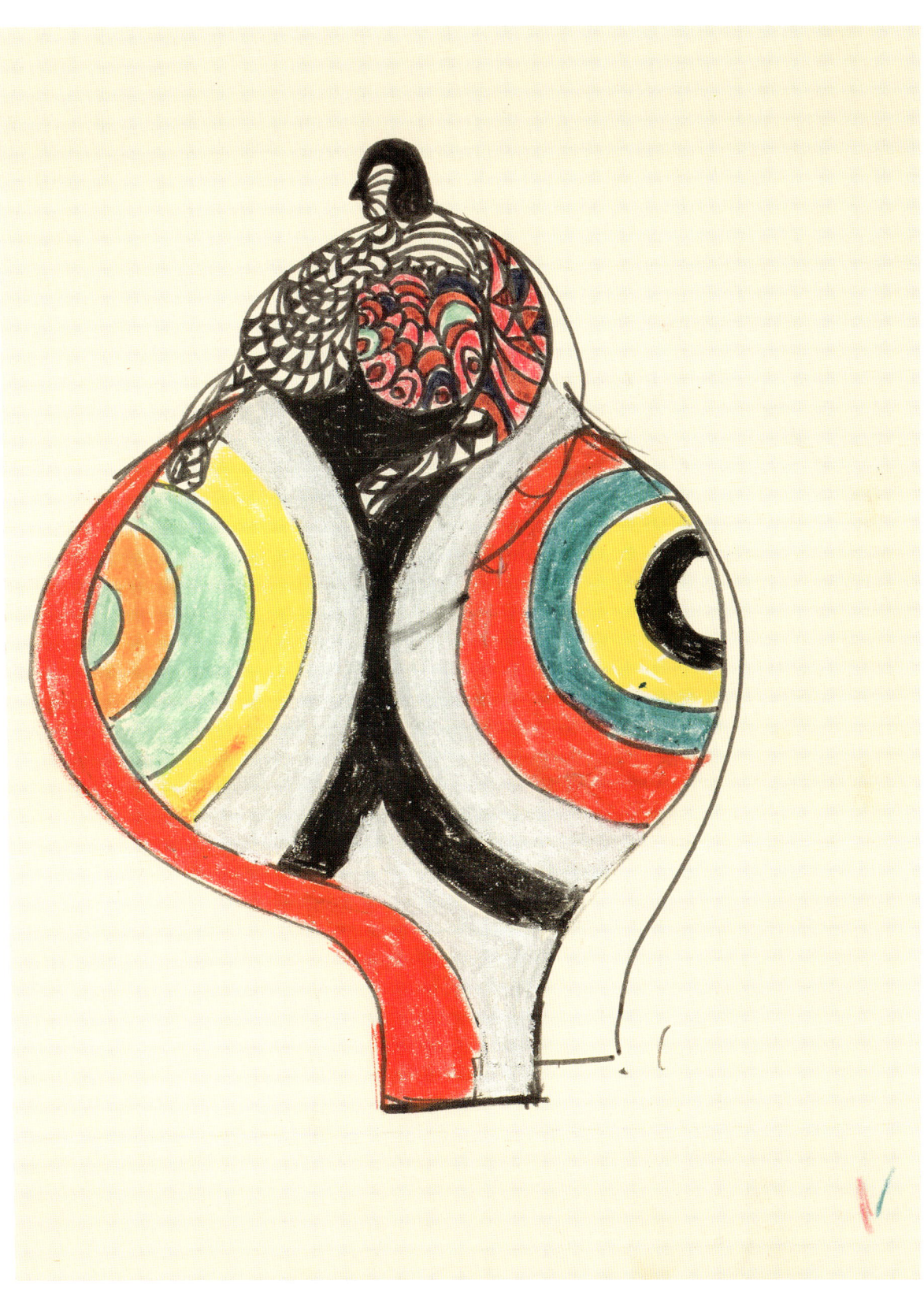

Nana enceinte (Pregnant Nana), n.d.
Pastel and felt-tip pen on paper (spiral bound book)
10 $^{15}/_{16}$ x 8 $^{7}/_{16}$ inches (27.8 x 21.4 cm)

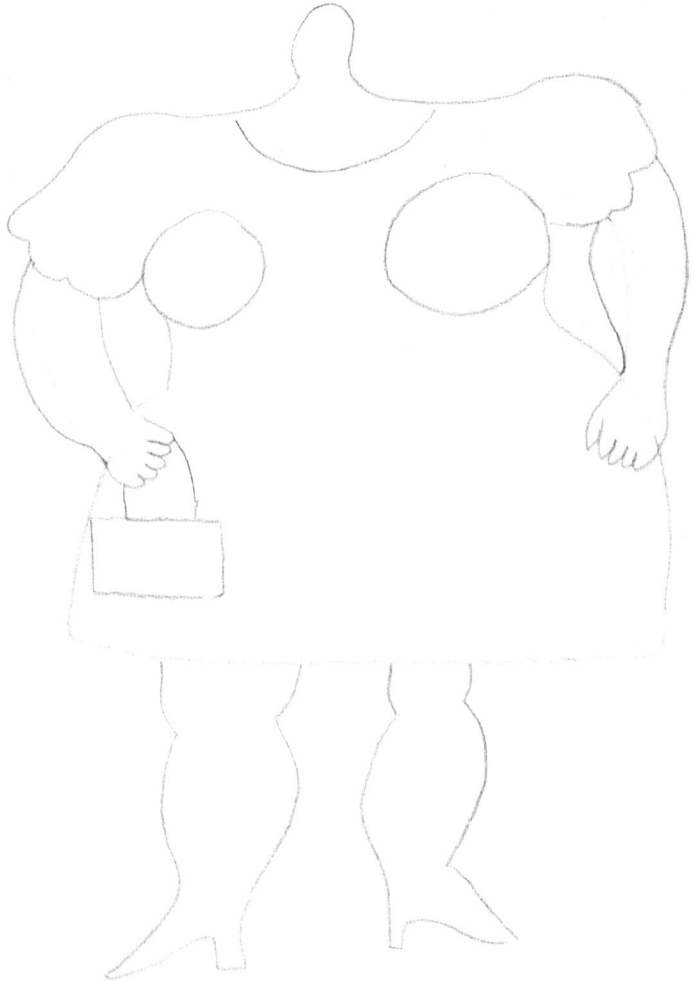

My love do you like my new dress?, 1970s
Pencil on paper
13 1/16 x 10 3/4 inches (33.1 x 27.3 cm)

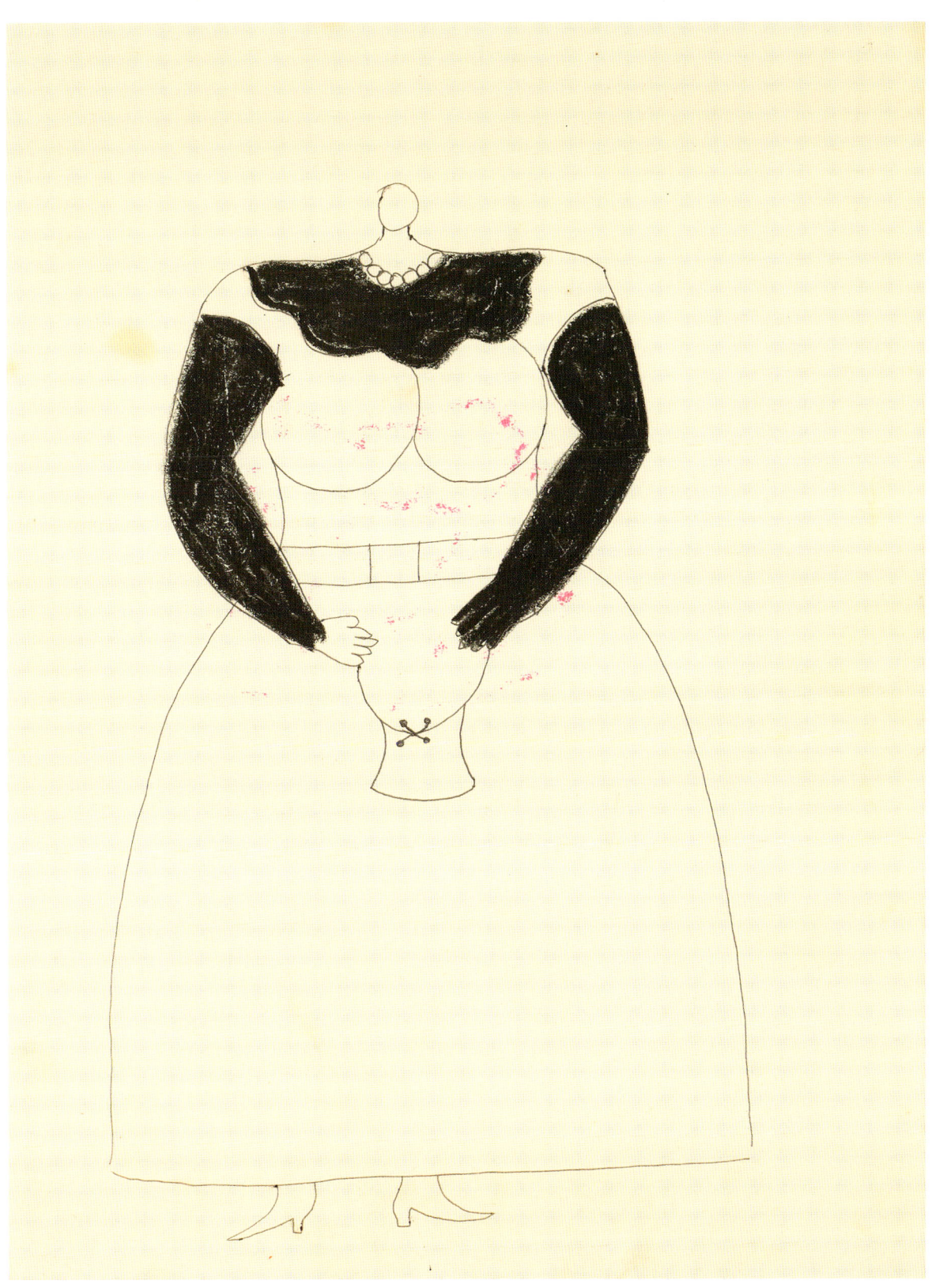

Nana & sac (Nana & Purse), n.d.
Black felt-tip pen, black pastel on paper (spiral bound book)
10 $^{15}/_{16}$ x 8 $^{7}/_{16}$ inches (27.8 x 21.4 cm)

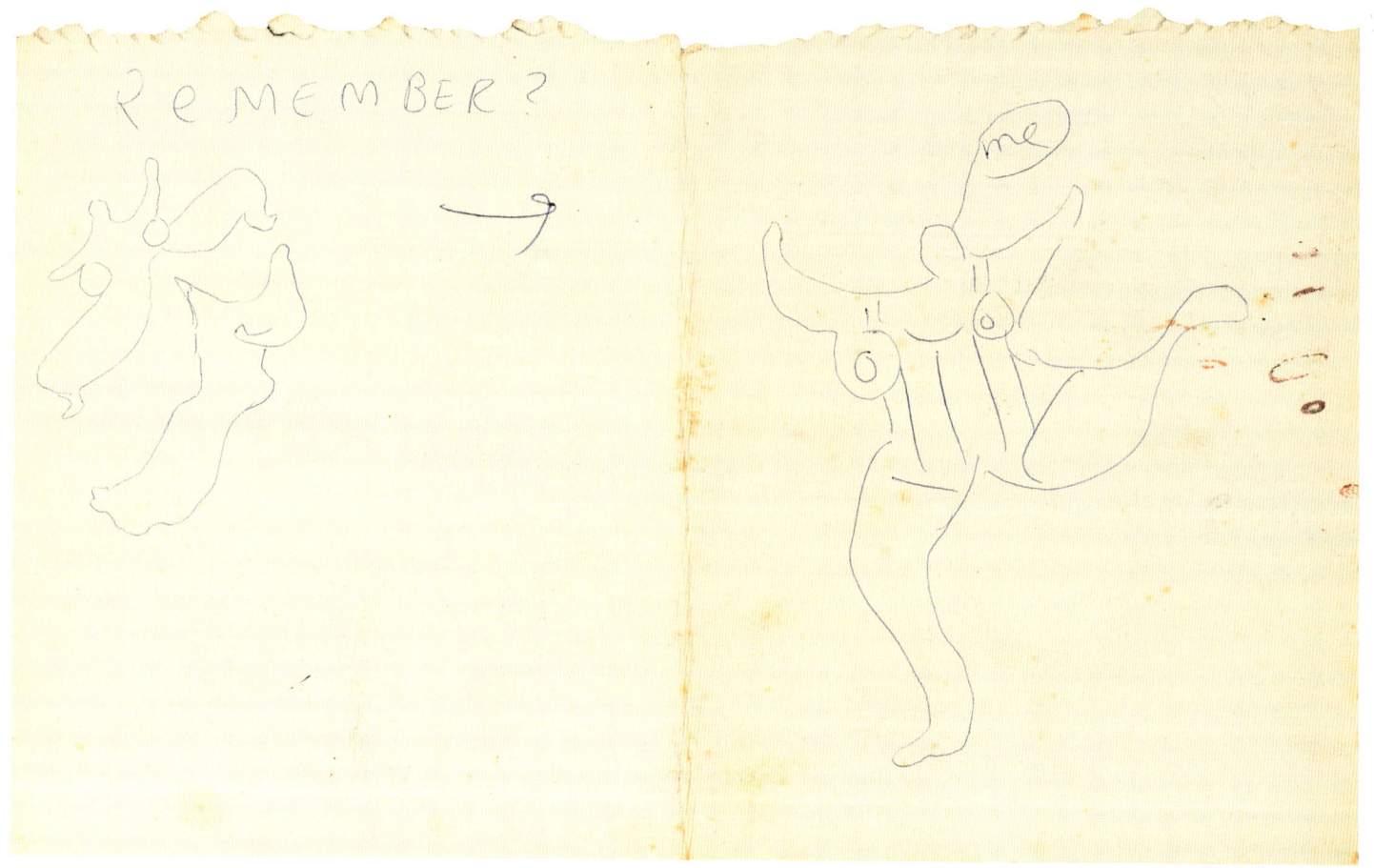

Remember? Me, c. 1970
Blue pen on paper (spiral bound book)
8 ¹/₄ x 13 inches (21 x 33 cm)

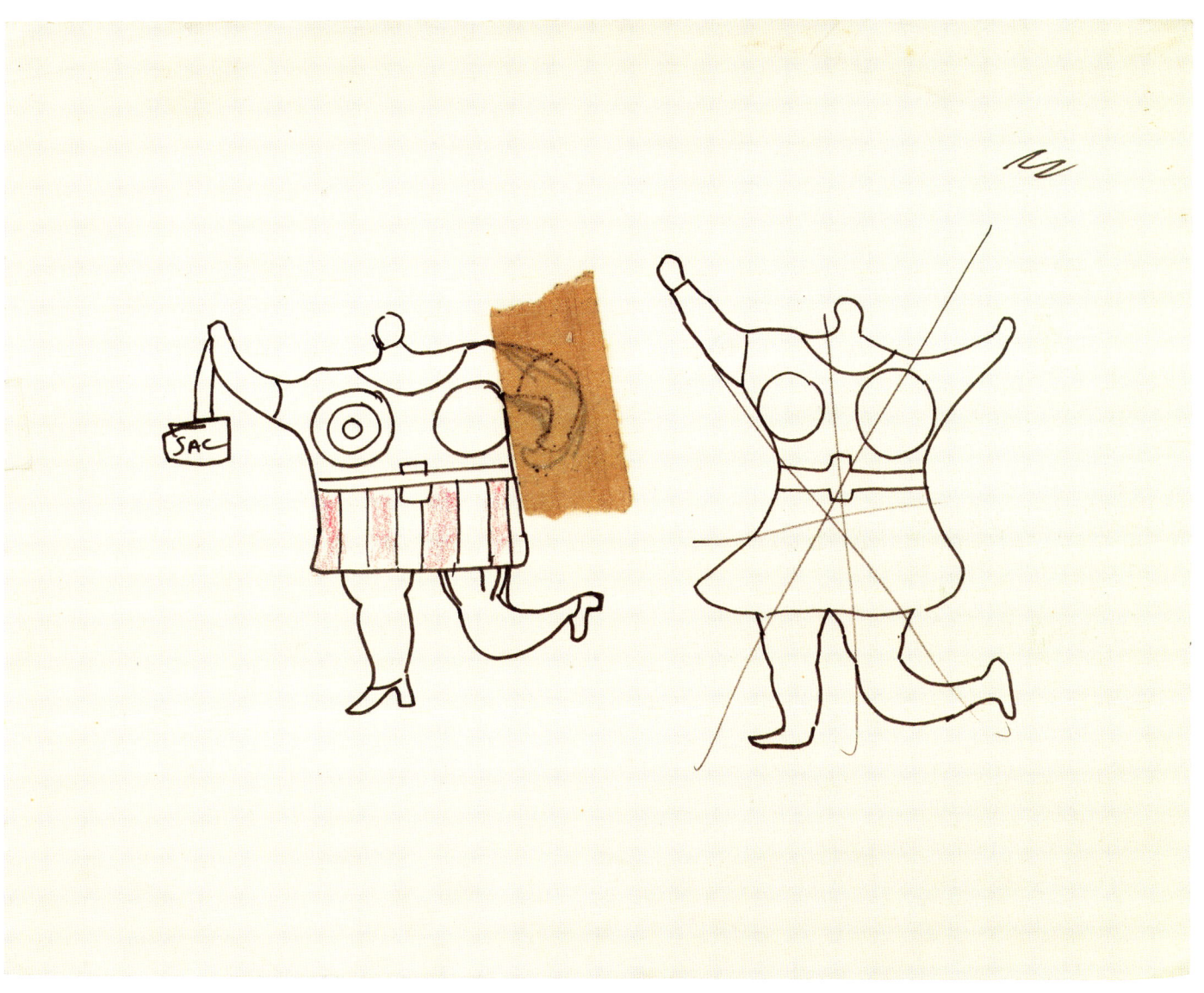

2 Nanas [Nana sac au main] (2 Nanas [Nana with Handbag]), 1960s
Black felt-tip pen, pink pastel, and tape on paper (spiral bound book)
10 $^5/_8$ x 13 $^{11}/_{16}$ inches (27 x 34.8 cm)

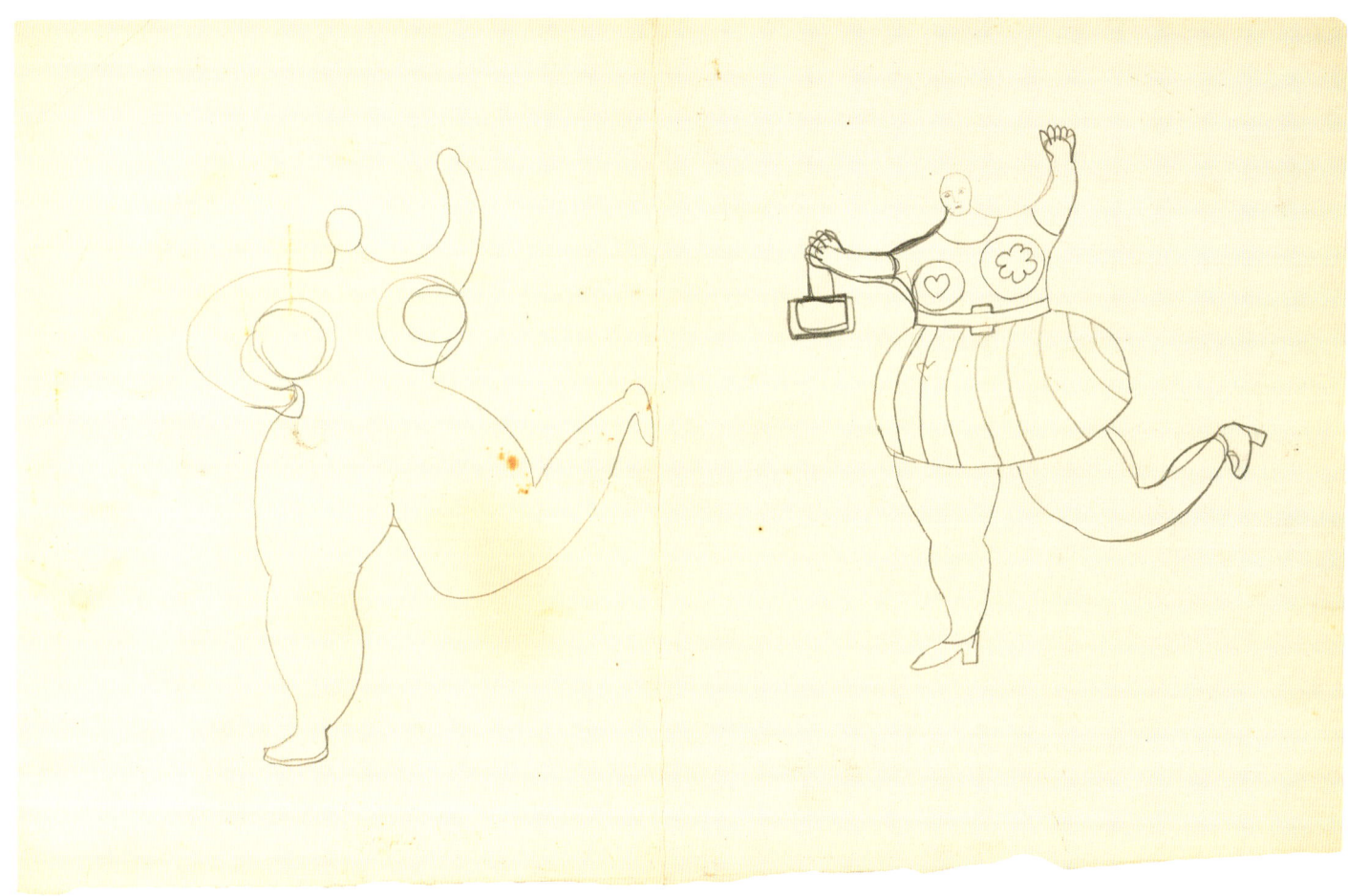

Nanas courant [2 d'un côté de la feuille, une de l'autre]
(Nanas Running [Two on one side of the sheet, one on the other], n.d.
Black pencil on paper (spiral bound book)
12 $^1/_2$ x 19 $^1/_2$ inches (31.8 x 49.5 cm)

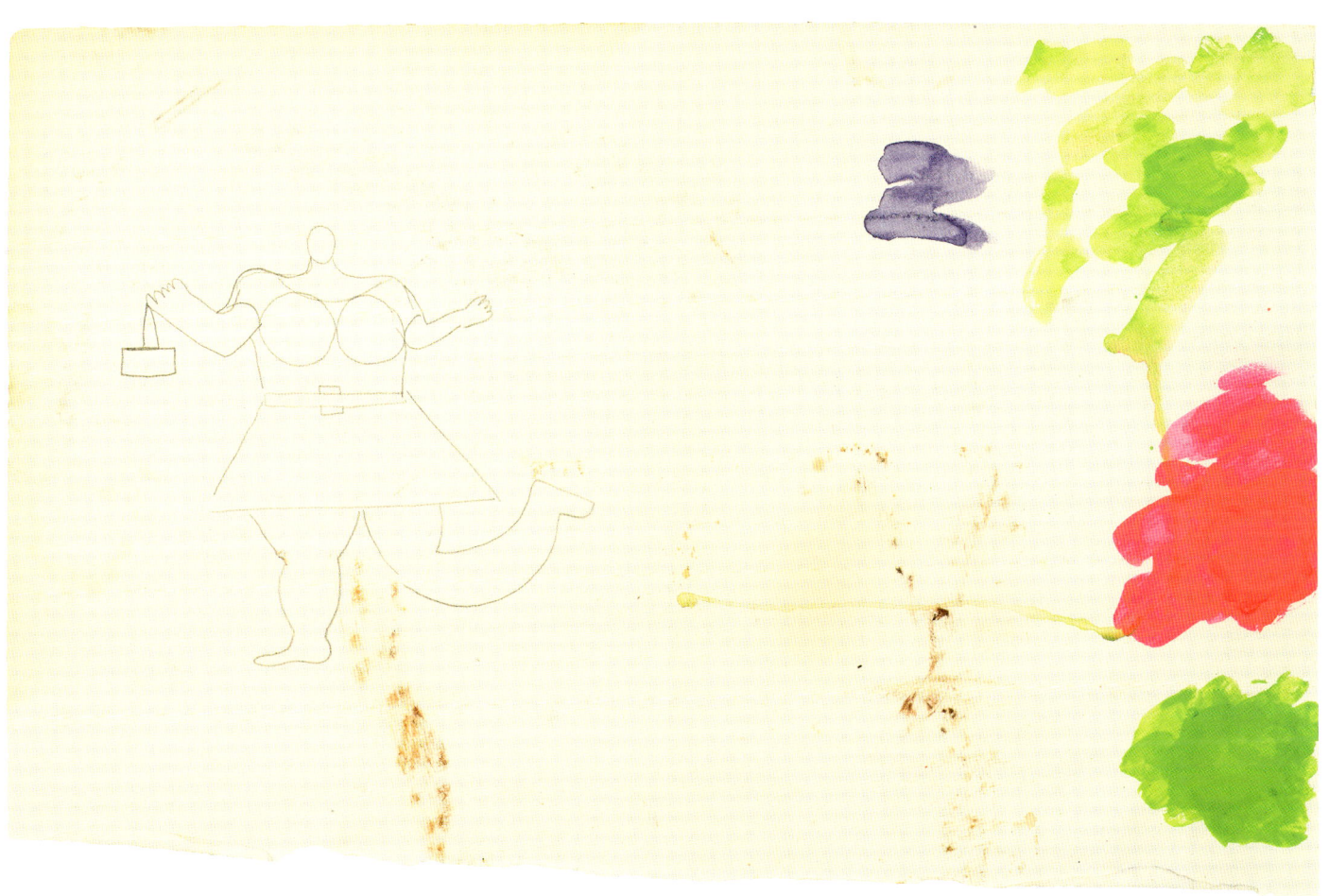

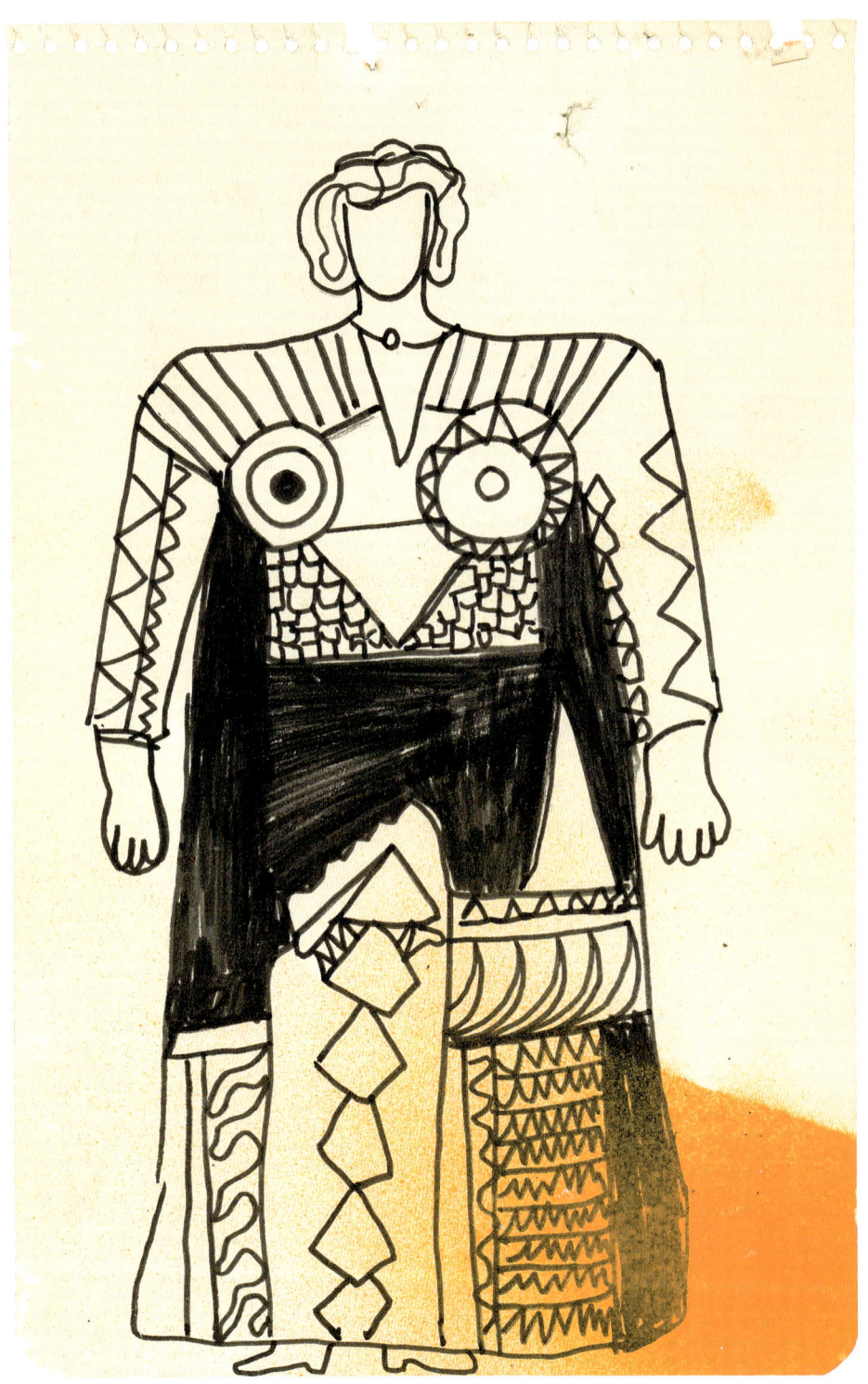

Femme (Woman), n.d.
Black felt-tip pen and orange paint stain on paper
8 ¹¹/₁₆ x 5 ¹/₂ inches (22 x 14 cm)

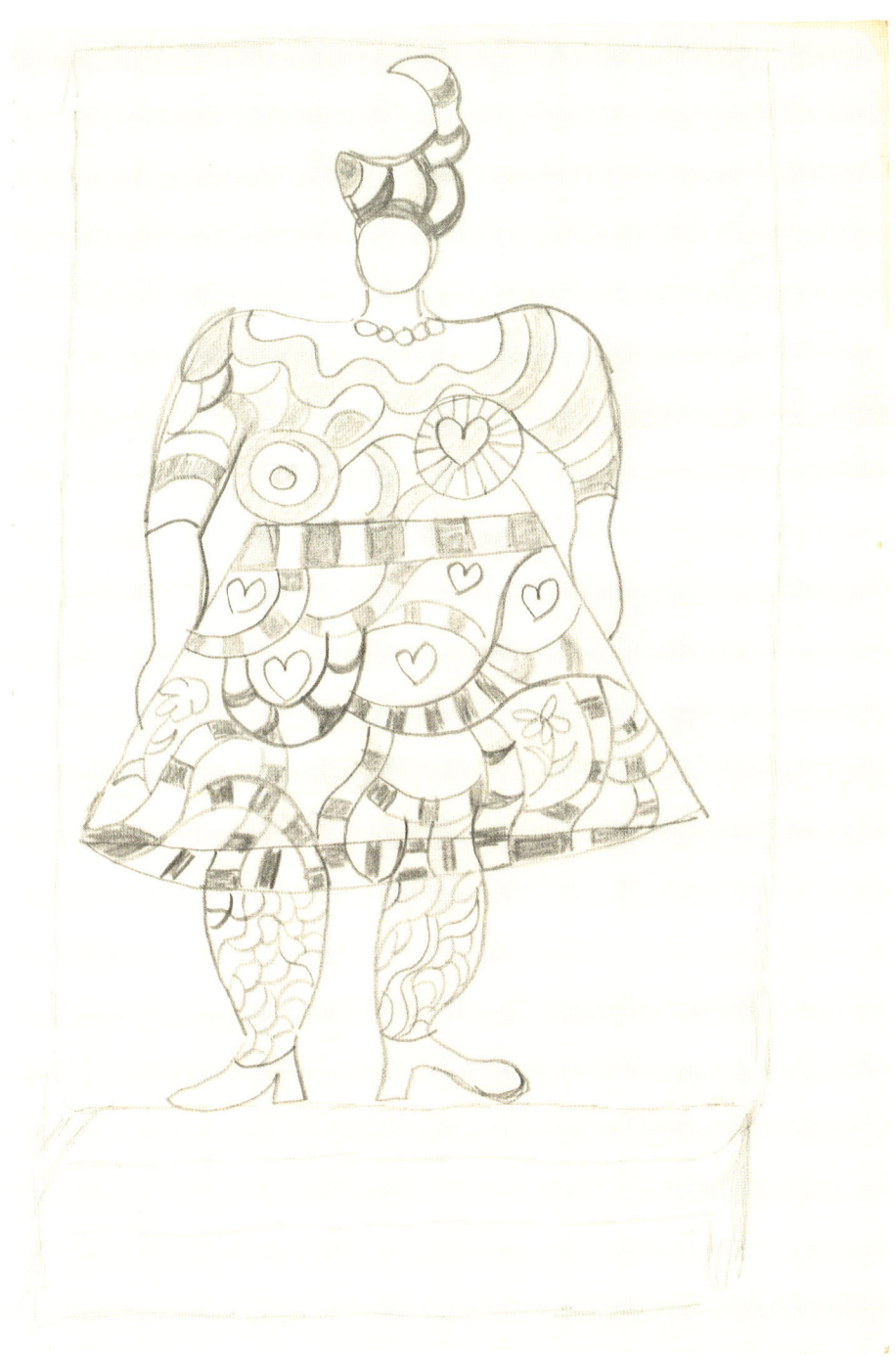

Page from Sennelier Paris Dessin sketchbook, n.d.
Pencil on white cardboard (spiral bound book)
6 $^5/_{16}$ x 4 $^5/_{16}$ inches (16 x 11 cm)

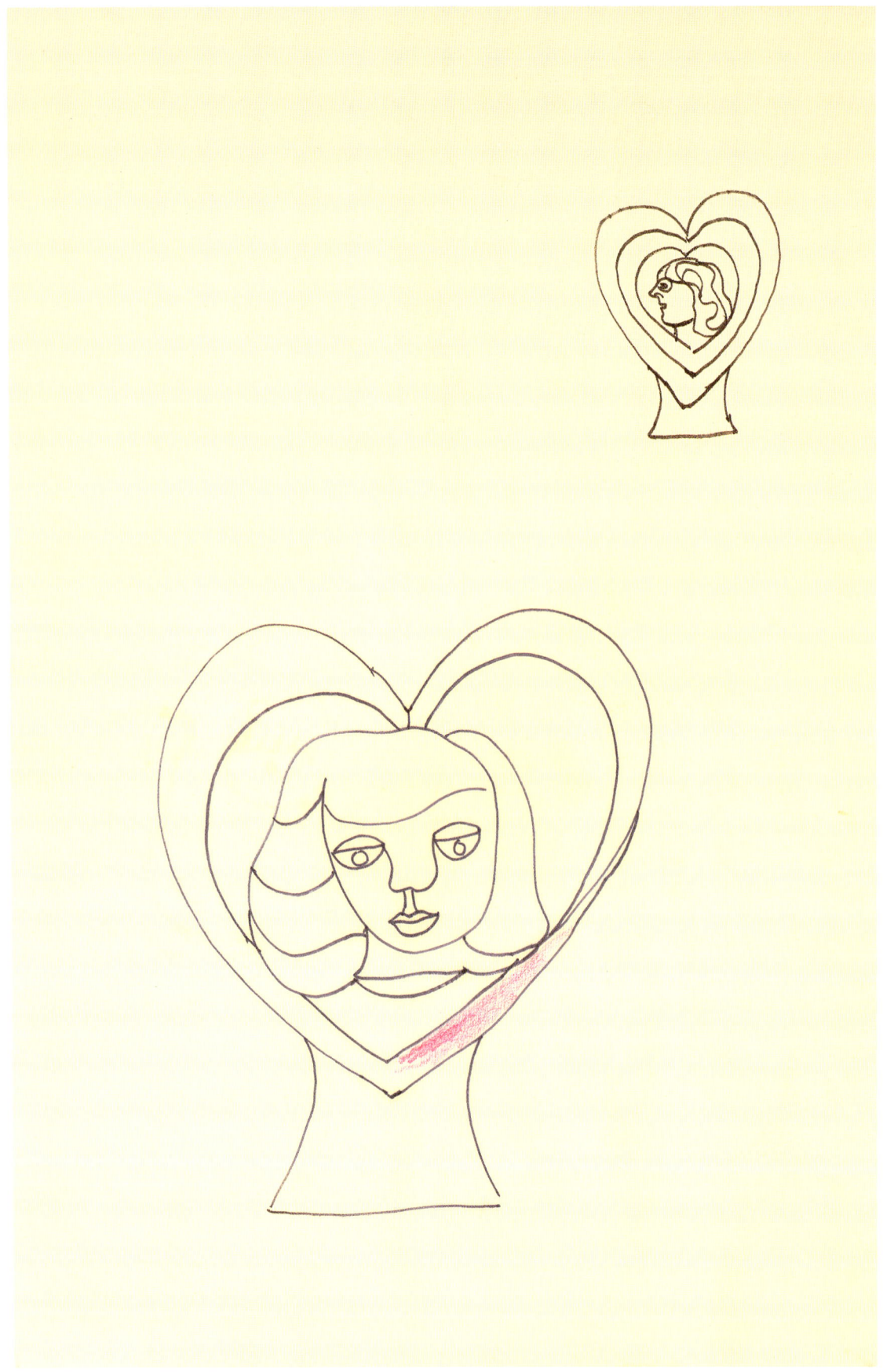

Page from Mal- u. Zeichenblock sketchbook, c. 1970
Colored crayon, watercolor, and black felt-tip pen on paper (spiral bound book)
18 $^7/_8$ x 12 $^5/_8$ inches (48 x 32 cm)

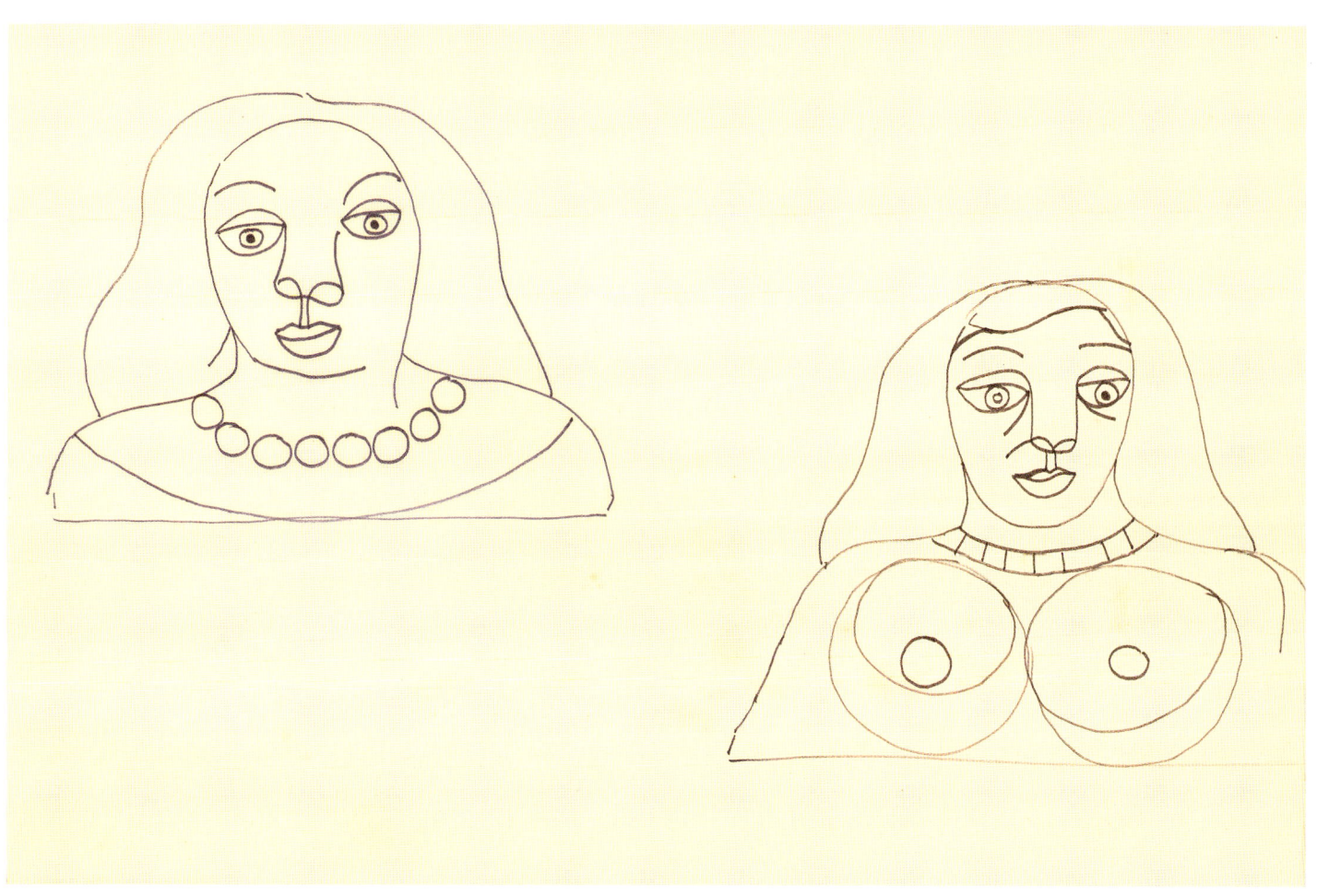

Page from Mal- u. Zeichenblock sketchbook, c. 1970
Felt-tip pen on paper (spiral bound book)
12 $^5/_8$ x 18 $^5/_8$ inches (32 x 48 cm)

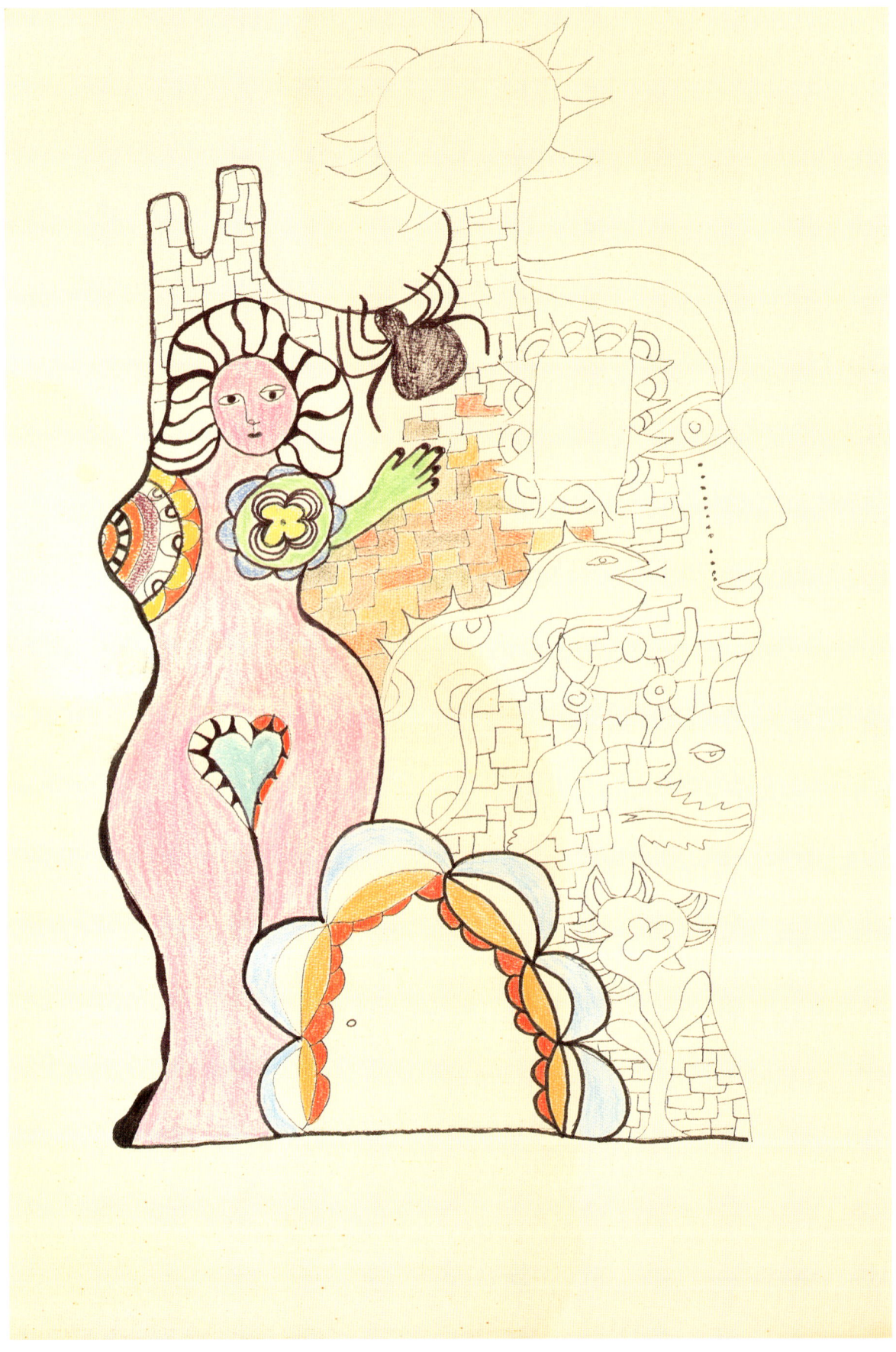

Page from Zeichenblock sketchbook (*Dannemois*), c. 1968–1970
Black felt-tip pen, fine-line pen, and colored crayon on paper (spiral bound book)
11 $^{13}/_{16}$ x 16 $^{9}/_{16}$ x $^{3}/_{16}$ inches (30 x 42 x 0.5 cm)

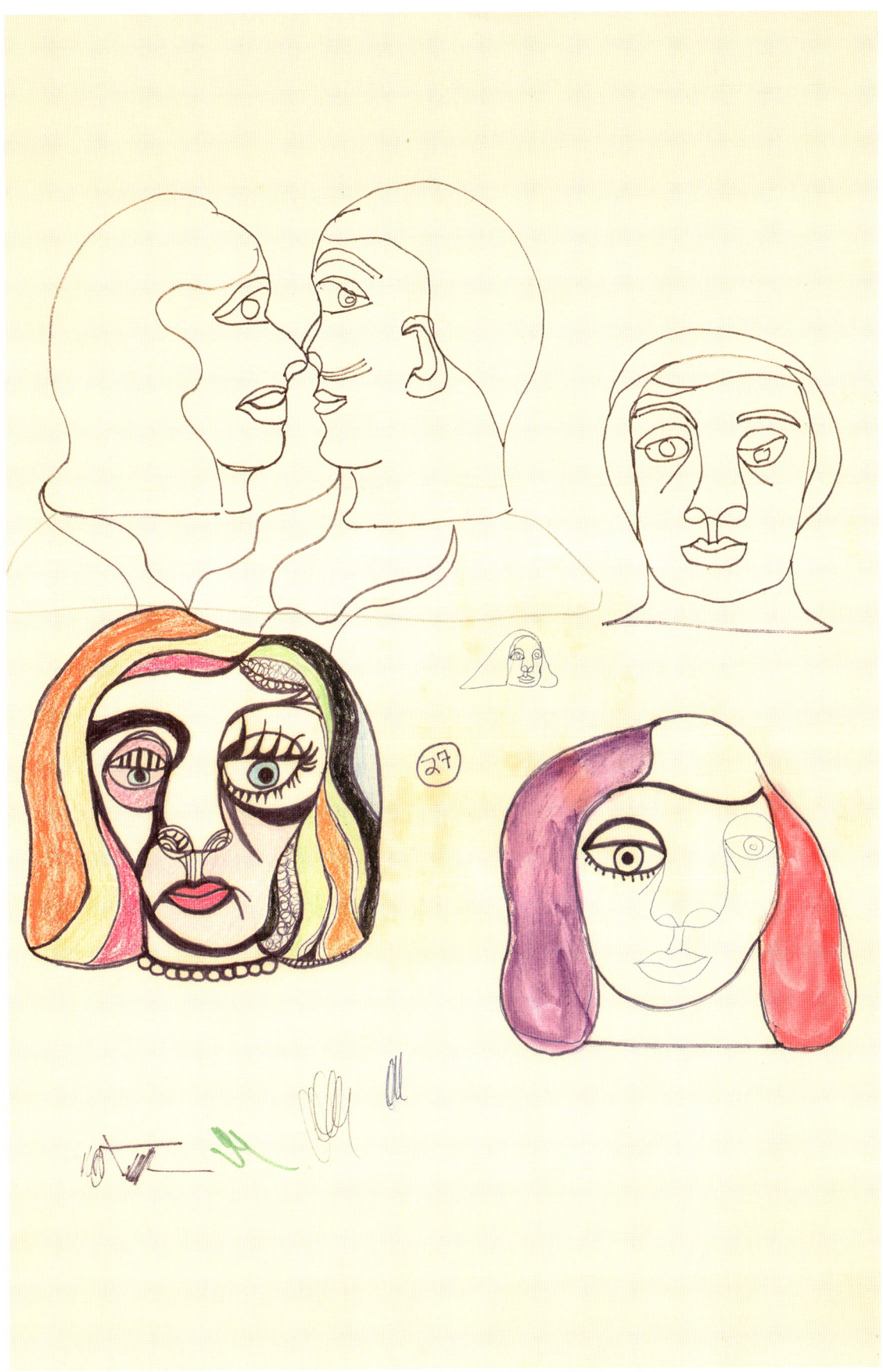

Page from Mal- u. Zeichenblock sketchbook, c. 1970
Colored crayon, watercolor, and black felt-tip pen on paper (spiral bound book)
18 $^7/_8$ x 12 $^5/_8$ inches (48 x 32 cm)

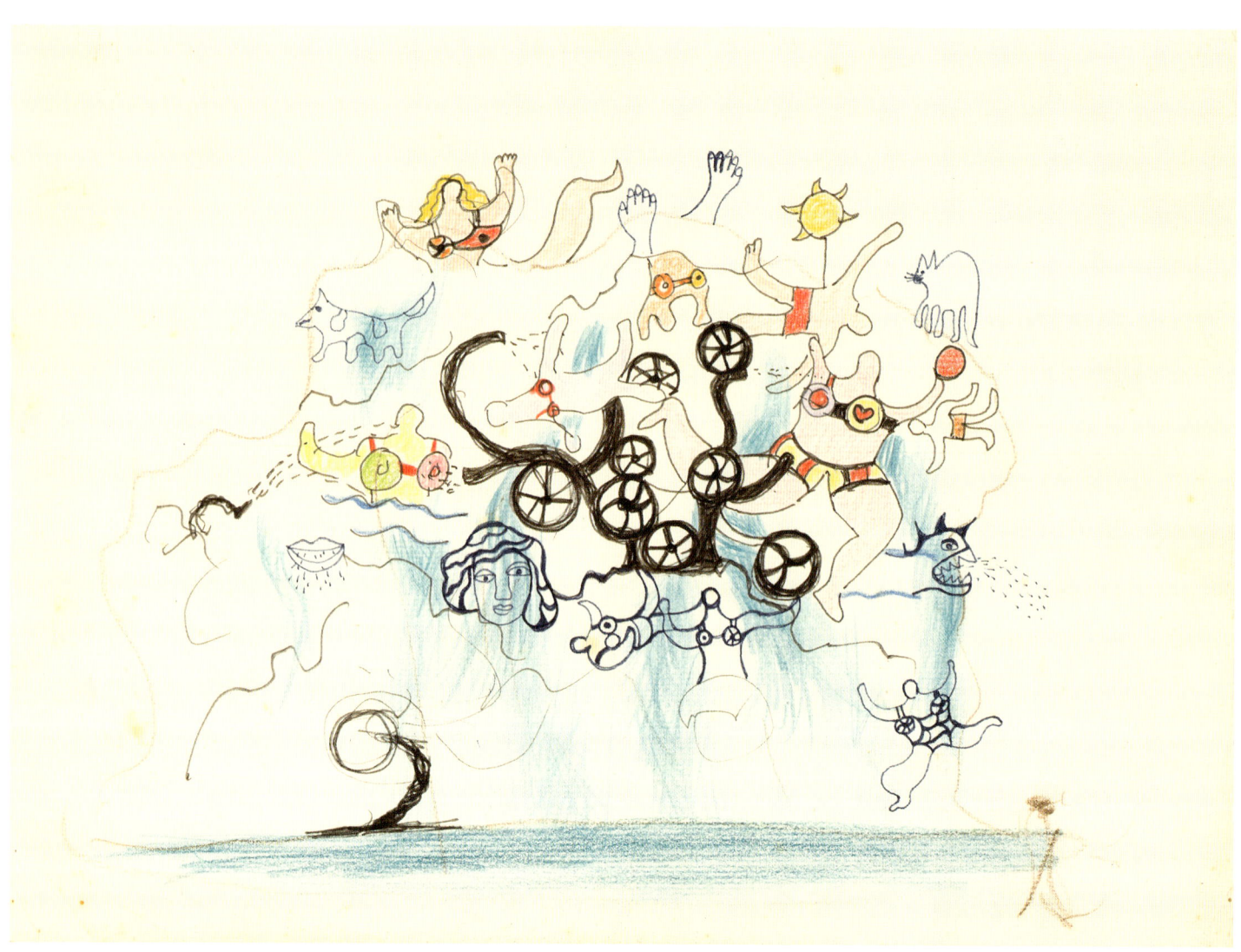

Fontaine Nana (Nana Fountain), *1978*
Marker, colored pencil, and pencil on paper (spiral boundbook)
7 ⁷/₈ x 11 inches (20 x 28 cm)

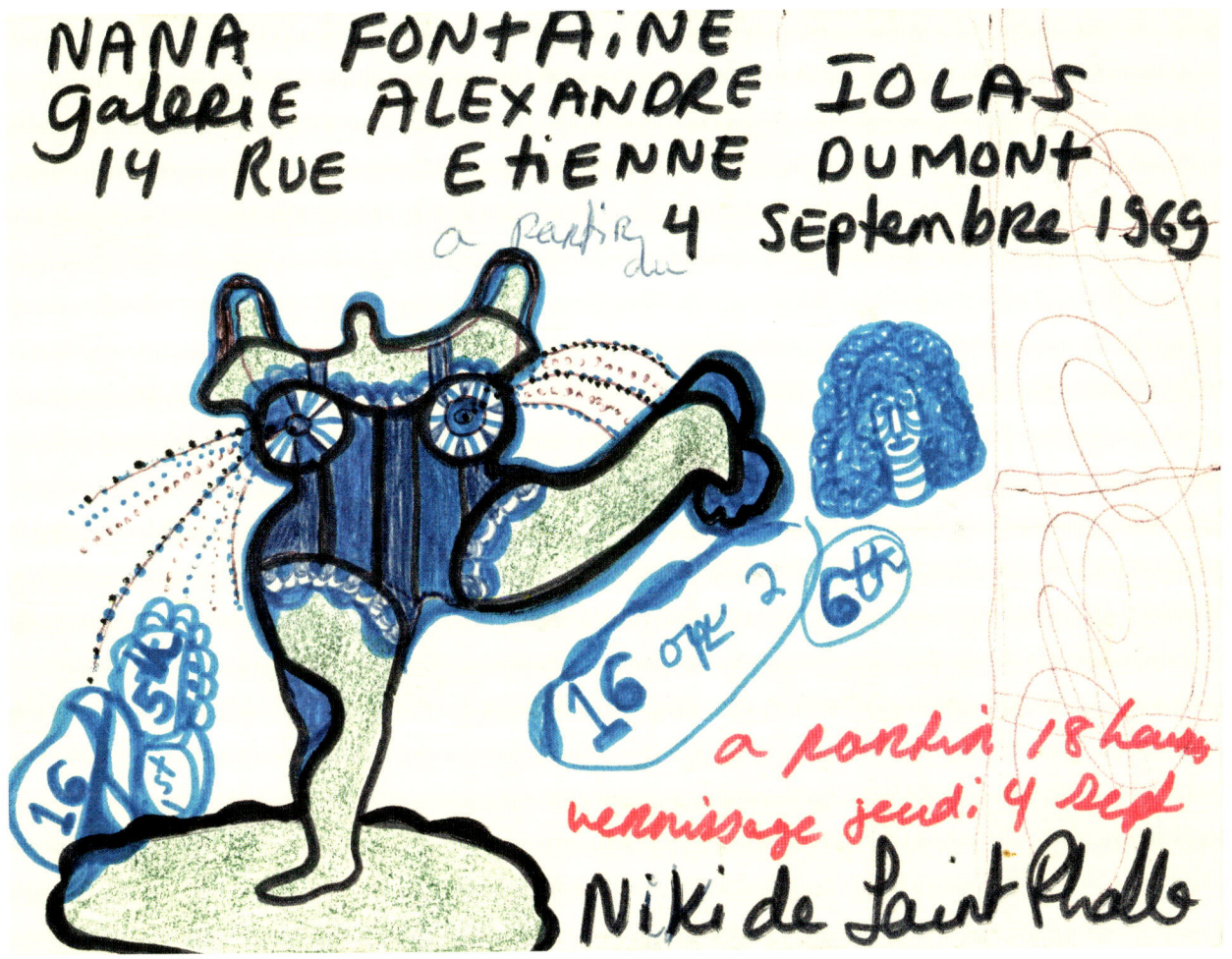

Esquisse pour carte nana fontaine (Sketch for nana fontaine card), c. 1969
Colored pencil, felt-tip pen on card
4 $^{15}/_{16}$ x 6 $^{1}/_{2}$ inches (12.5 x 16.5 cm)

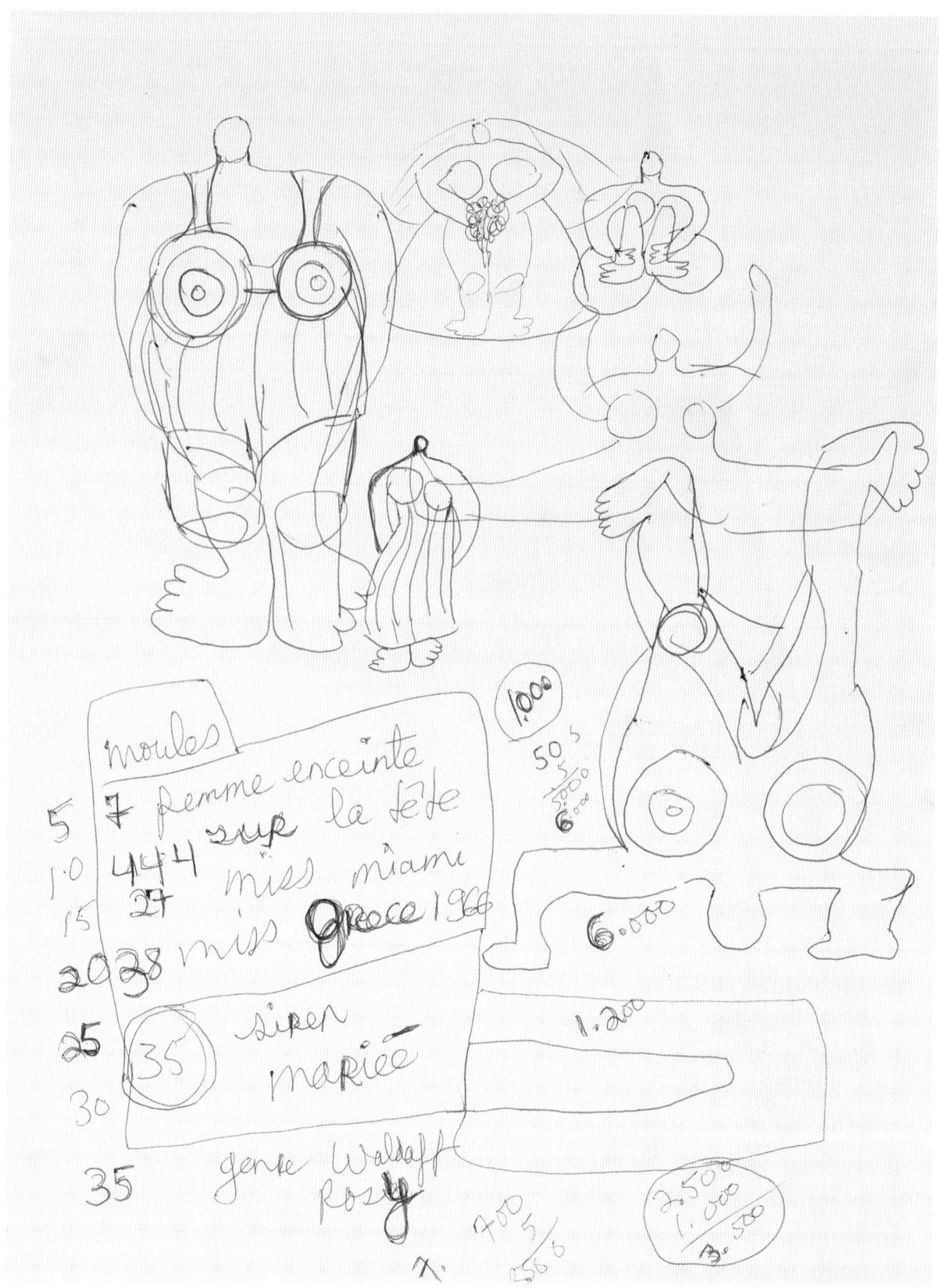

Moules... (Molds...), 1960s
Blue ballpoint pen on paper (spiral bound book)
11 x 9 ¹/₁₆ inches (28 x 23 cm)

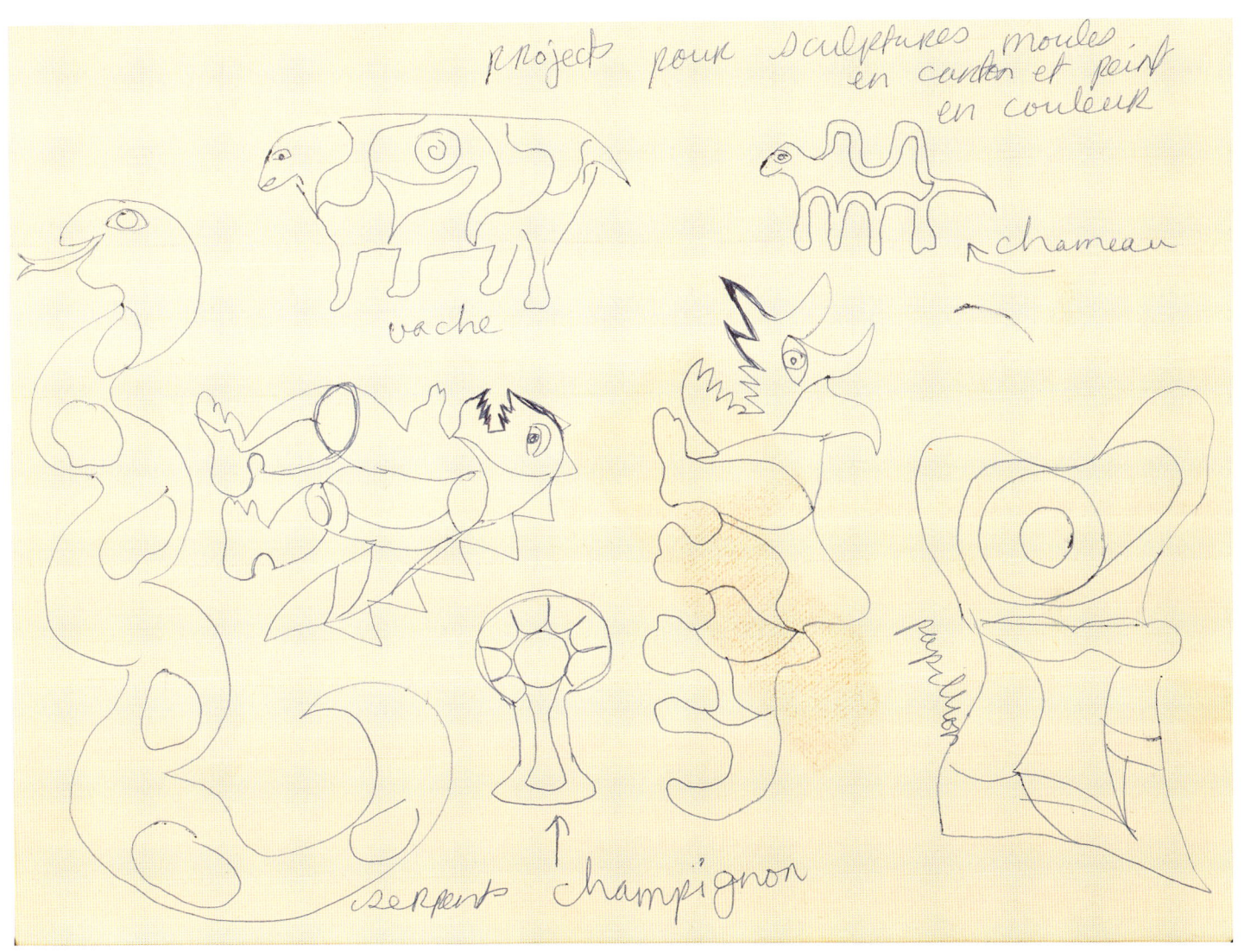

Projects pour sculptures... (Projects for sculptures...), 1960s
Blue ballpoint pen on paper (spiral bound book)
9 $\frac{1}{16}$ x 11 inches (23 x 28 cm)

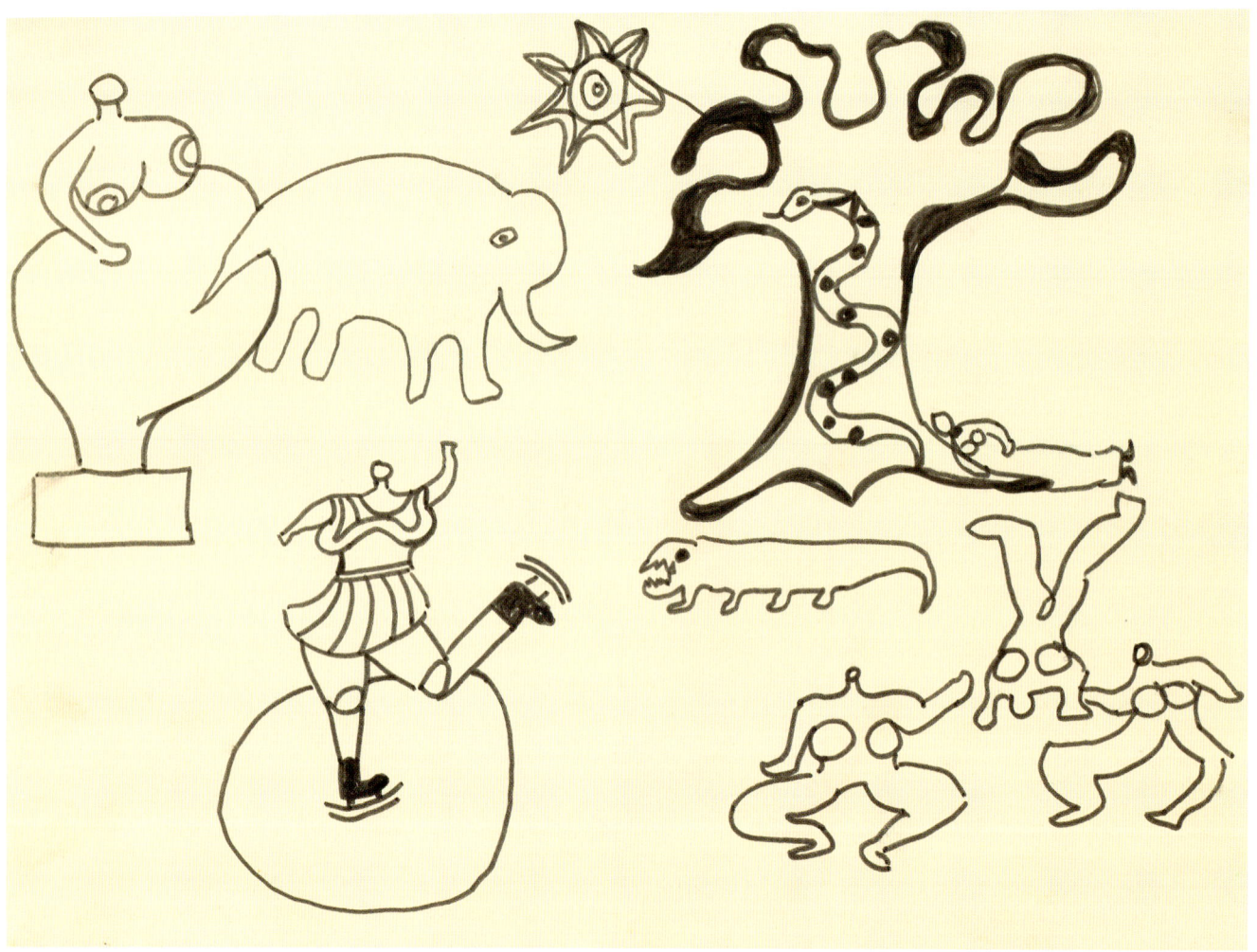

Femme enceinte, Patineuse, arbre, éléphant... (Pregnant Woman, Skater, Tree, Elephant...), 1960s
Felt-tip pen on paper (spiral bound book)
9 $^1/_{16}$ x 11 inches (23 x 28 cm)

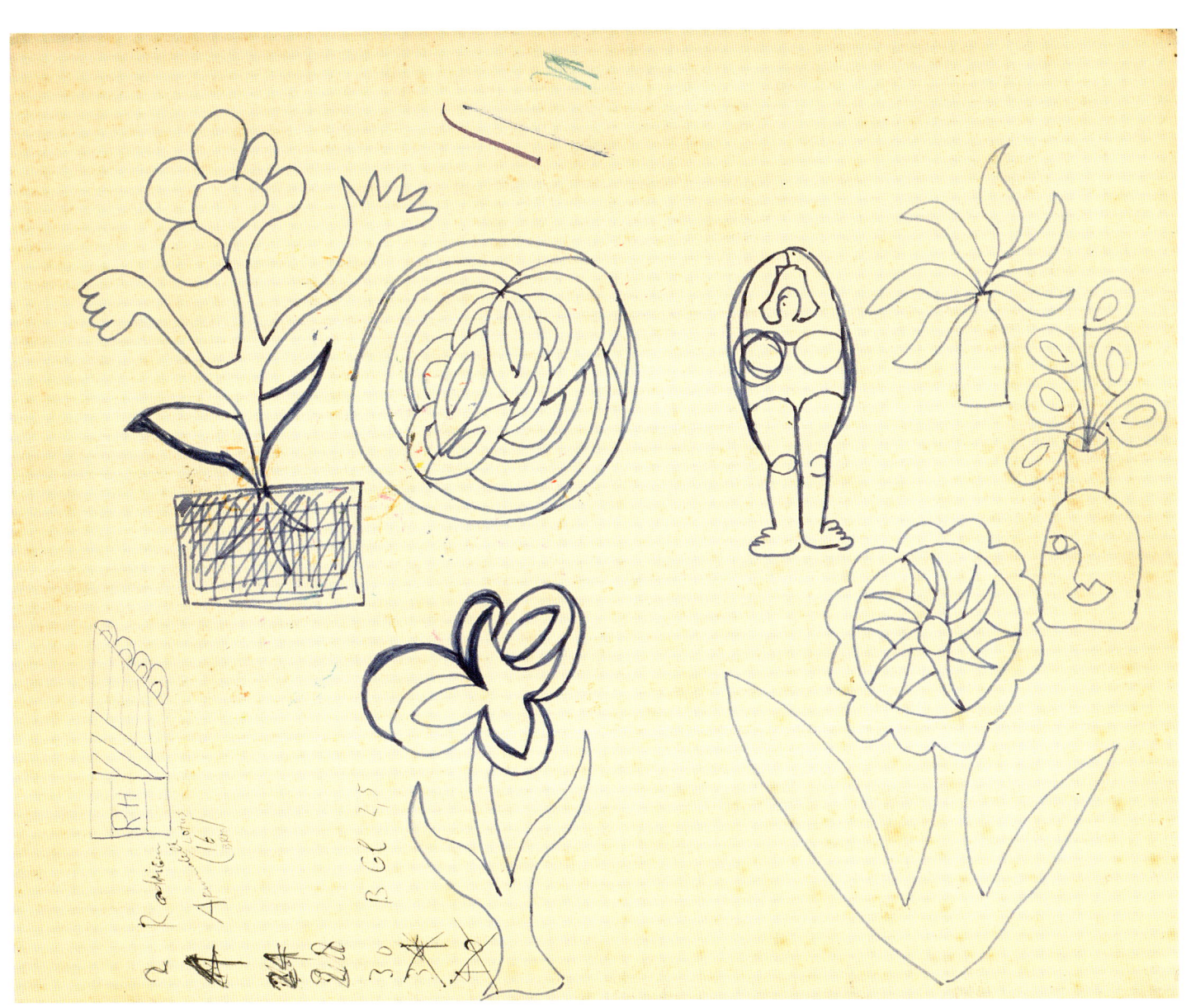

Page from Lavis Aquarelle sketchbook, 1965
Blue felt-tip pen on paper (spiral bound book)
12 $\frac{1}{2}$ x14 $\frac{1}{2}$ inches (31.8 x 36.8 cm)

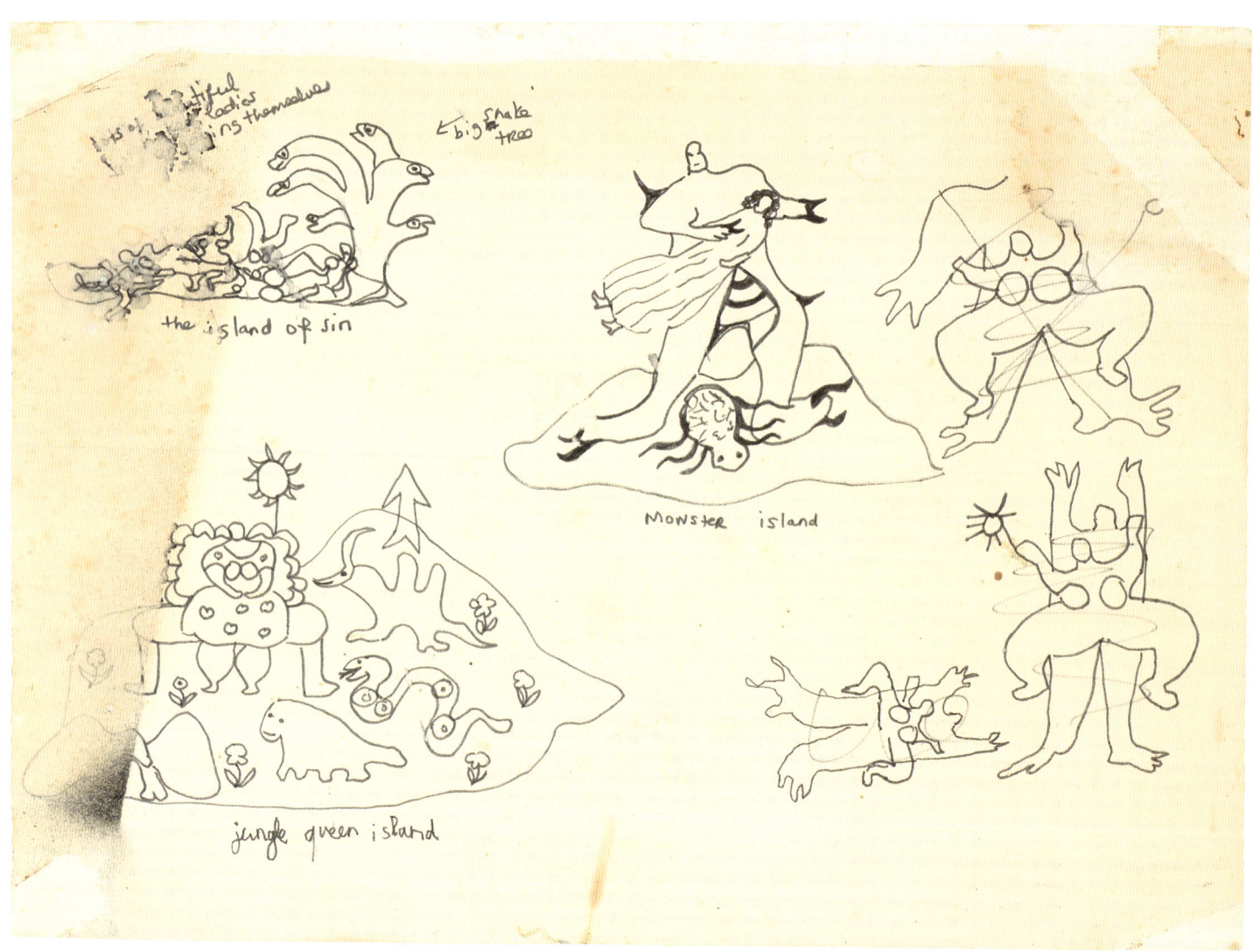

Studies for islands, n.d.
Black felt-tip pen on paper
15 ³/₁₆ x 11 inches (38.5 x 28 cm)

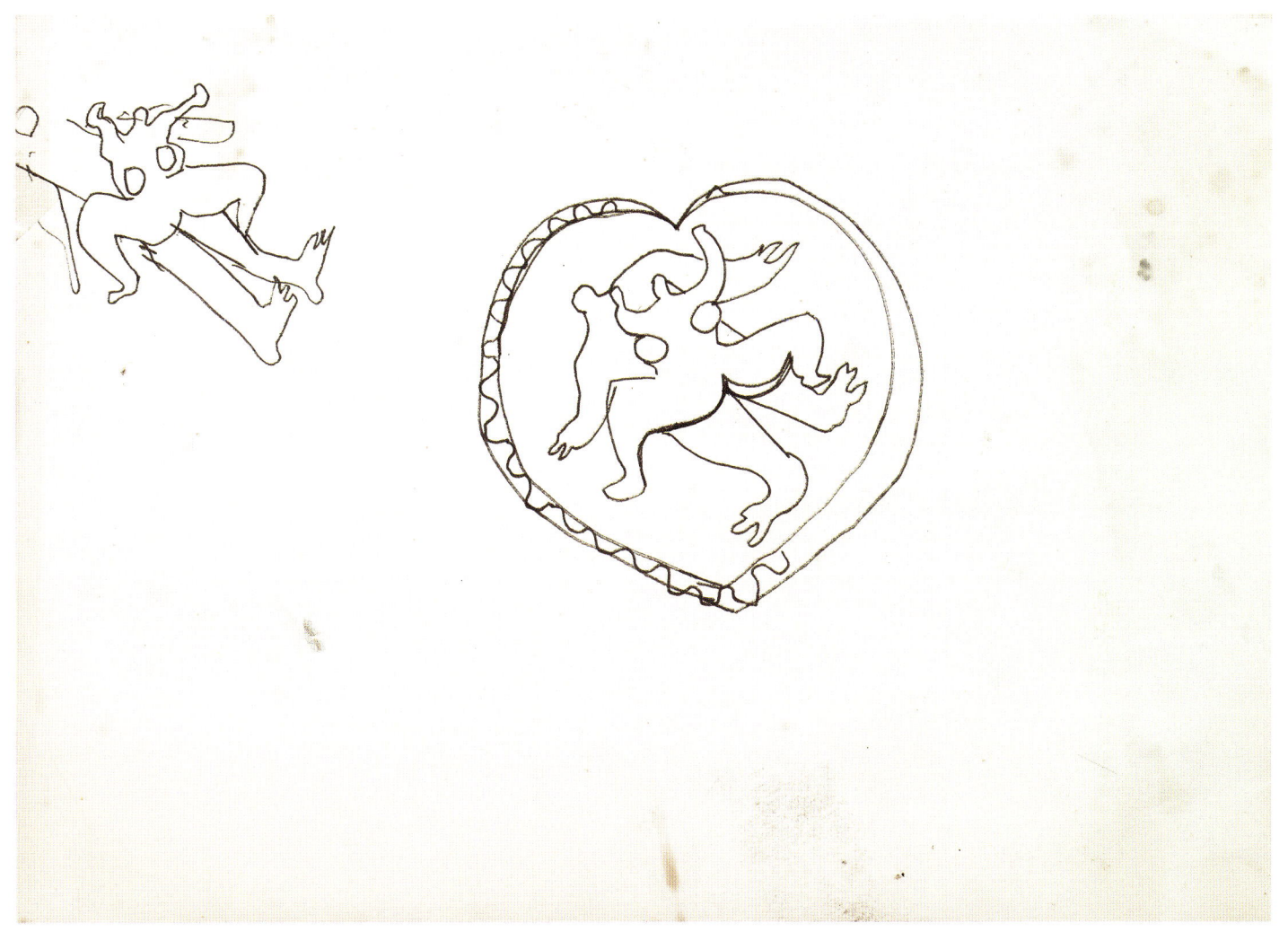

Couples, n.d.
Black felt-tip pen on paper
15 3/16 x 11 inches (38.5 x 28 cm)

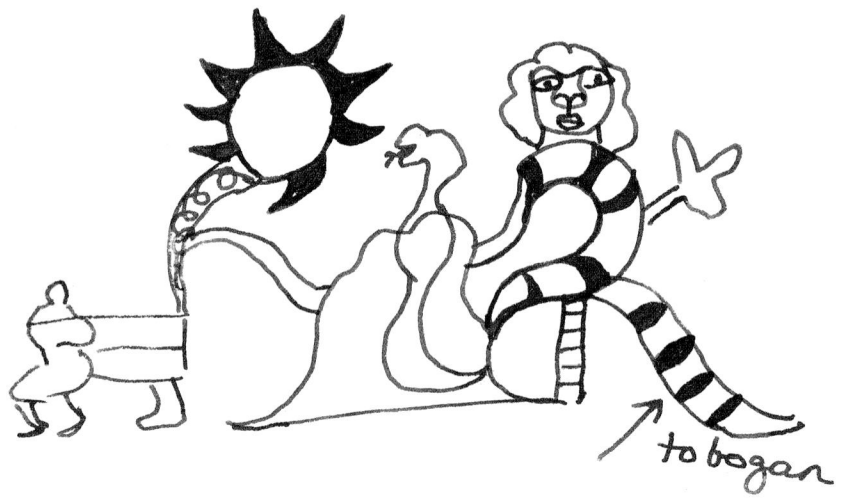

Study (tobogan), n.d.
Black marker on paper
4 $\frac{1}{8}$ x 6 $\frac{7}{8}$ inches (10.5 x 17.5 cm)

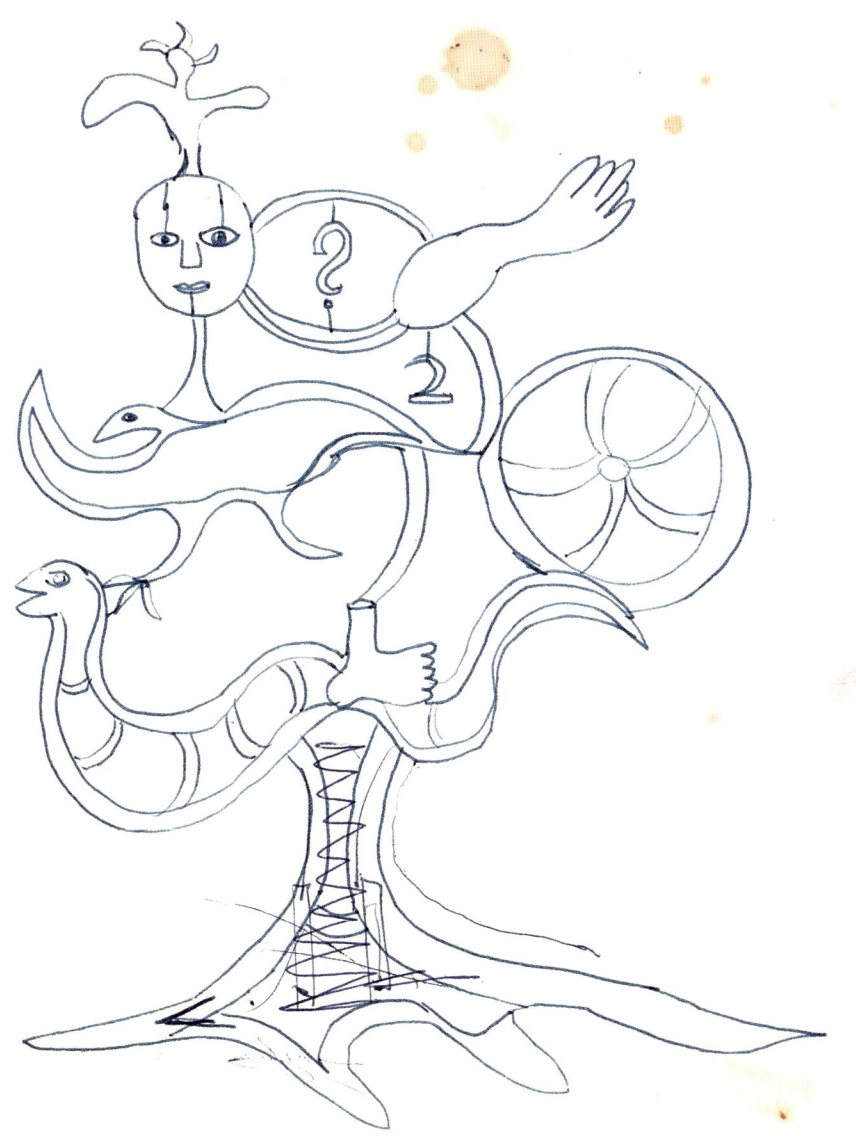

Tree Skinny, n.d.
Blue fine-line pen on paper
8 $\frac{1}{16}$ x 10 $\frac{1}{16}$ inches (20.4 x 25.5 cm)

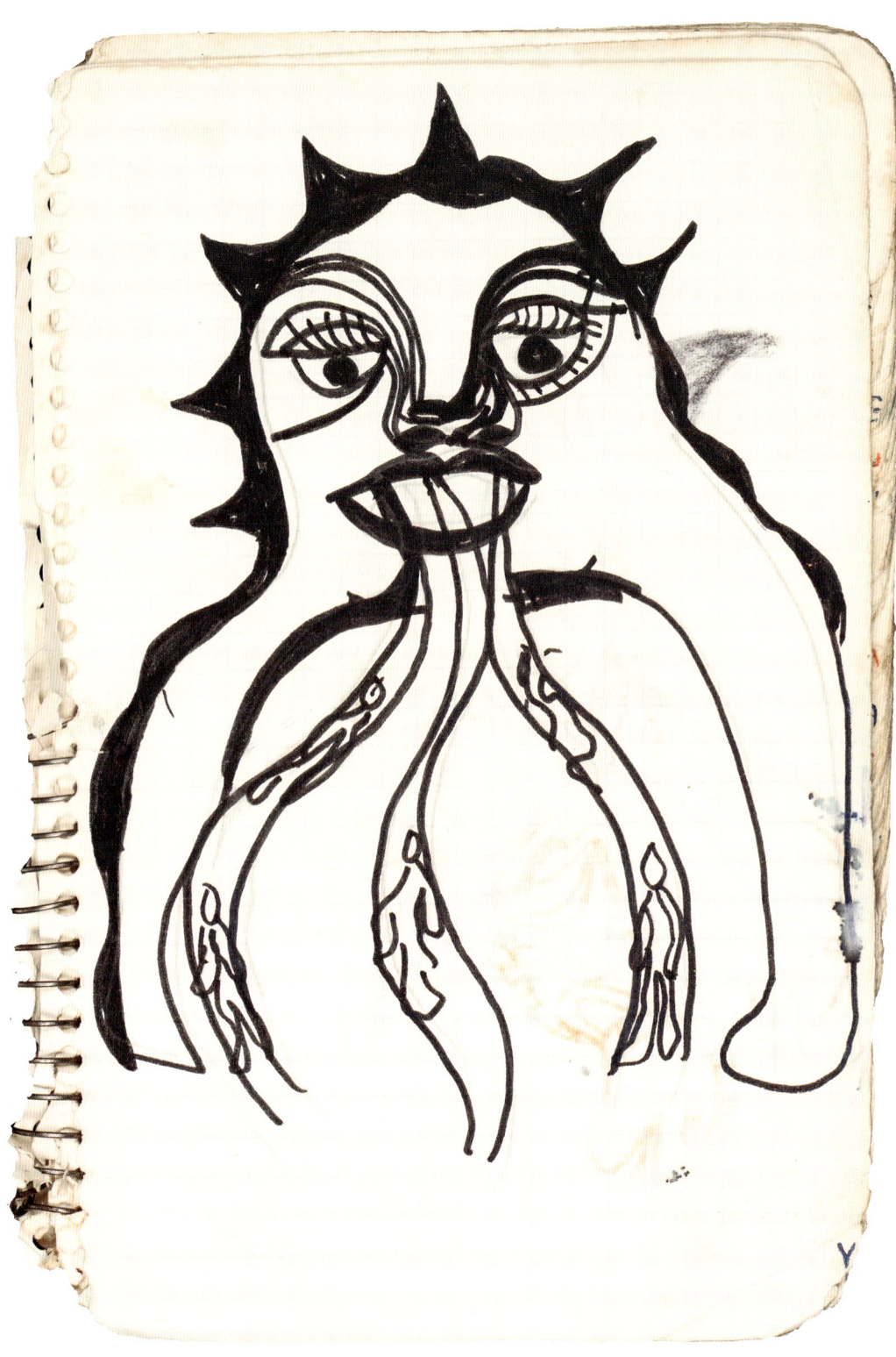

Notebook page, n.d.
Pencil and marker on quadrille paper (spiral bound book)
6 $\frac{1}{2}$ x 4 $\frac{5}{16}$ inches (16.5 x 11 cm)

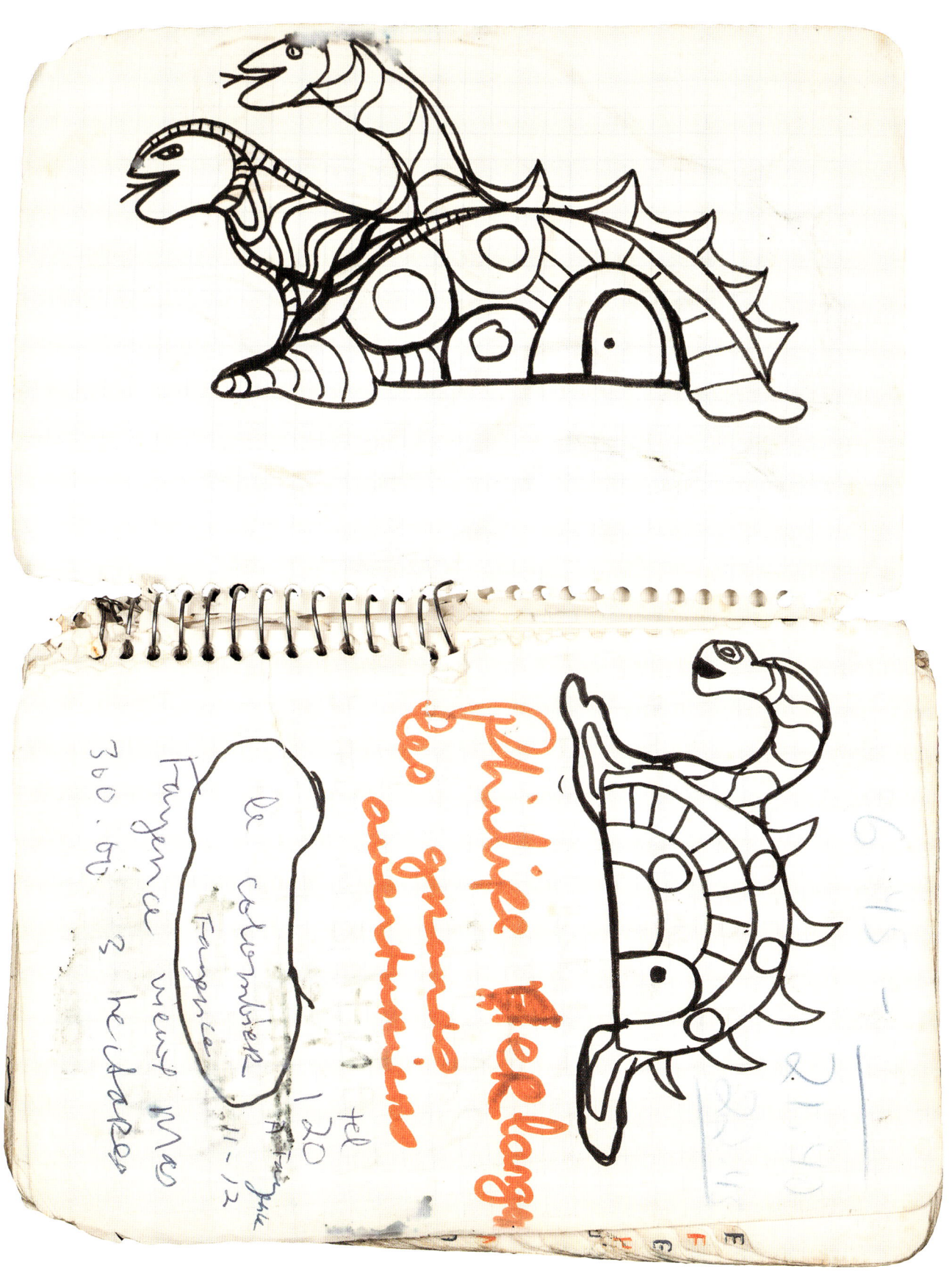

Notebook pages, n.d.
Pencil and marker on quadrille paper (spiral bound book)
6 ¹/₂ x 4 ⁵/₁₆ inches (16.5 x 11 cm) each page

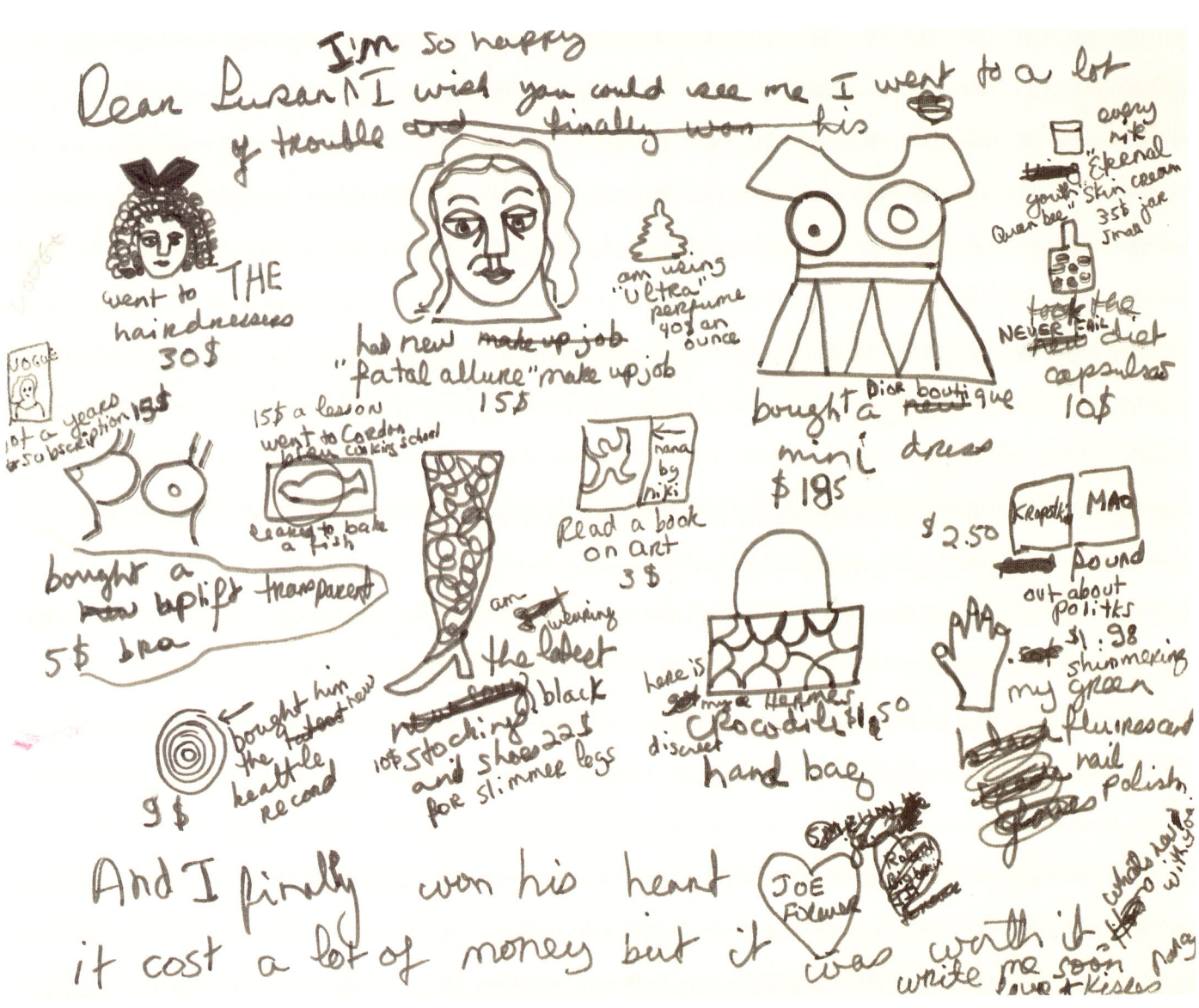

I'm so happy

Dear Susan I wish you could see me I went to a lot of trouble and finally won his

went to THE hairdressers 30$

had new make up job "fatal allure" make up job 15$

am using "Ultra" perfume 40$ an ounce

bought a Dior boutique mini dress $195

every nite "Ekenal" youth "skin cream 35$ jar small

took the NEVER FAIL diet capsules 10$

VOGUE got a years subscription 15$

15$ a lesson went to Cordon bleu cooking school learning to bake a fish

nana by niki Read a book on art 3$

$2.50 Kropotkin MAC found out about politics

bought a uplift transparent 5$ bra

am wearing the latest black 10$ stocking and shoes 22$ for slimmer legs

bought him the latest new seattle record 9$

here is my Crocodile $1.50 discreet hand bag

$1.98 shimmering my green fluirescent nail polish

And I finally won his heart it cost a lot of money but it was worth it

JOE FOXXER

what's happening with you write me soon love + kisses

Sketchbook page, n.d.
Marker, pencil, and crayon on cardboard (spiral bound book)
8 ¼ x 10 ¹³/₁₆ inches (21 x 27.5 cm)

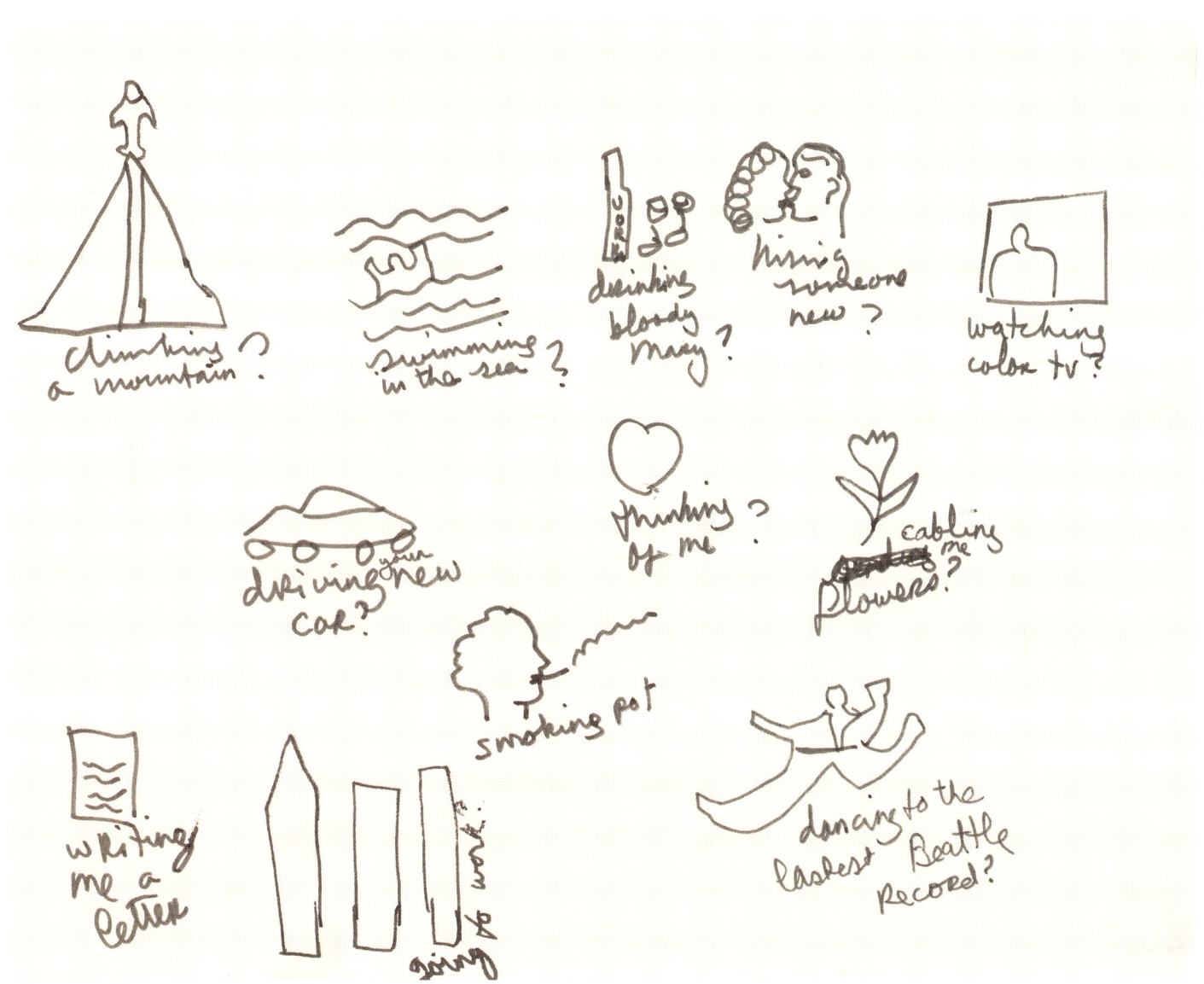

climbing? a mountain.

swimming in the sea?

drinking bloody mary?

kissing someone new?

watching color tv?

driving your new car?

thinking of me?

calling me

sending me flowers?

smoking pot

writing me a letter

going to work

dancing to the lastest Beattle record?

Sketchbook page, n.d.
Marker, pencil, and crayon on cardboard (spiral bound book)
8 1/4 x 10 13/16 inches (21 x 27.5 cm)

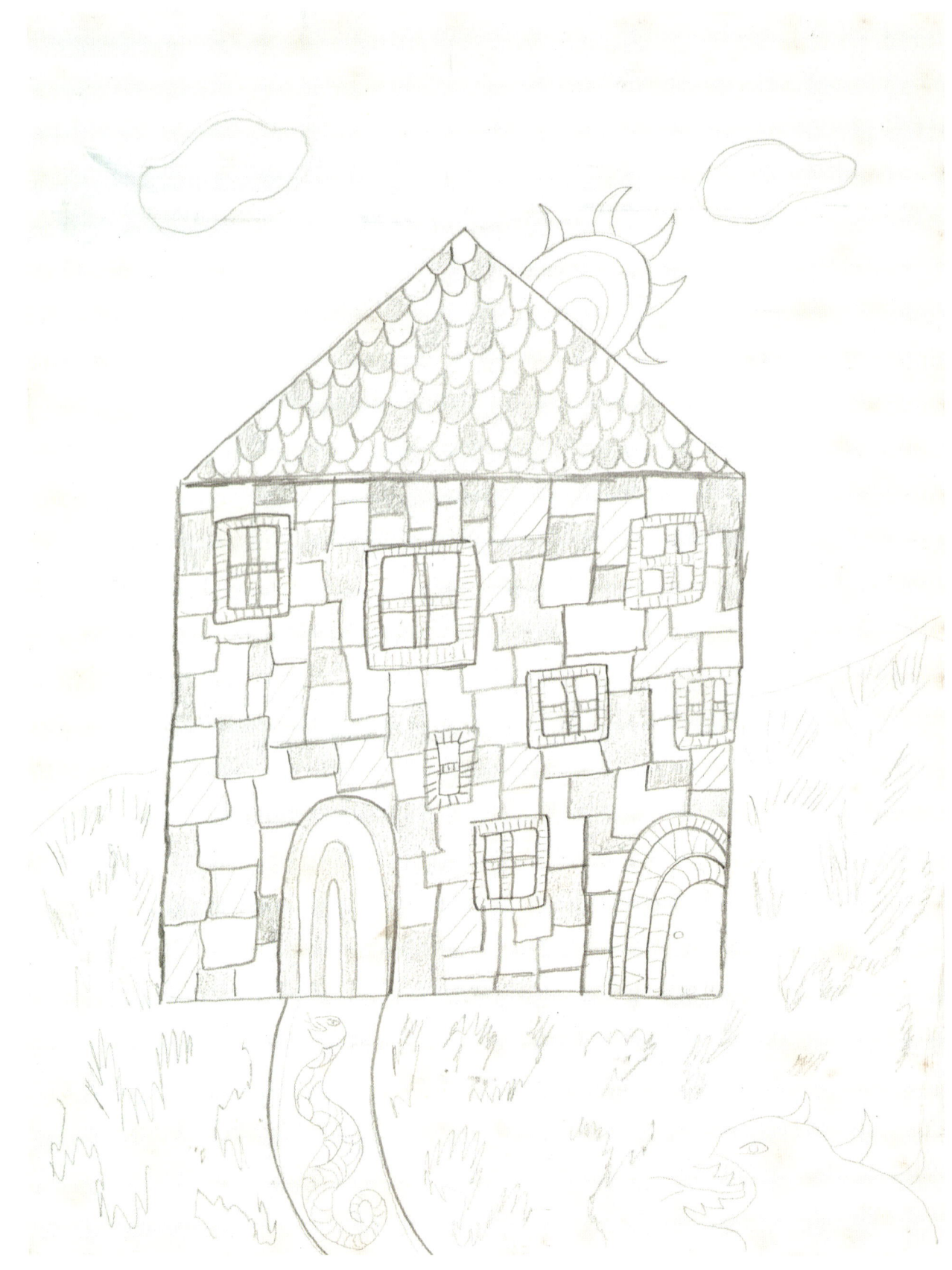

La Maison [house, dragon], n.d.
Pencil on cardboard
12 $^5/_8$ x 9 $^7/_{16}$ inches (32 x 24 cm)

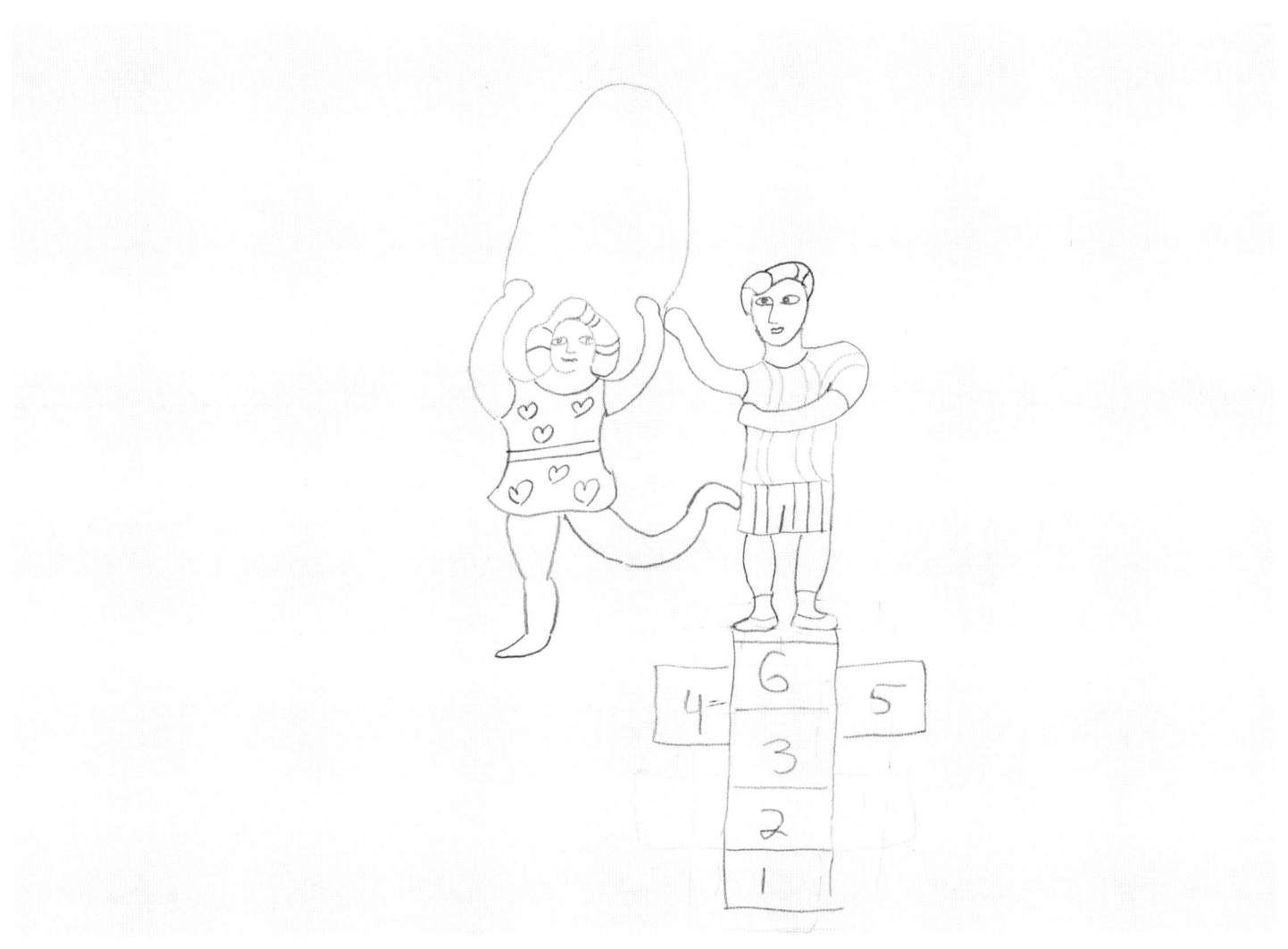

Children Playing, 1980s
Pencil on paper
8 1/4 x 11 5/8 inches (21 x 2-9.6 cm)

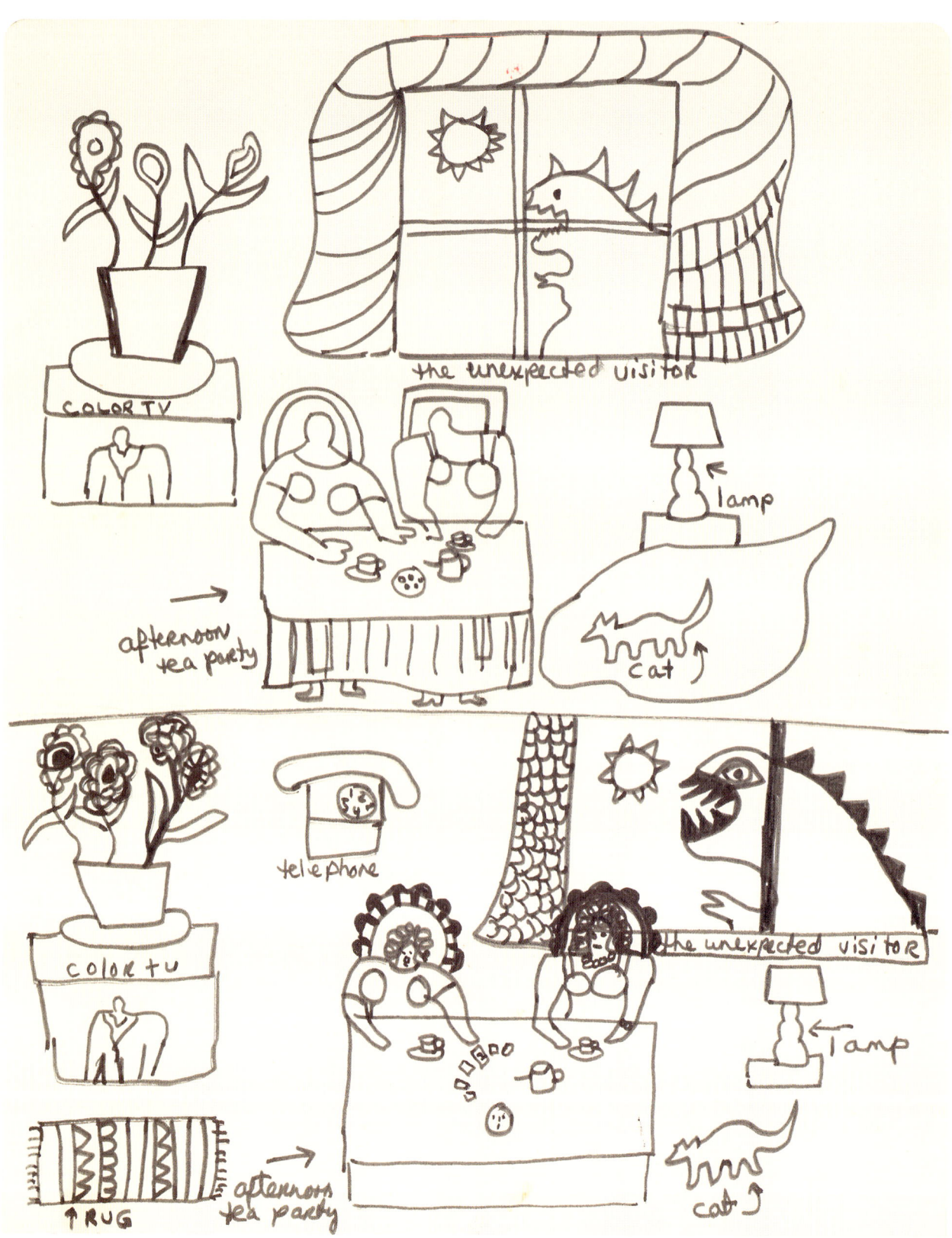

Sketchbook page, n.d.
Marker, pencil, and crayon on cardboard (spiral bound book)
10 $^{13}/_{16}$ x 8 $^{1}/_{4}$ inches (27.5 x 21 cm)

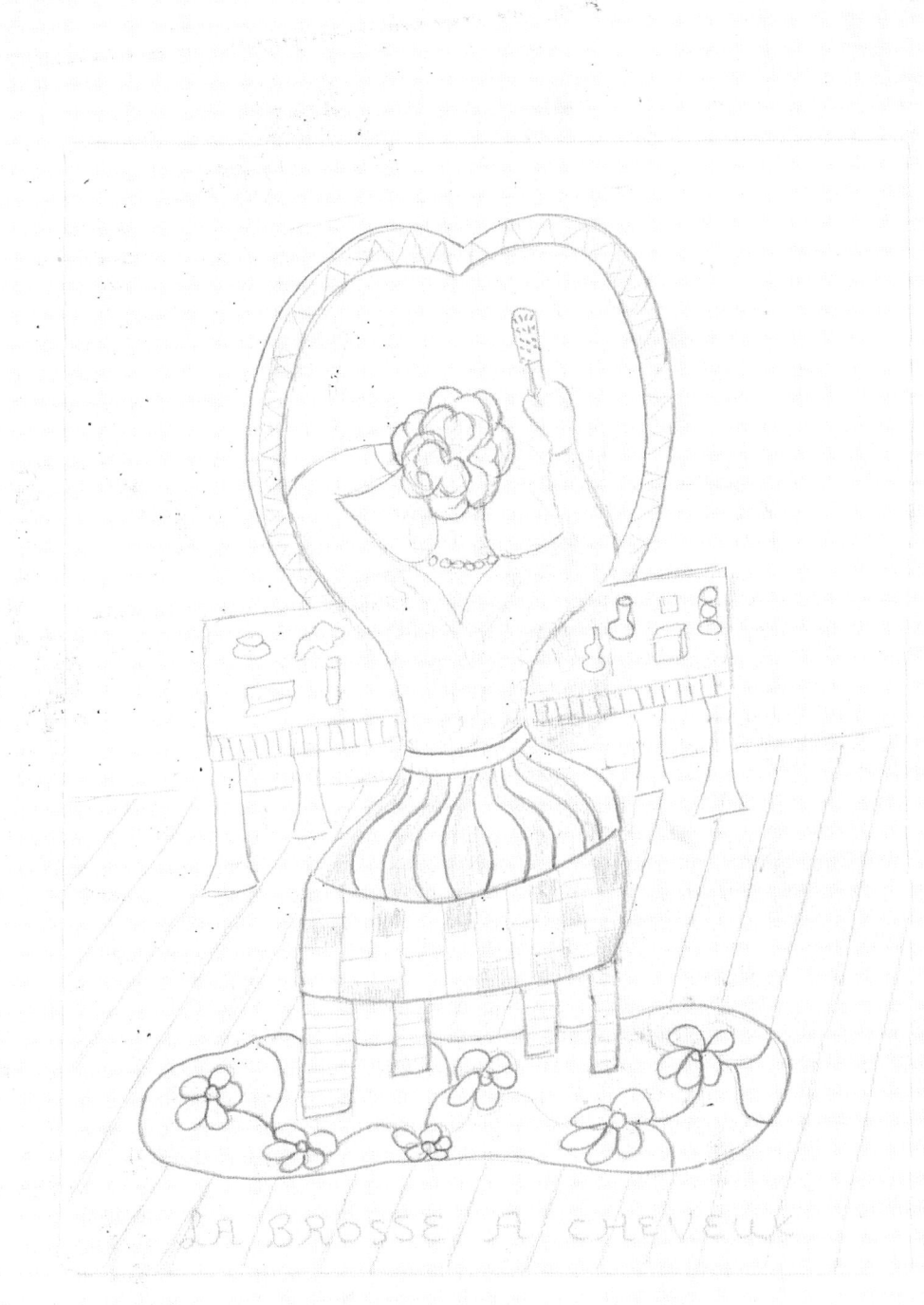

La toilette [la brosse a cheveux] (Grooming [The Hairbrush]), n.d.
Pencil on paper
12 ⁵/₈ x 9 ⁷/₁₆ inches (32 x 24 cm)

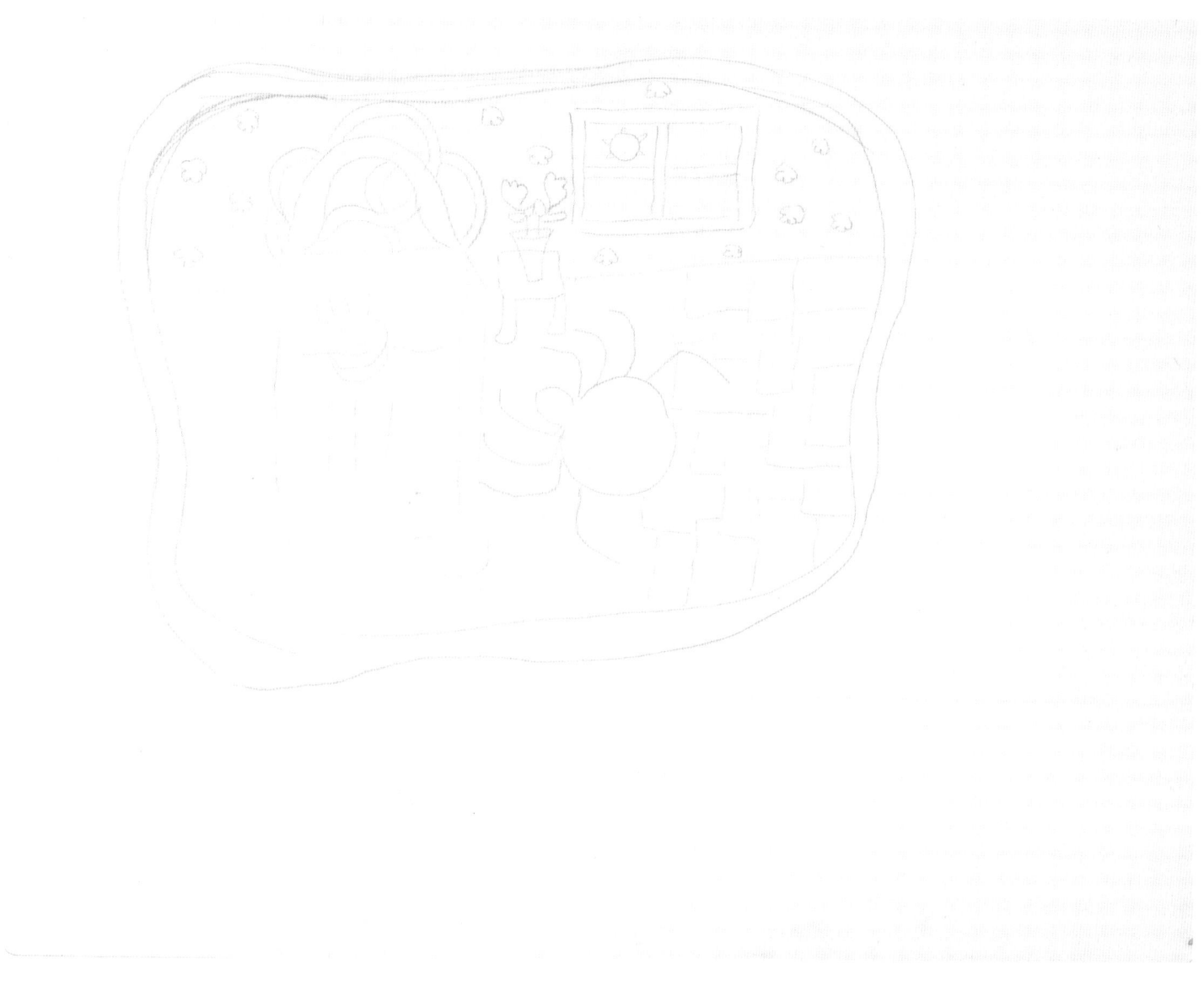

Woman in Room, Spider, n.d.
Pencil on paper
10 $^5/_8$ x 13 $^3/_8$ inches (27 x 34 cm)

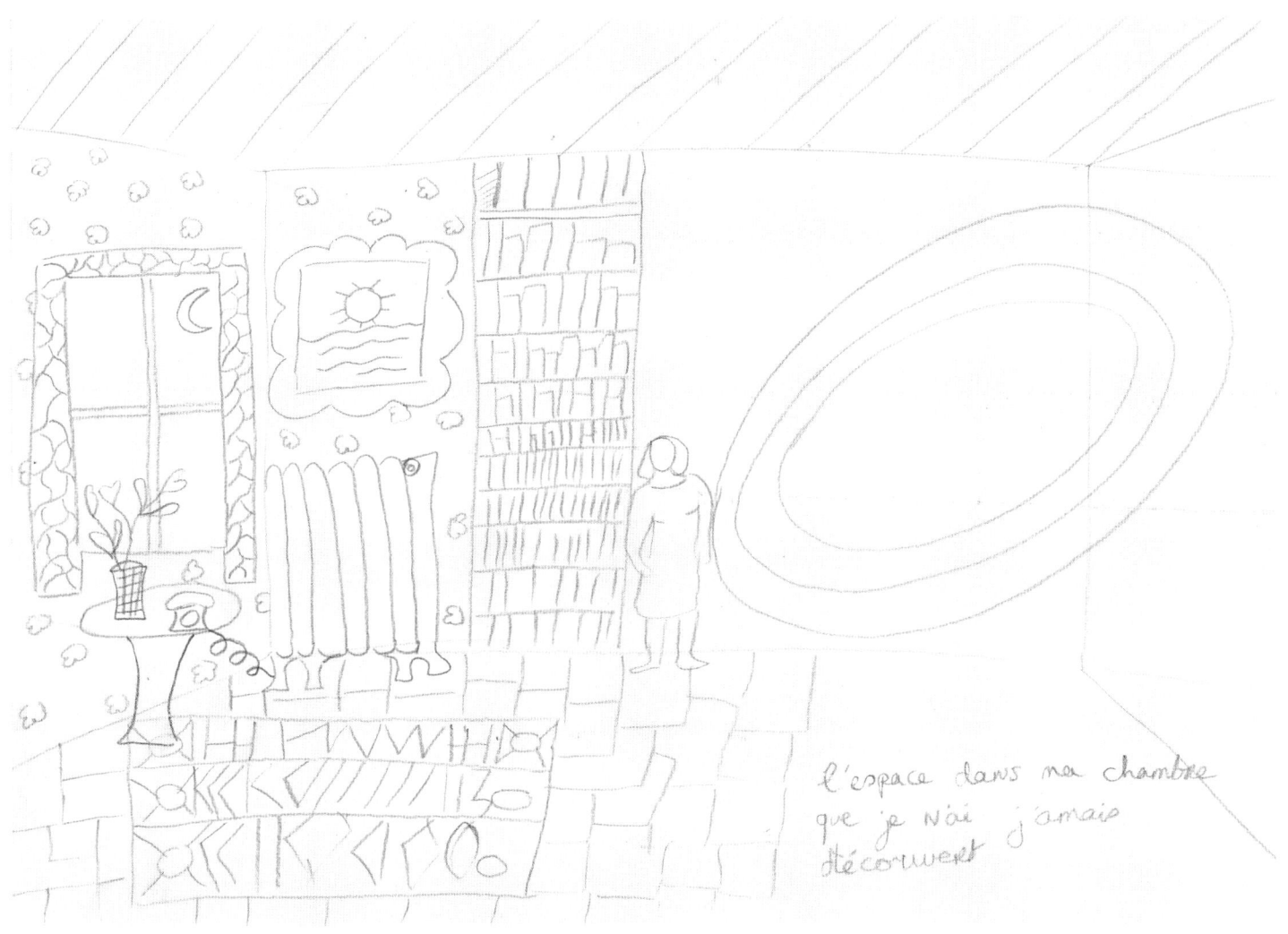

L'espace dans ma chambre que je n'ai jamais découvert
(The space in my room that I never discovered), n.d.
Pencil on paper
8 ¹/₄ x 10 ¹³/₁₆ inches (21 x 27.5 cm)

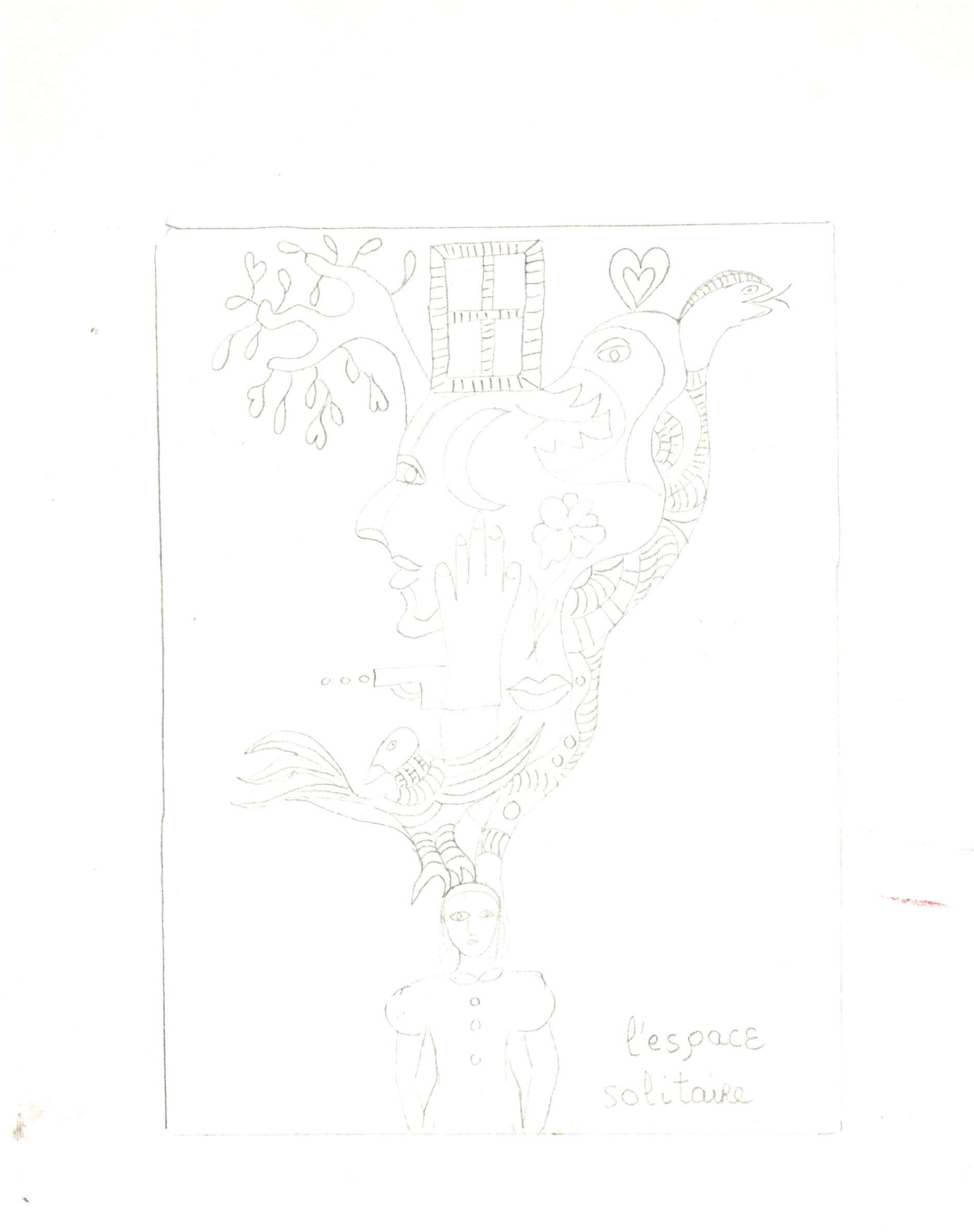

L'espace solitaire (The Solitary Space), n.d.
Pencil on paper
12 ⁵/₈ x 9 ⁷/₁₆ inches (32 x 23.9 cm)

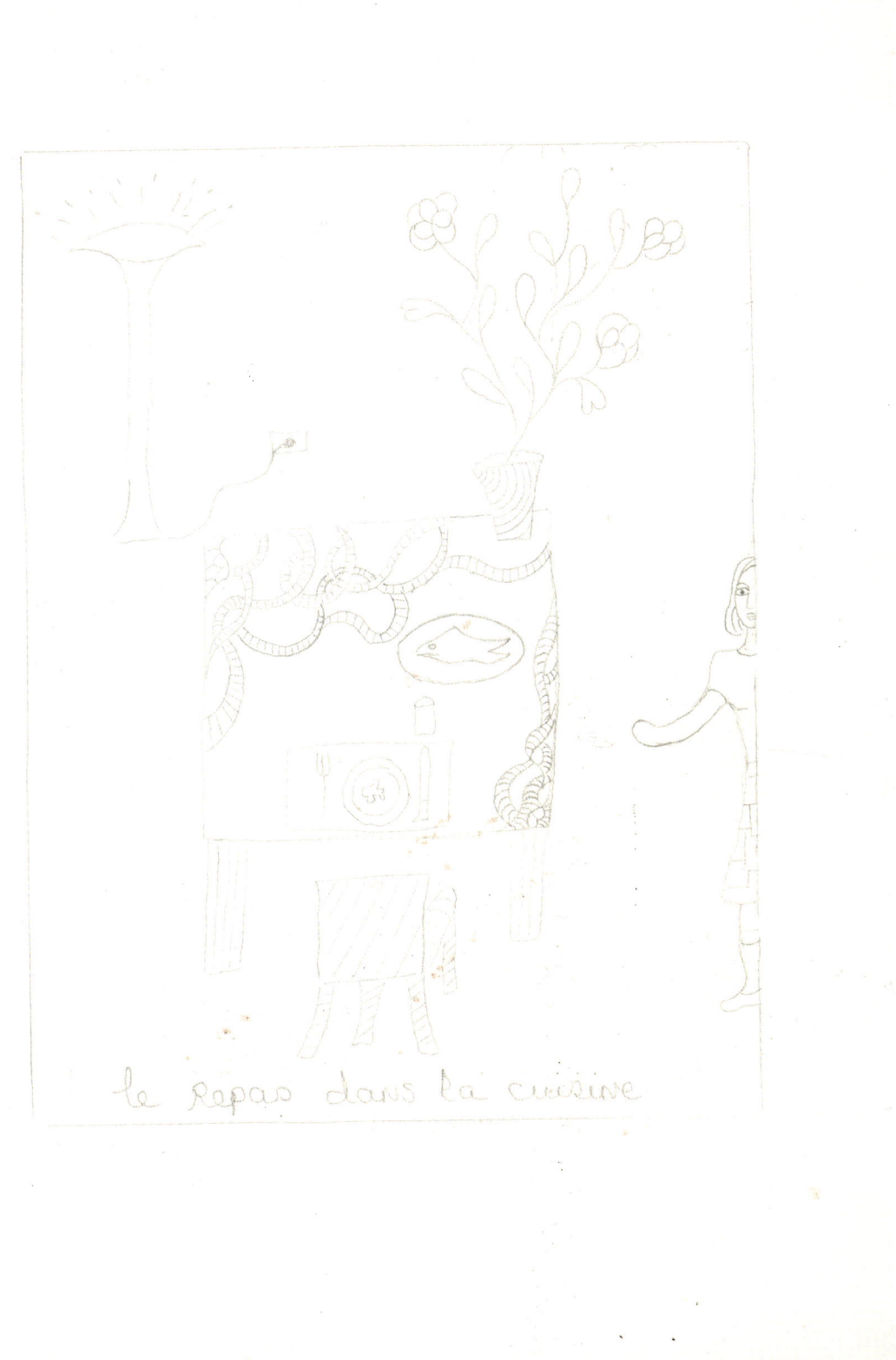

Le repas dans la cuisine (The Meal in the Kitchen), n.d.
Pencil on paper
12 ⁵/₈ x 9 ⁷/₁₆ inches (32 x 24 cm)

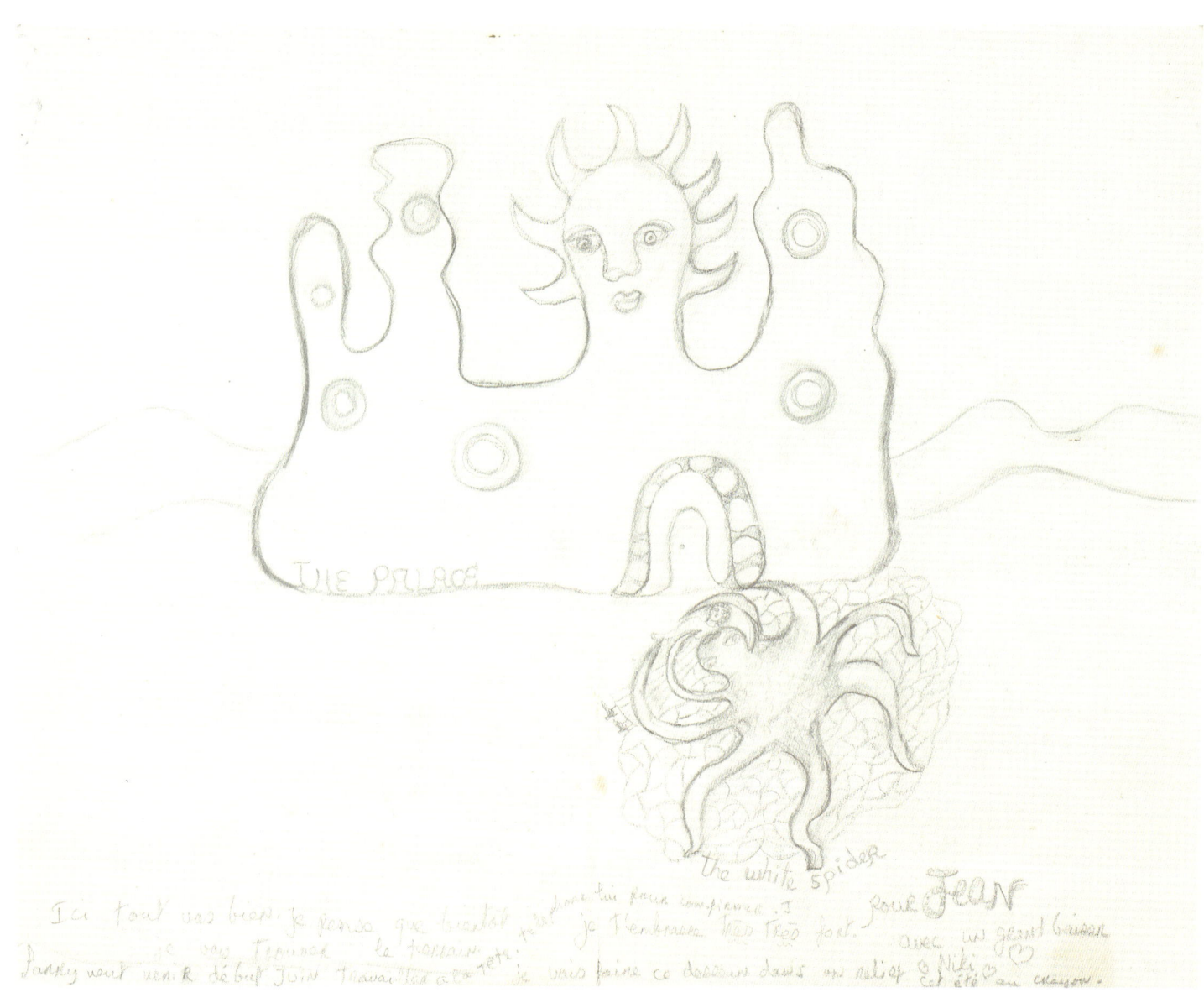

The Palace, the White Spider..., 1970s
Pencil on paper
8 1/16 x 10 inches (20.4 x 25.4 cm)

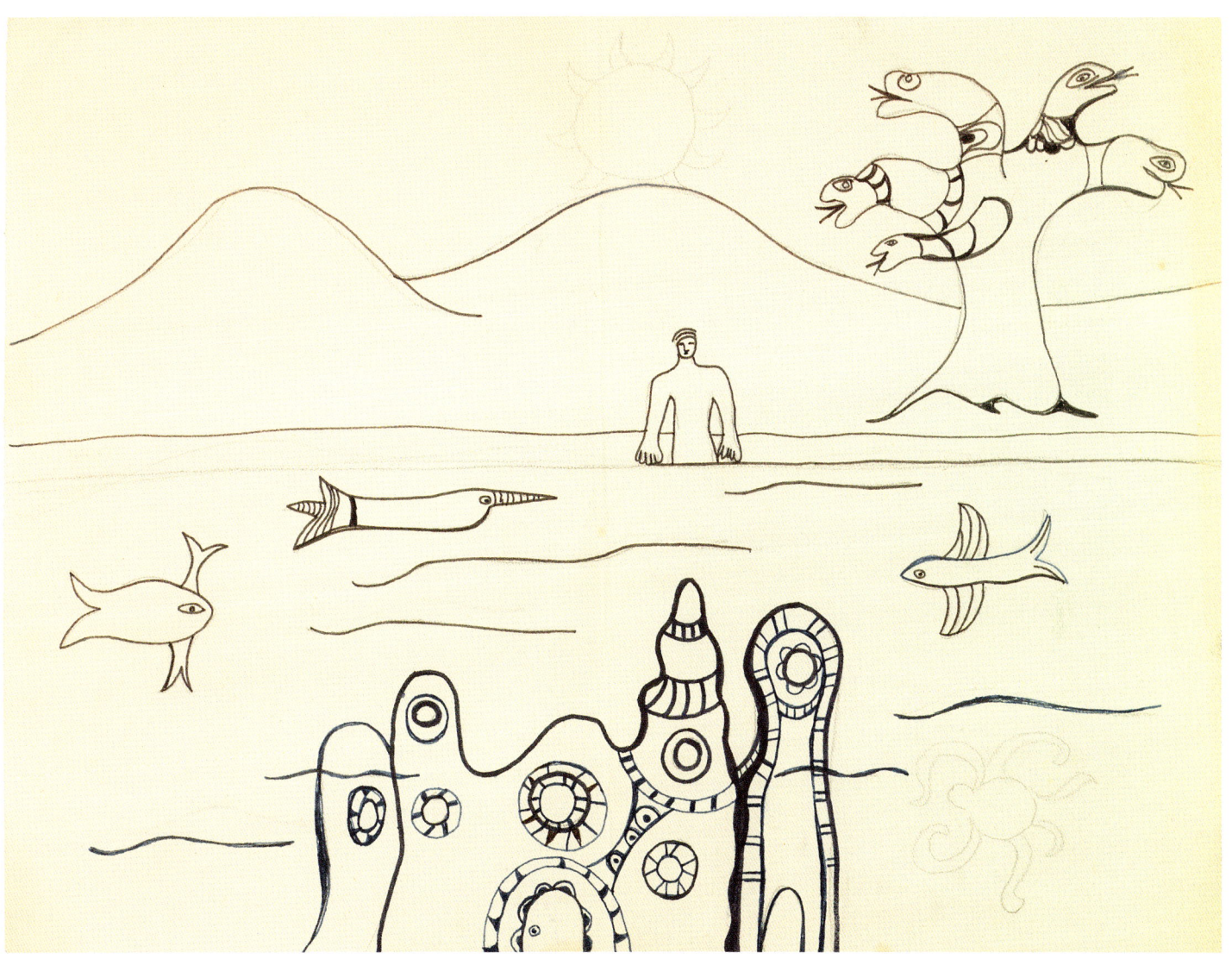

Mer, homme, arbre de vie, château, poissons (Sea, Man, Tree of Life, Castle, Fish), 1970s
Pencil, felt-tip pen and ink on drawing pad sheet
14 x 10 $^{13}/_{16}$ inches (35.5 x 27.5 cm)

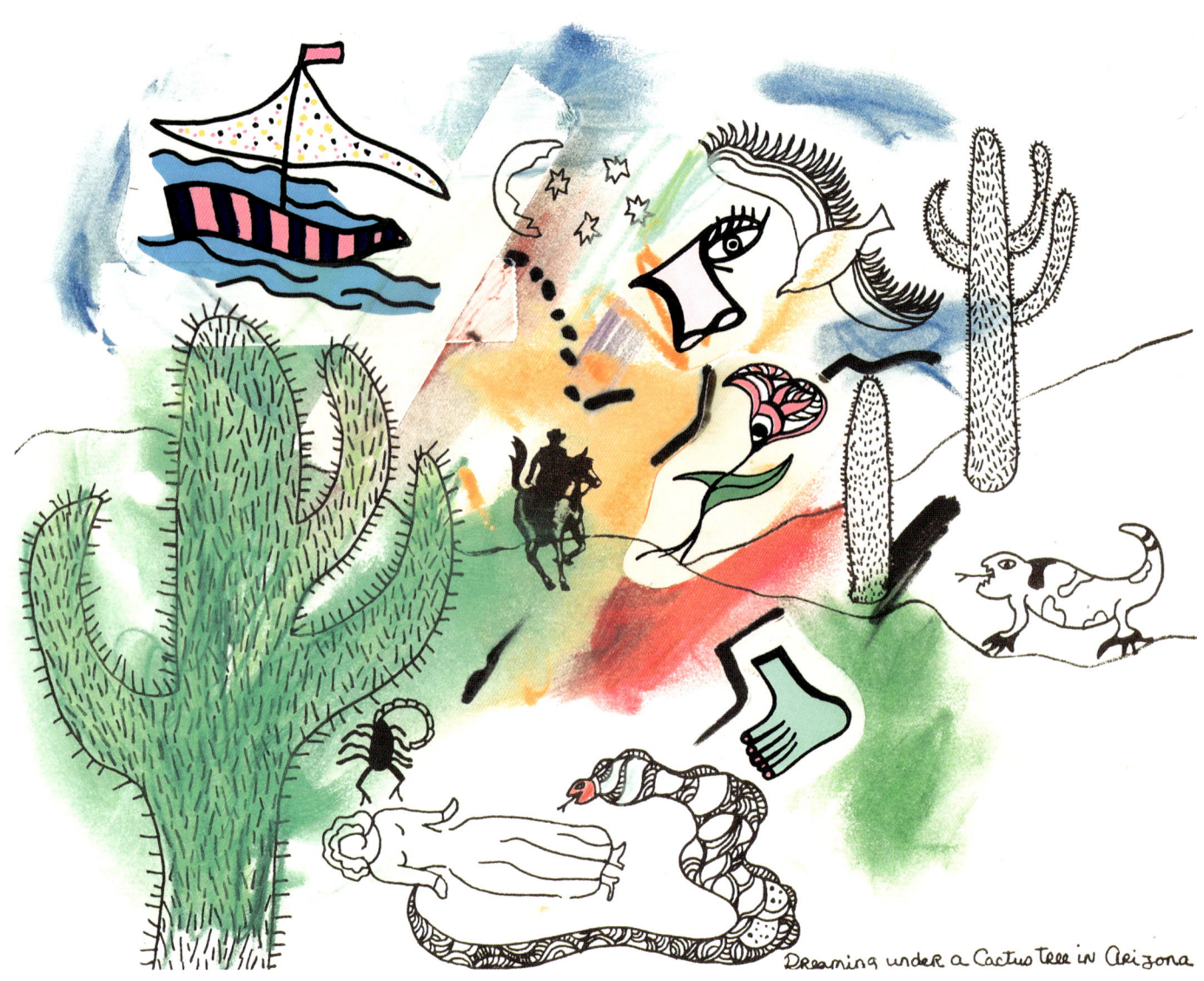

Dreaming under a Cactus Tree in Arizona

Dreaming under a Cactus Tree in Arizona, n.d.
Felt-tip pen, pastel, gouache, and stickers on print
8 1/2 x 11 inches (21.6 x 28 cm)

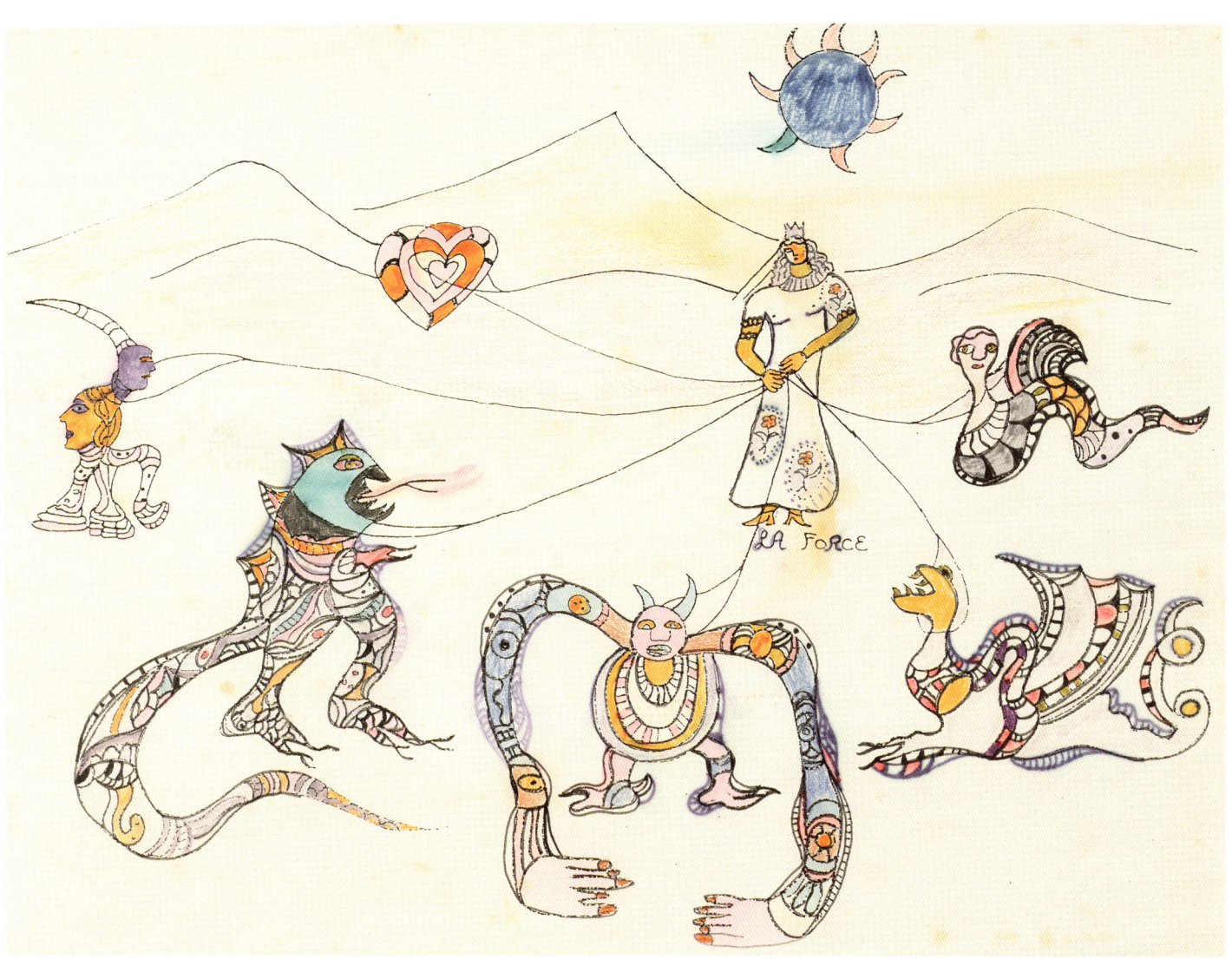

La Force (Strength), 1978
Ink, felt-tip pen, and colored pencil on paper
9 $\frac{7}{16}$ x 12 $\frac{5}{8}$ inches (24 x 32 cm)

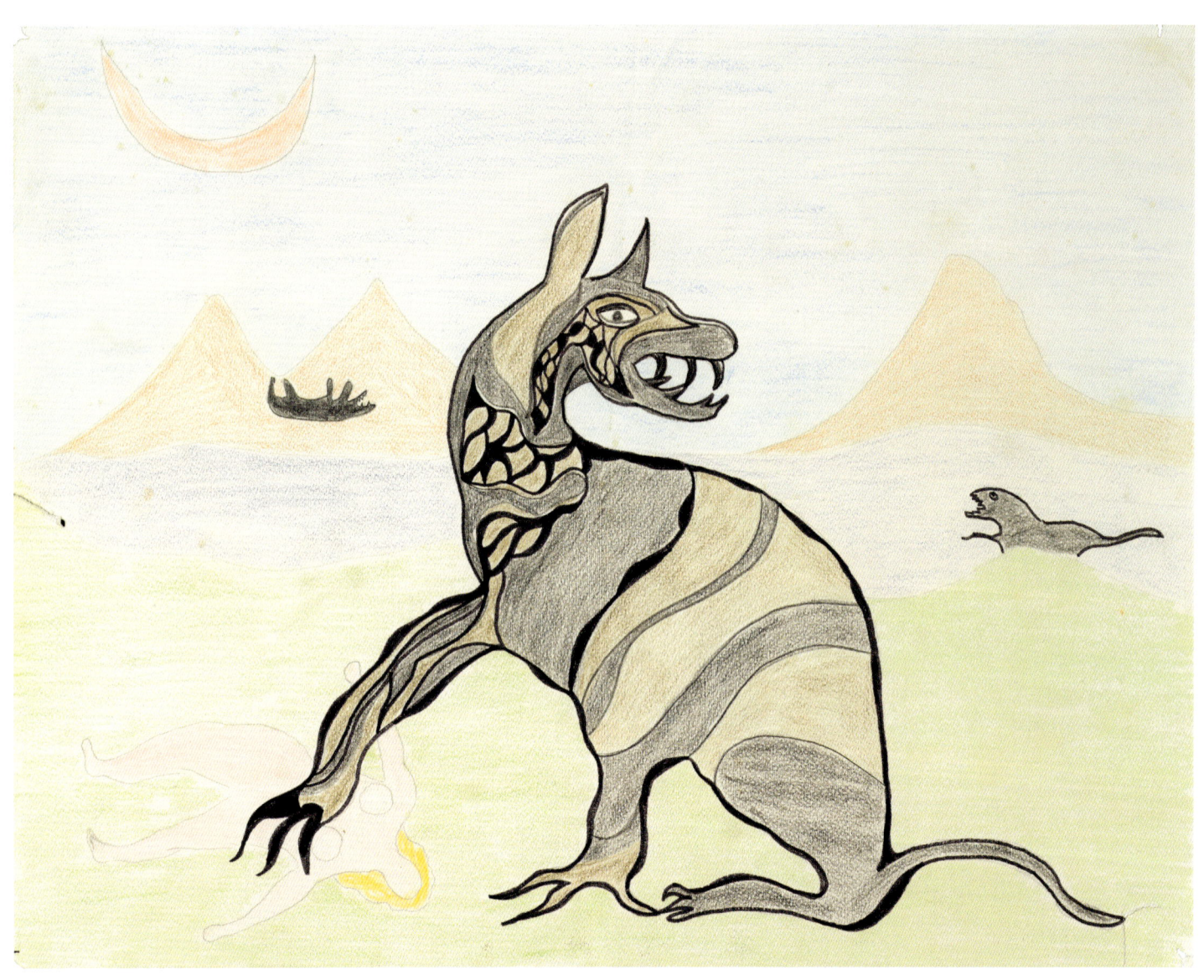

Wolf in the Desert, n.d.
Black felt-tip pen, colored pencil on Canson paper
15 ¹/₄ x 16 ¹/₈ inches (38.8 x 41 cm)

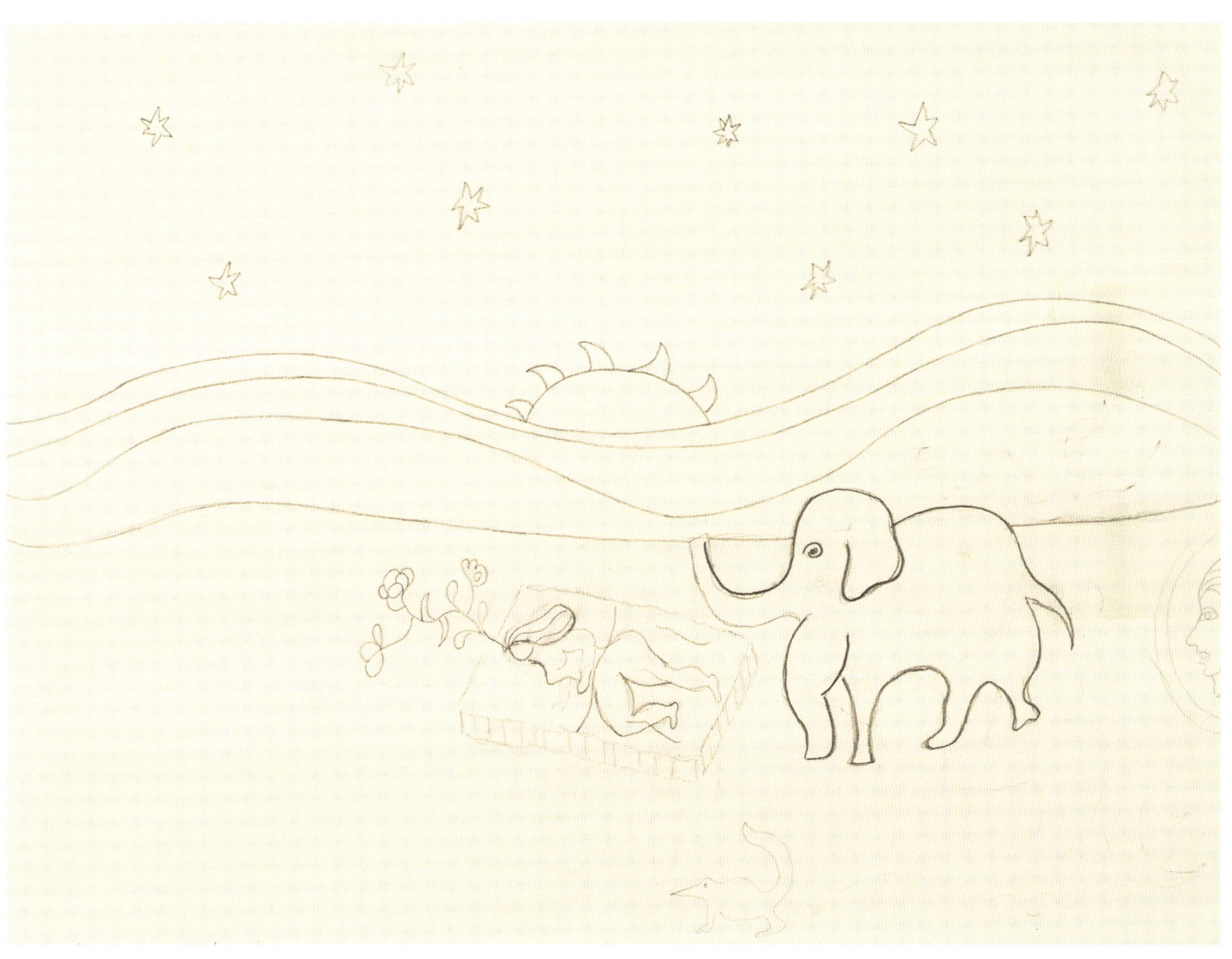

Study for *Bepe's Arizona Dream*, 1993
Pencil on cardboard
11 $^{13}/_{16}$ x 15 $^{3}/_{4}$ inches (30 x 40 cm)

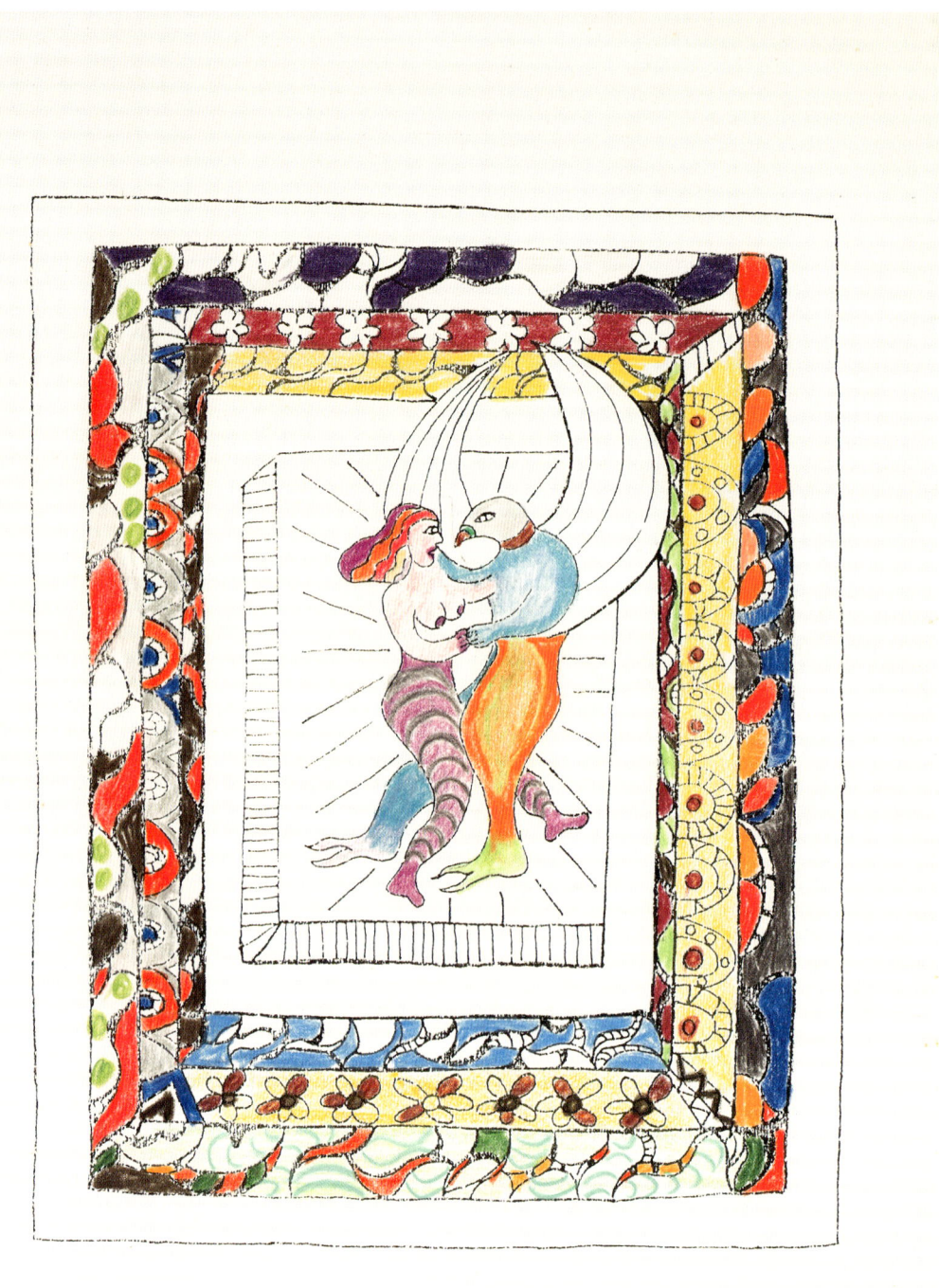

Woman and Bird, n.d.
Colored pencil on photocopy
12 $^5/_8$ x 9 $^7/_{16}$ inches (32 x 24 cm)

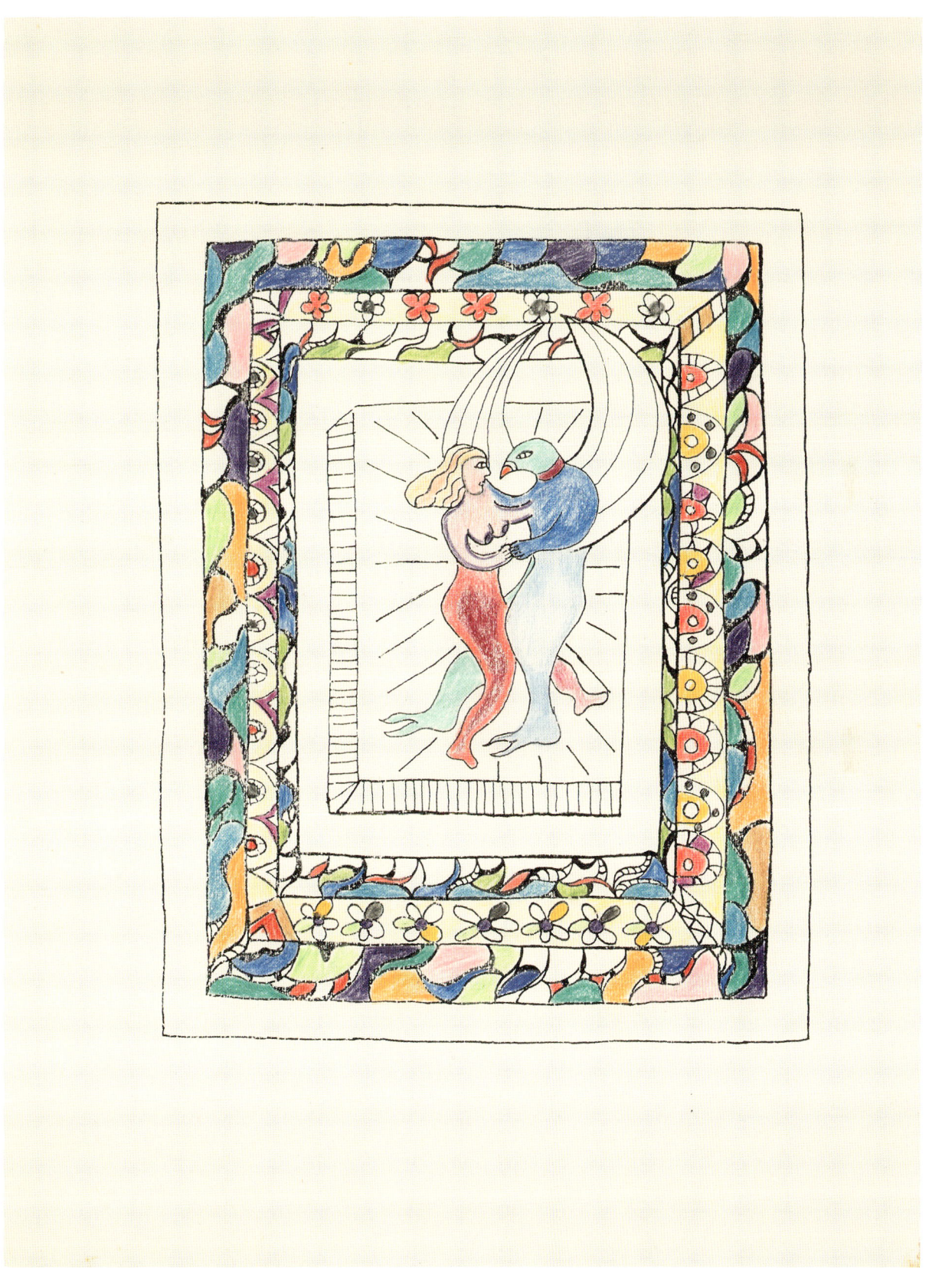

Woman and Bird, n.d.
Colored pencil on photocopy
12 $\frac{5}{8}$ x 9 $\frac{7}{16}$ inches (32 x 24 cm)

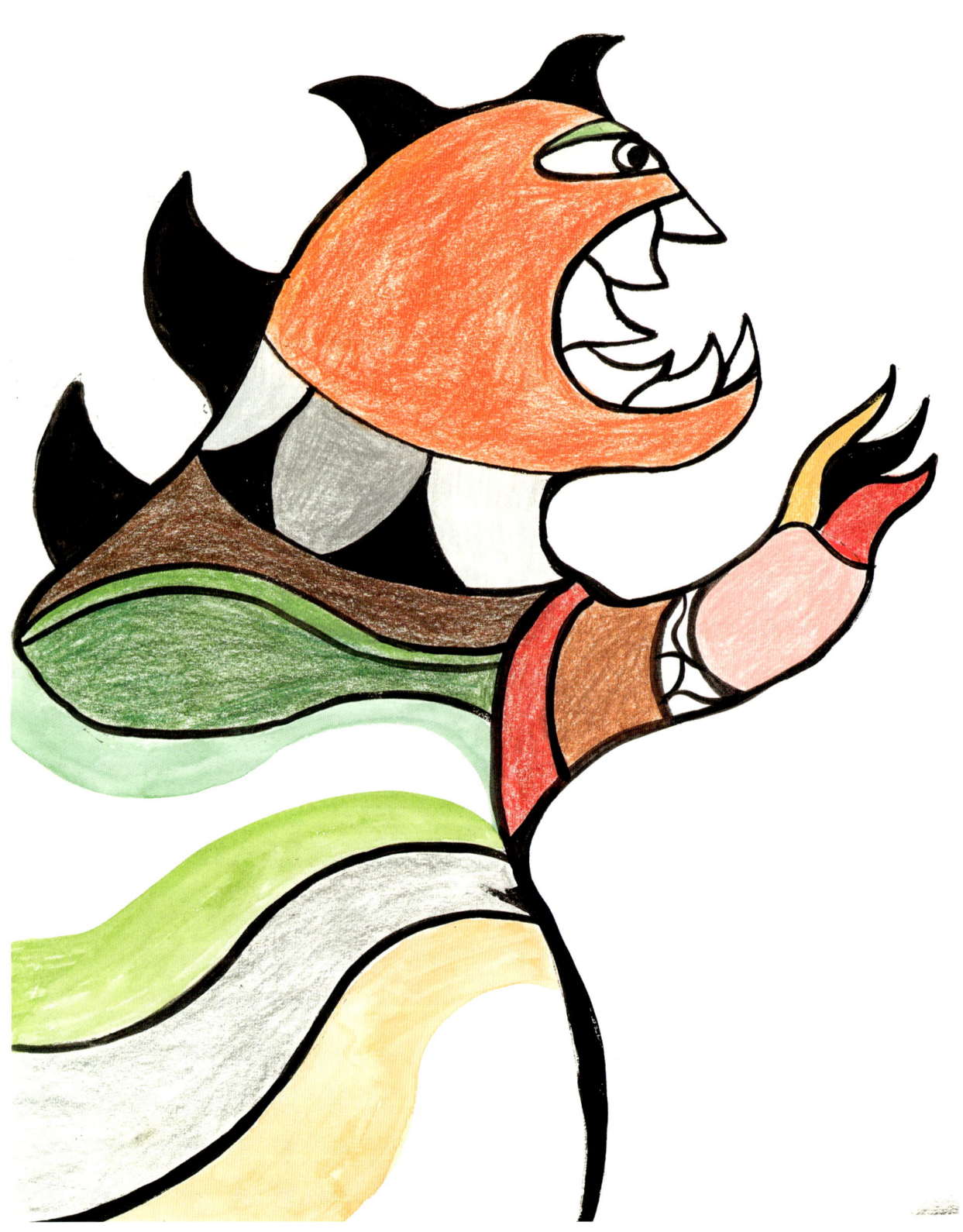

Dragon, n.d.
Watercolor and crayon on paper
11 $^{13}/_{16}$ x 8 1/4 inches (30 x 21 cm)

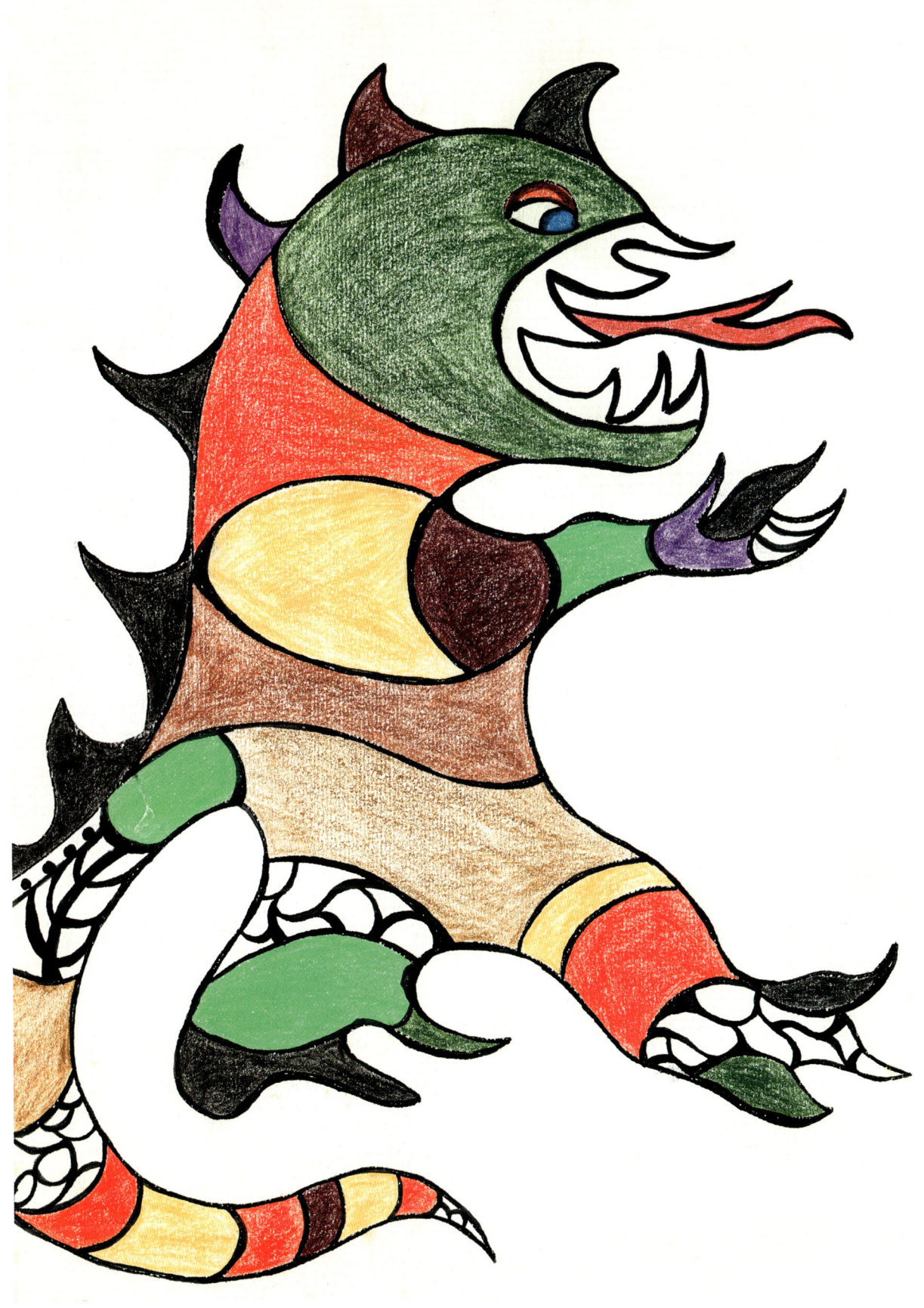

Dragon, n.d.
Watercolor and crayon on paper
11 ¹³/₁₆ x 8 1/4 inches (30 x 21 cm)

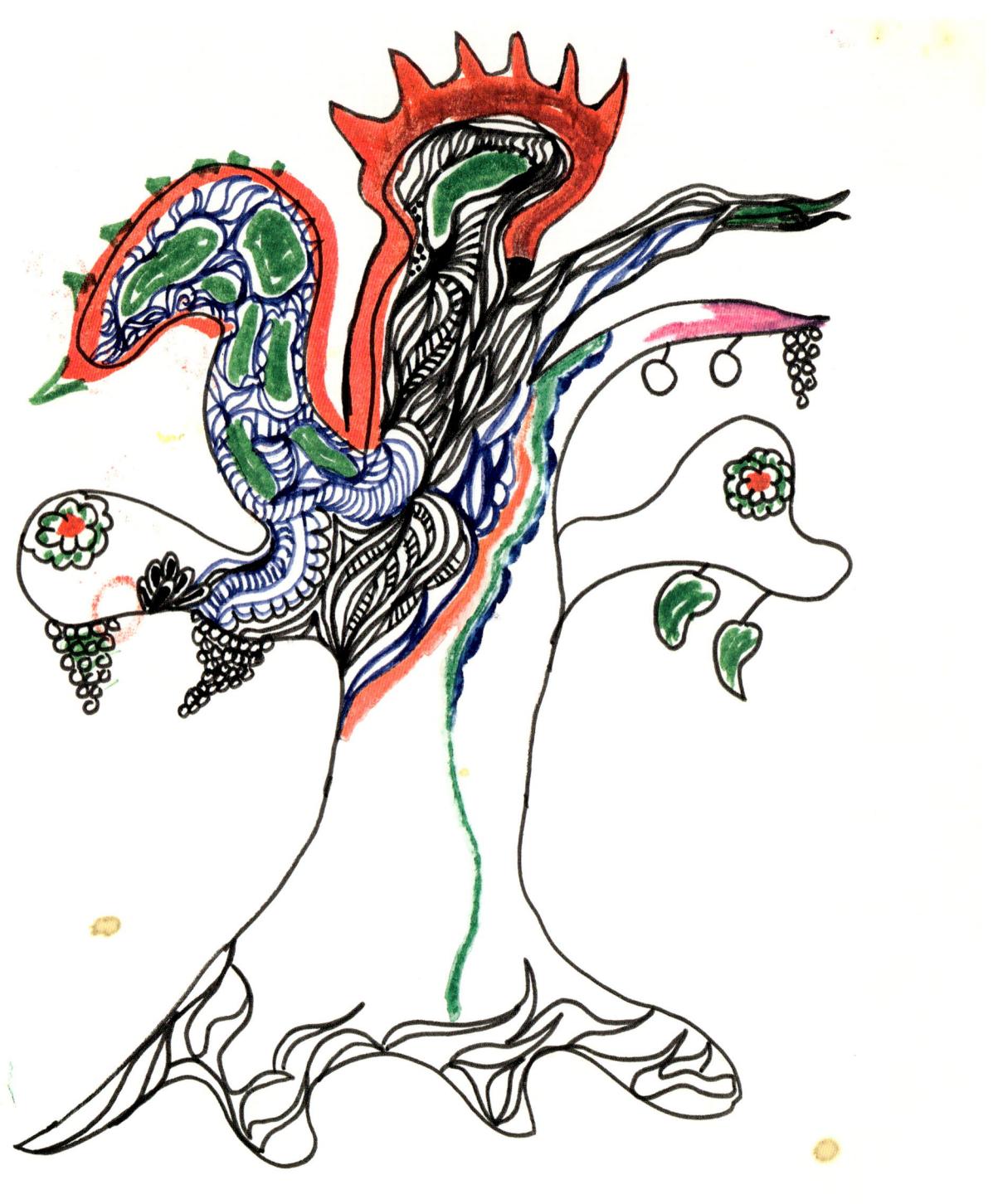

Tree, n.d.
Colored marker on translucent paper
10 $^5/_8$ x 8 $^1/_4$ inches (27 x 21 cm)

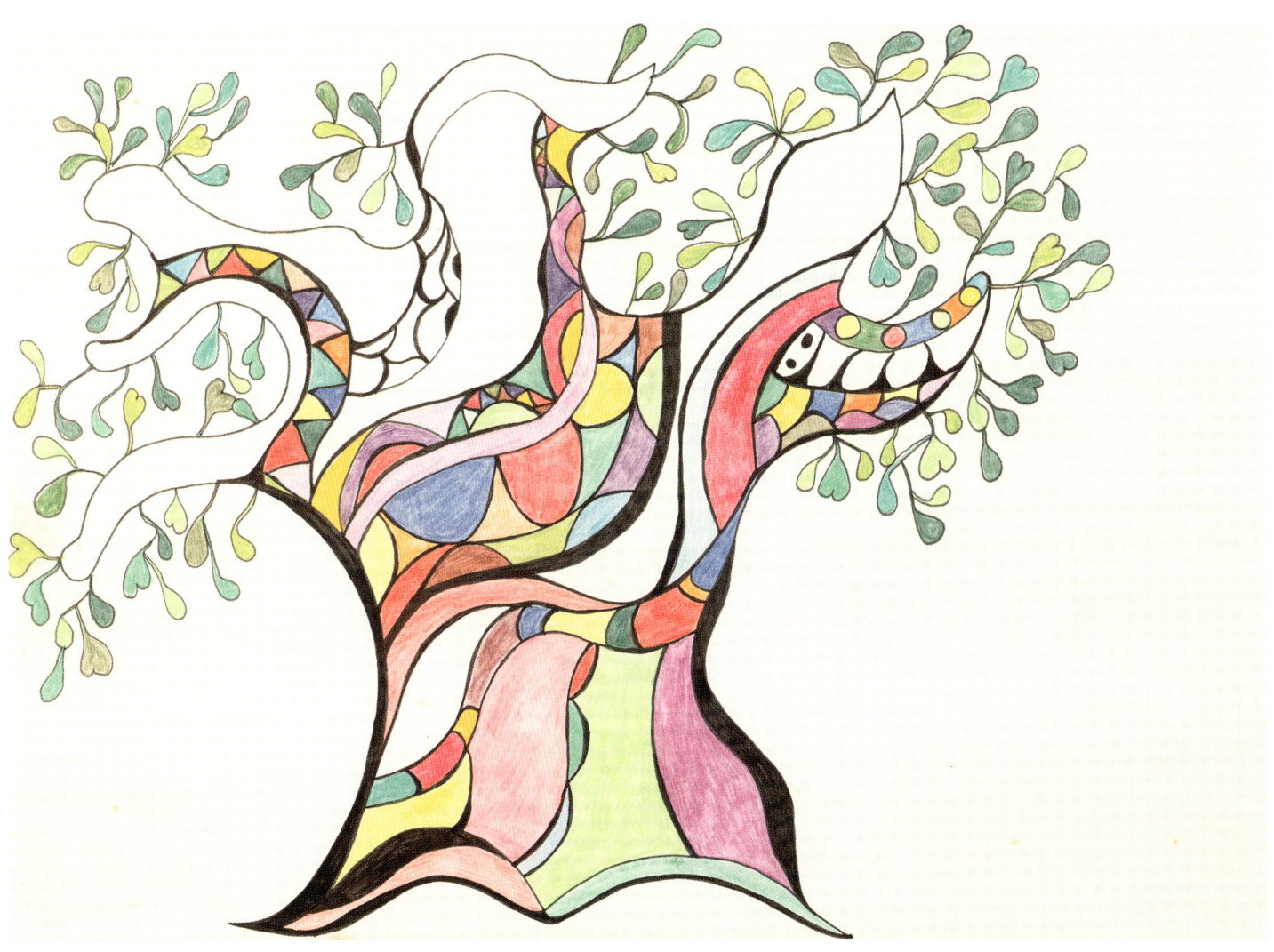

Tree, c. 1985
Colored marker on cardboard
9 $^{13}/_{16}$ x 13 $^{3}/_{4}$ inches (25 x 35 cm)

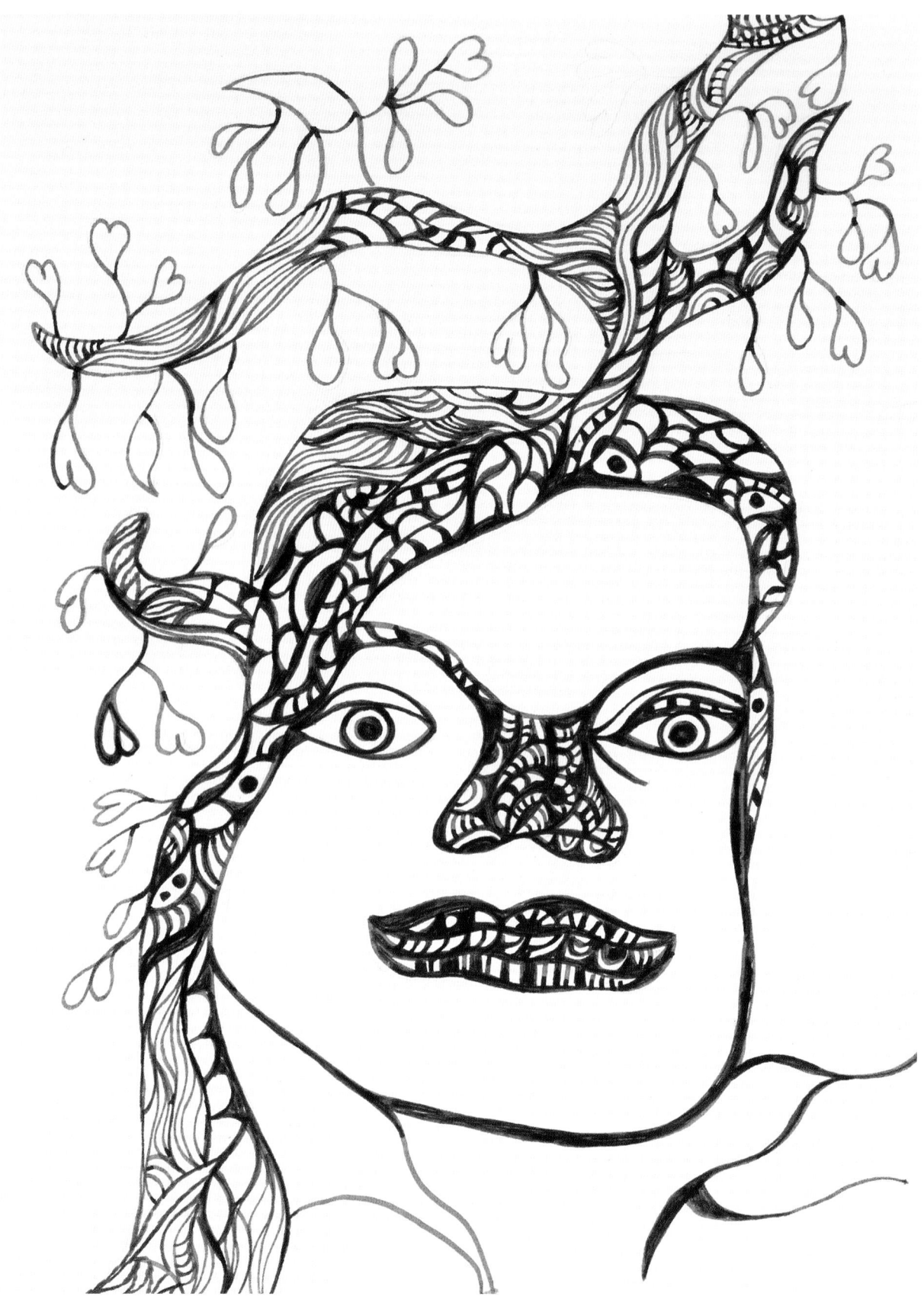

Head with Branches, n.d.
Black fine-line pen and marker on paper
12 $\frac{1}{16}$ x 9 inches (30.7 x 22.9 cm)

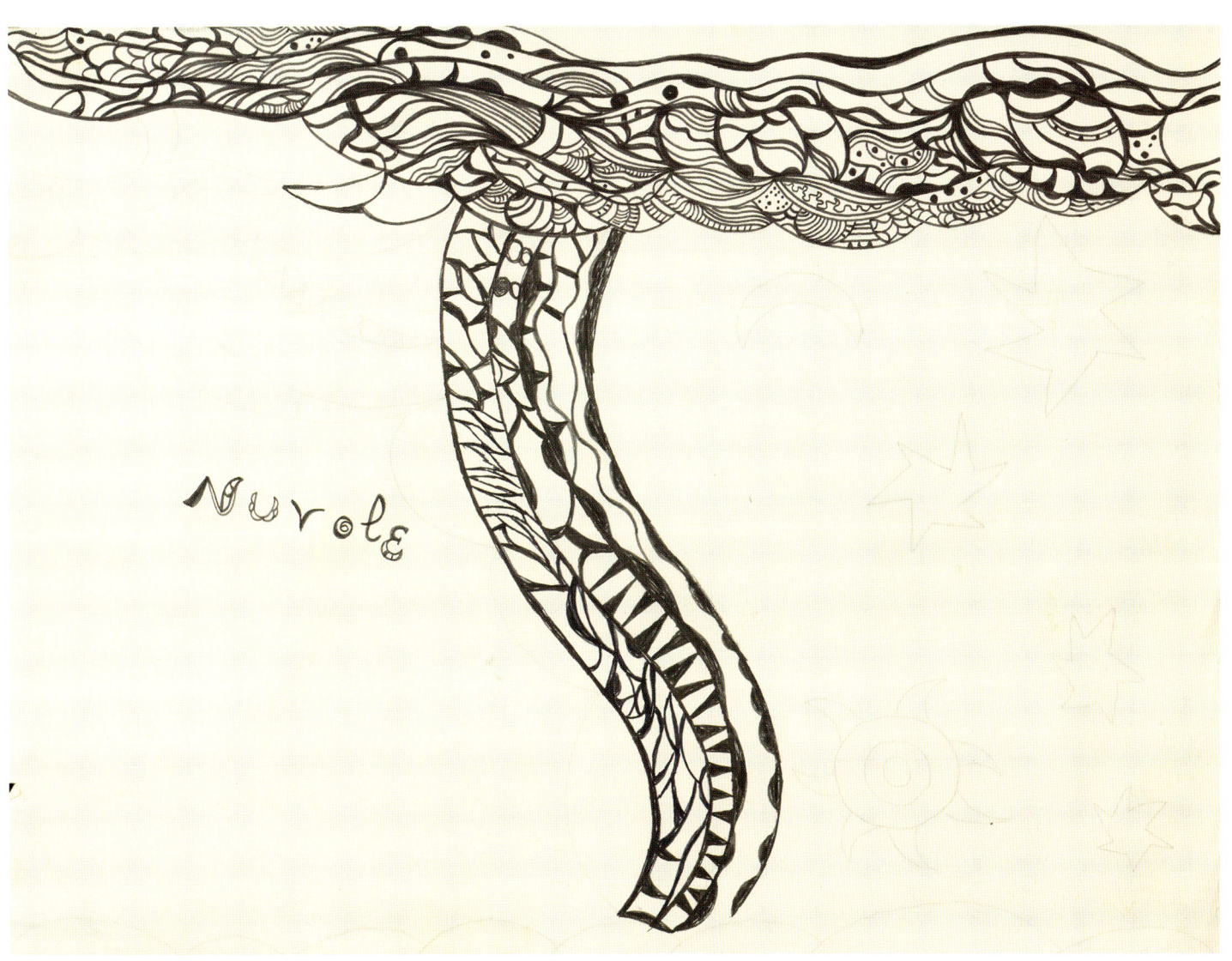

Nuvole (Cloud), n.d.
Black felt-tip pen and black pencil on paper
11 7/8 x 15 15/16 inches (30.2 x 40.5 cm)

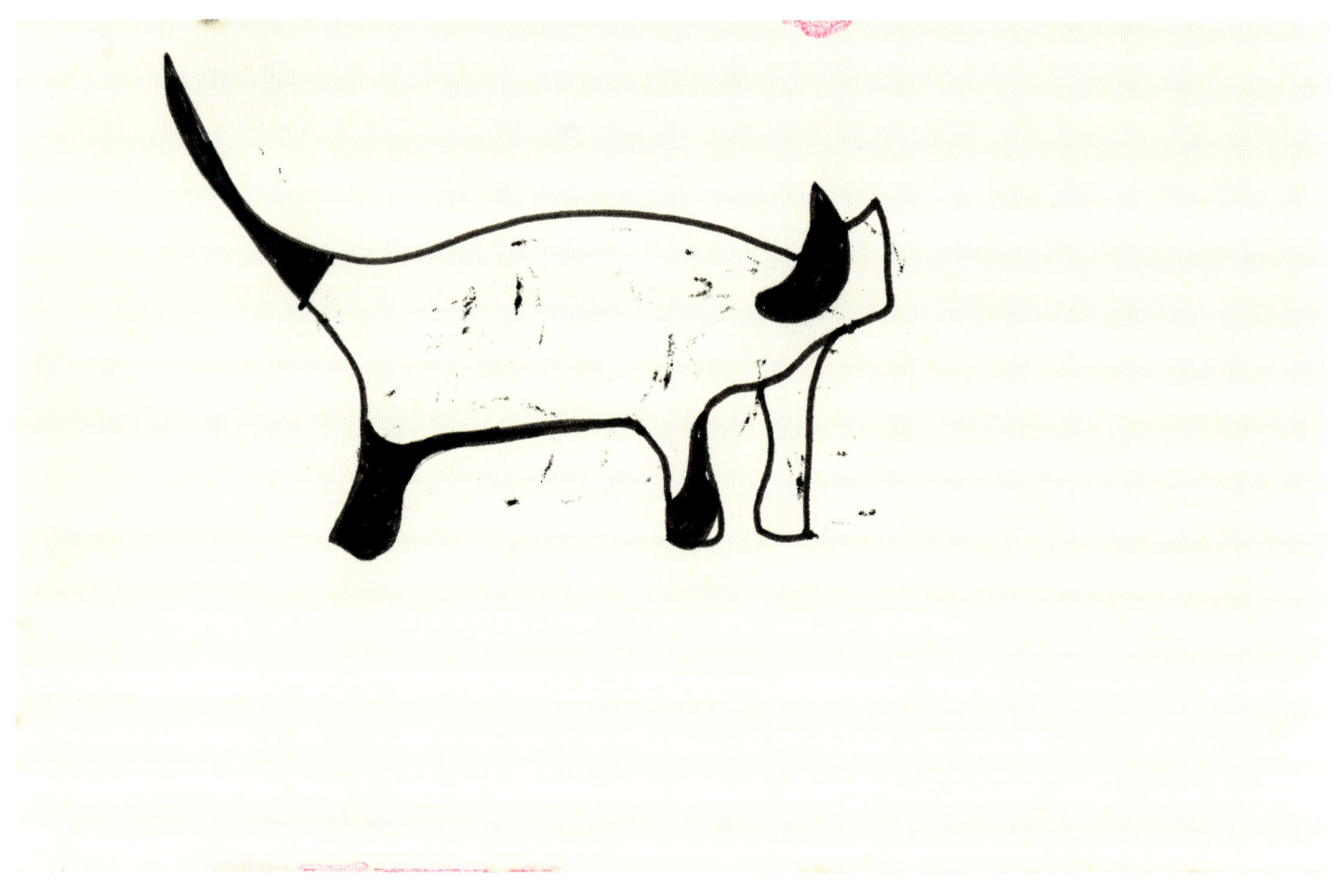

Chat (Cat), 1966–1967
Black marker on paper
5 $\frac{1}{4}$ x 8 $\frac{1}{4}$ inches (13.3 x 21 cm)

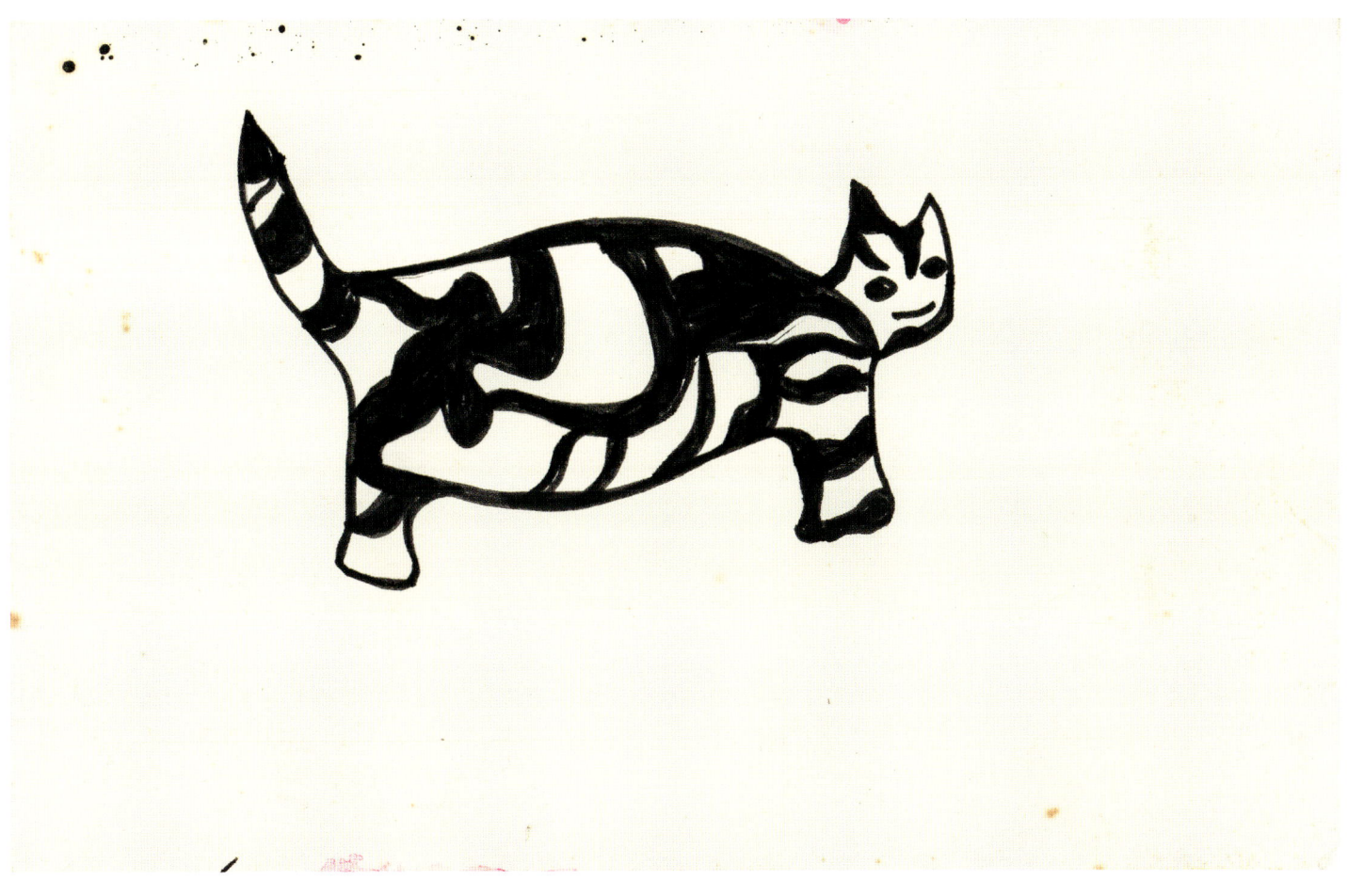

Chat (Cat), 1966–1967
Black marker on paper
5 ¹/₄ x 8 ¹/₄ inches (13.3 x 21 cm)

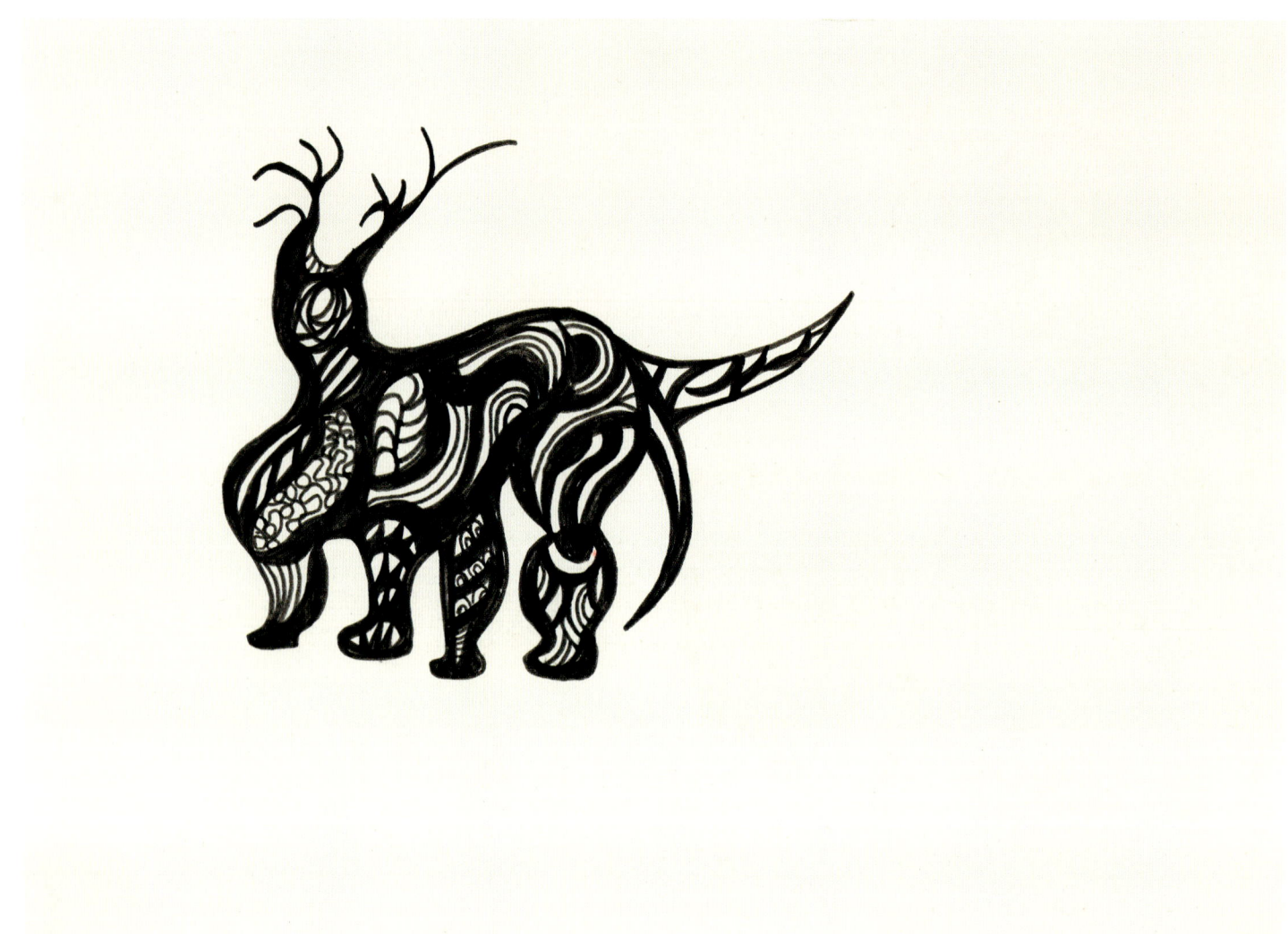

Animal, n.d.
Black felt-tip pen on paper
8 $^5/_{16}$ x 10 $^5/_8$ inches (21.1 x 27 cm)

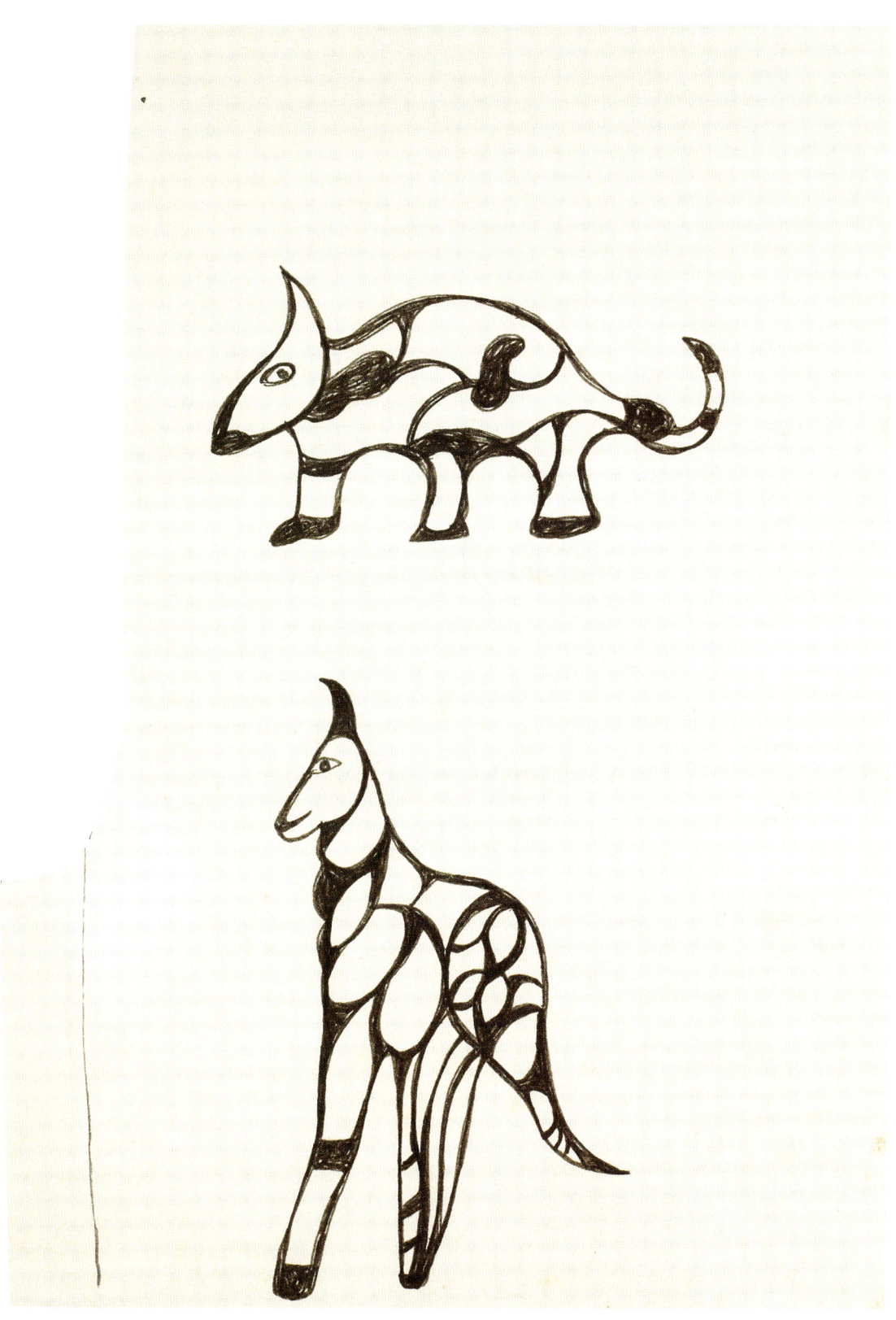

Animaux (Animals), c. 1967
Black ink on paper
9 $^{7}/_{16}$ x 6 $^{9}/_{16}$ inches (24 x 16.7 cm)

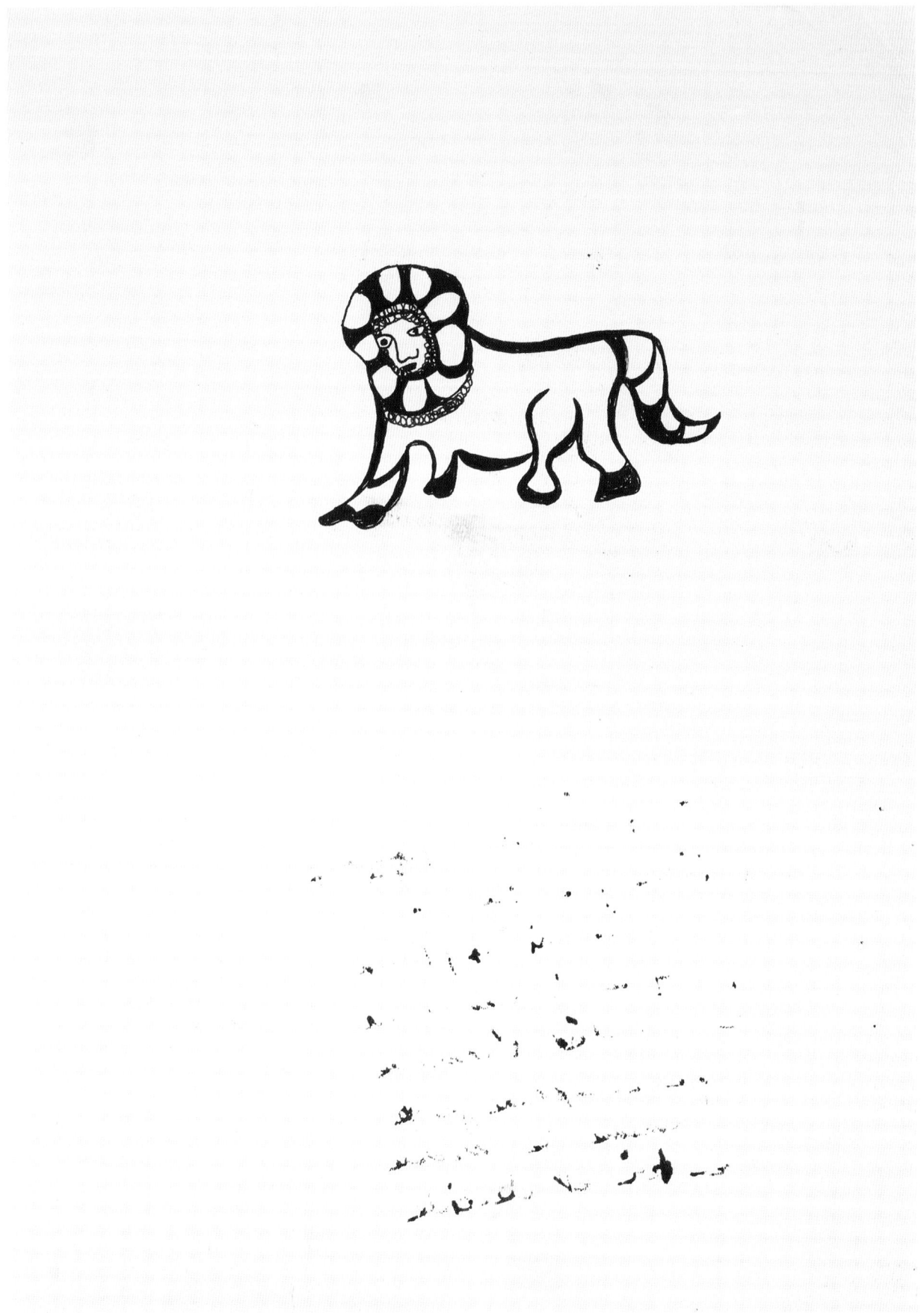

Lion, n.d.
Black fine-line pen on cardboard
16 $^9/_{16}$ x 11 $^3/_4$ inches (42 x 29.8 cm)

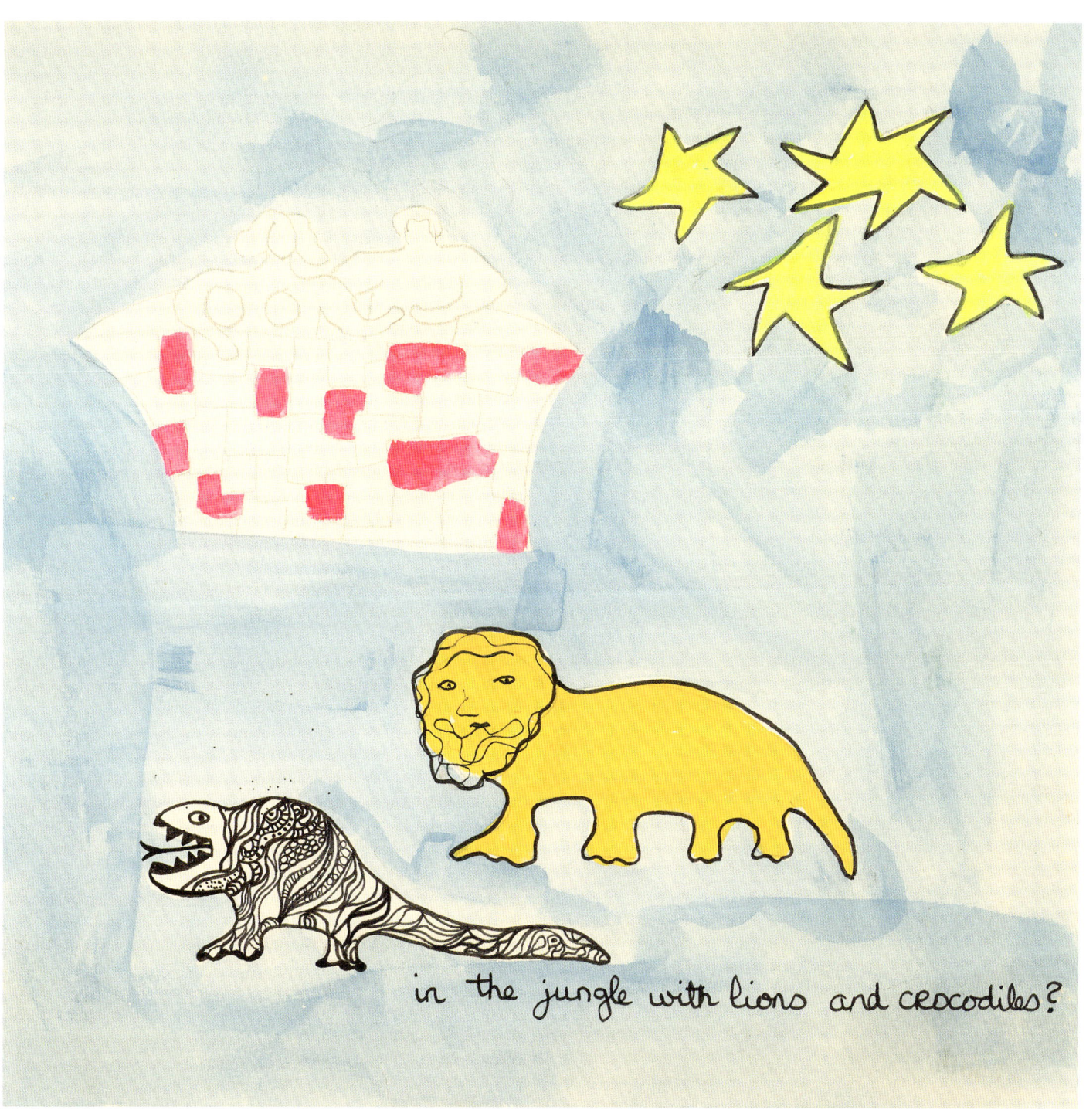

In the jungle with lions and crocodiles?, n.d.
Watercolor on paper
12 ⁵/₈ x 12 ⁵/₈ inches (32 x 32 cm)

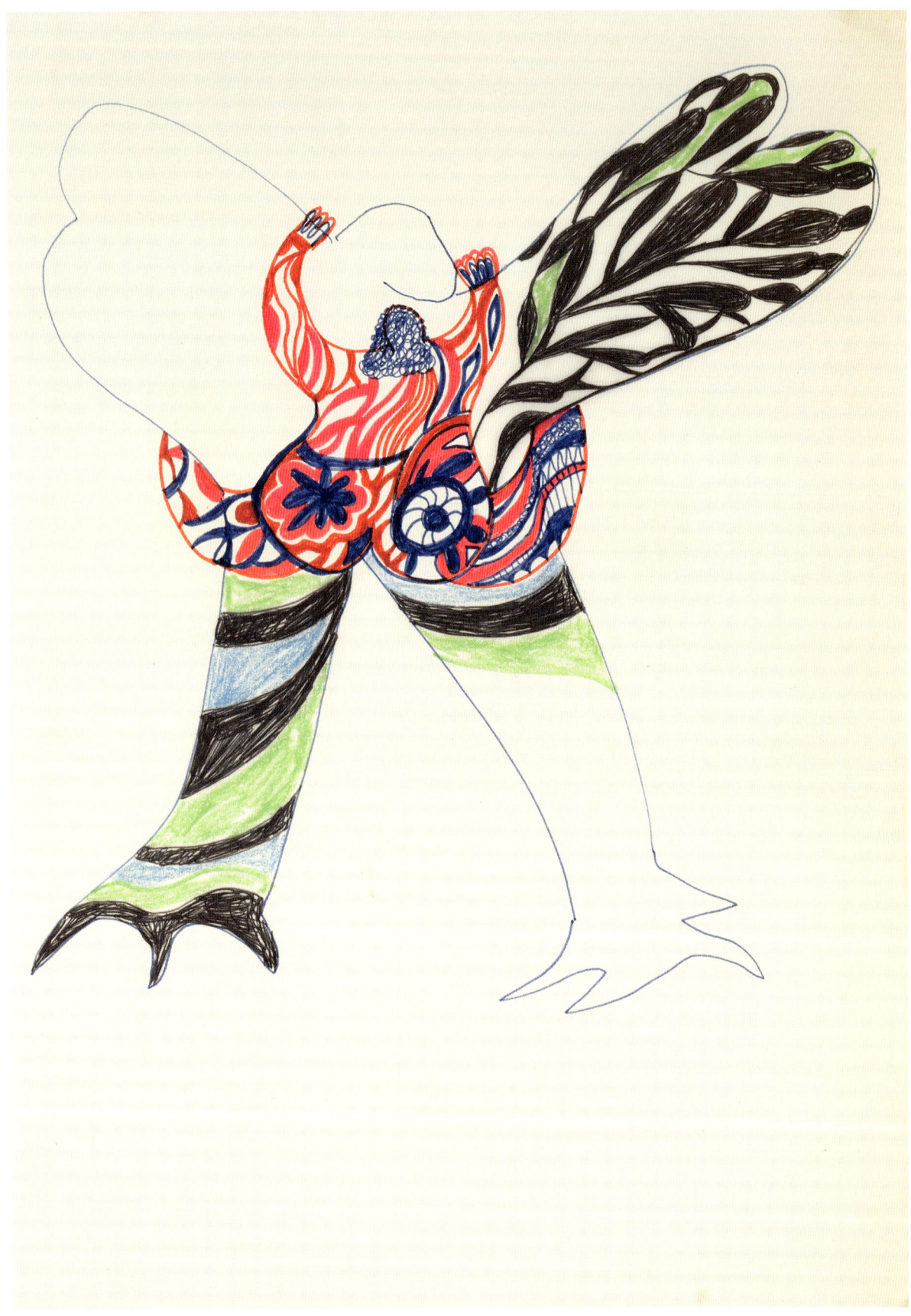

Oiseau Amoureux (Bird in Love), c. 1972
Colored pencil, black and blue fine-line pen, and colored felt-tip pen on paper
13 $^9/_{16}$ x 9 $^5/_8$ inches (34.5 x 24.5 cm)

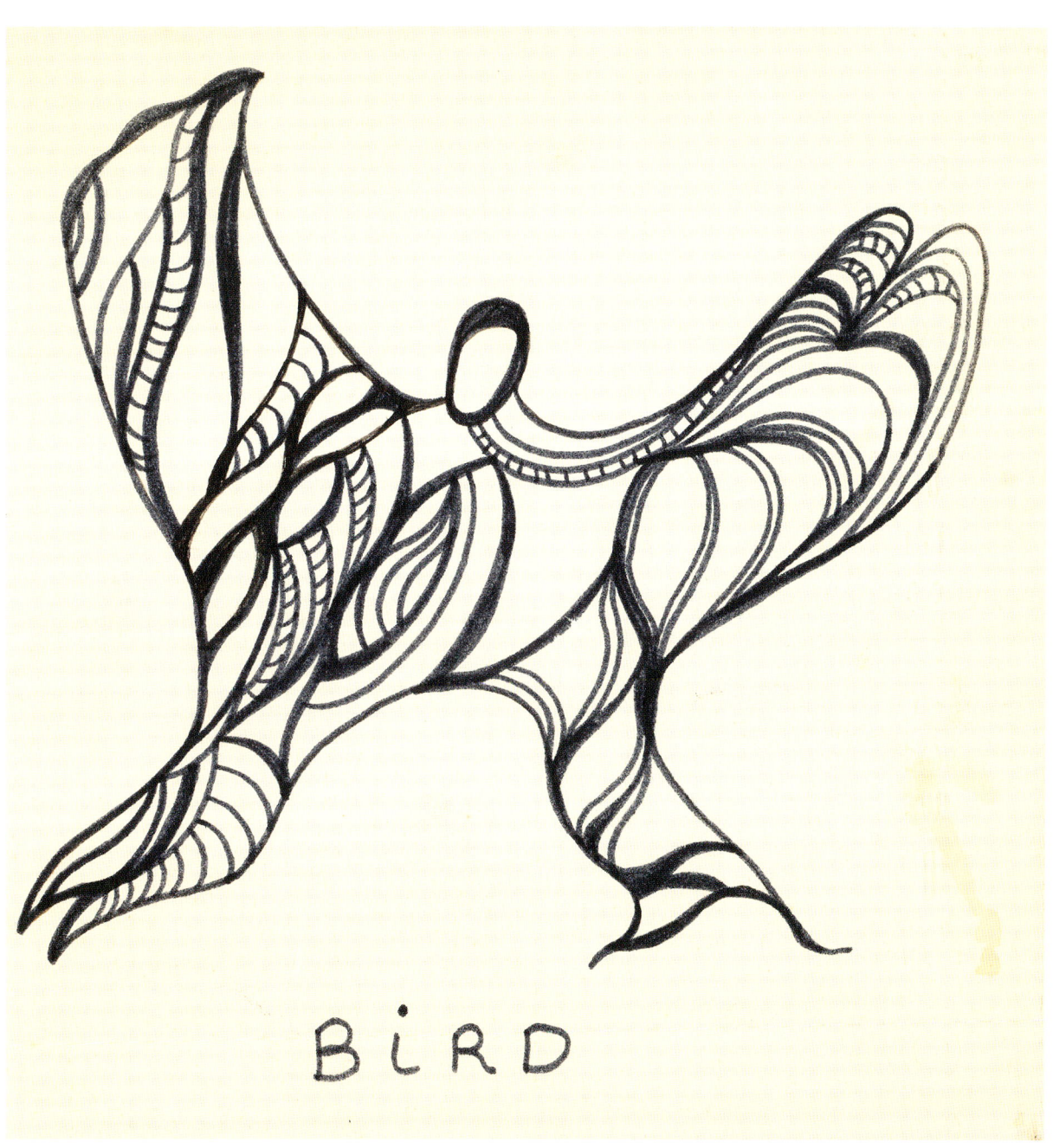

Bird, cover image for unrealized book maquette for *Daddy*, c. 1972
Marker on Canson paper and print
7 x 7 $\frac{1}{4}$ x $\frac{1}{2}$ inches (17.8 x 18.4 x 1.3 cm)

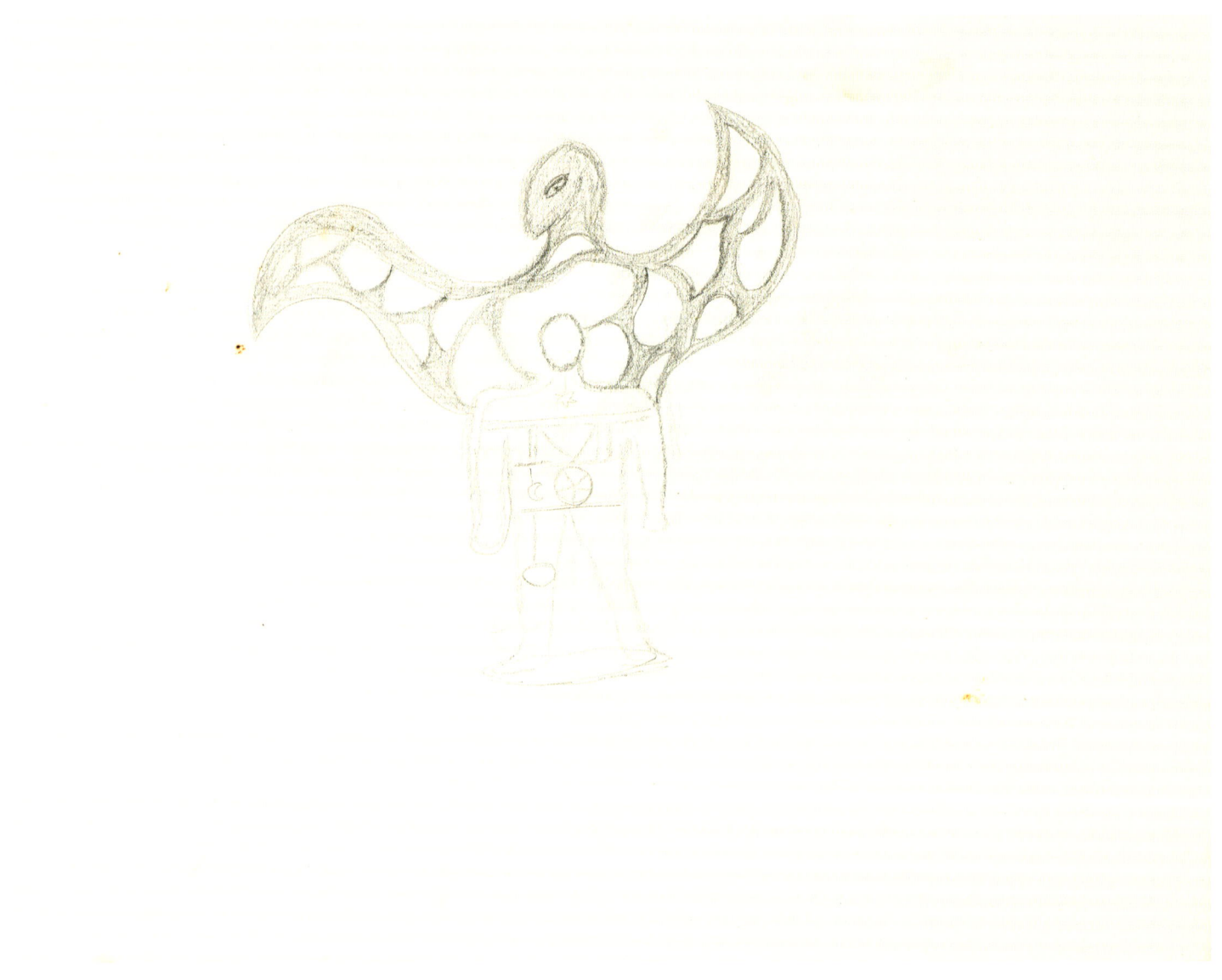

Homme skinny et rossignol ("Skinny" Man and Nightingale), n.d.
Pencil on paper
10 $^5/_8$ x 13 $^3/_8$ inches (27 x 34 cm)

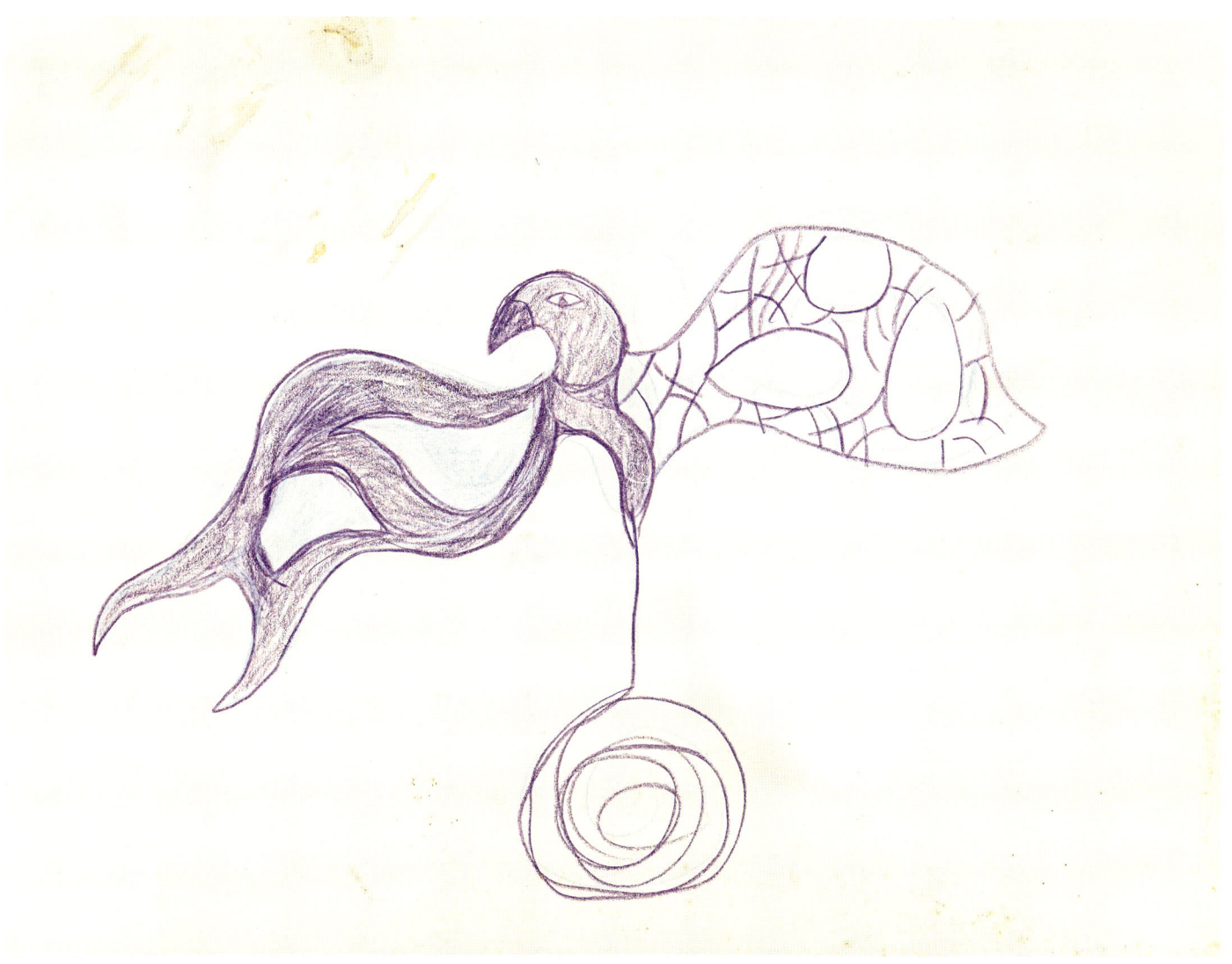

Rossignol (Nightingale), n.d.
Colored pencil on Canson paper "CA grain" (spiral bound book)
9 ¹/₁₆ x 12 ³/₁₆ inches (23 x 31 cm)

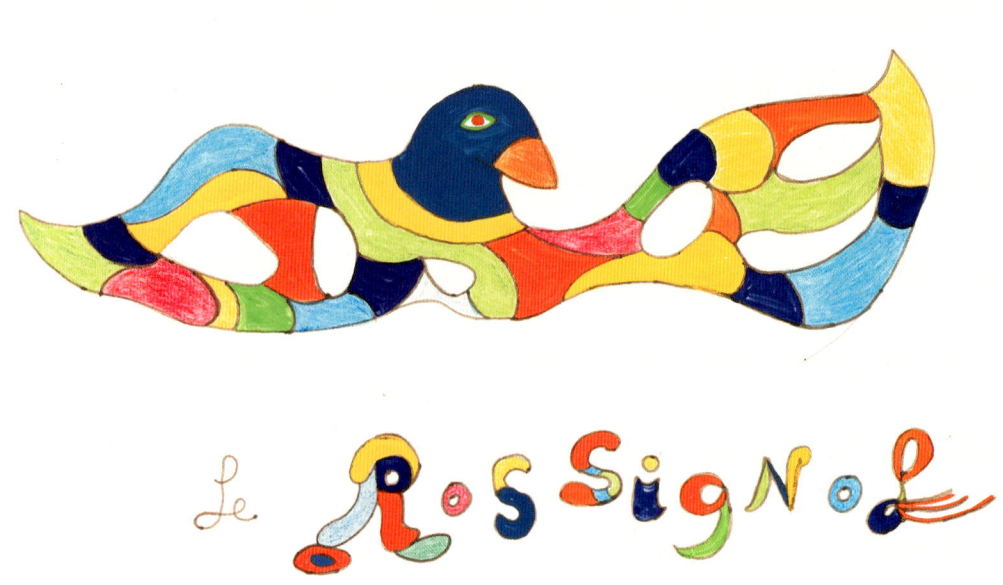

Le rossignol [Esquisse pour Fontaine Stravinsky]
(The Nightingale) [Sketch for Stravinsky Fountain], c. 1983
Felt-tip pen, gouache, and colored pencil on glossy paper
9 $^{1}/_{16}$ x 11 $^{1}/_{4}$ inches (23 x 28.5 cm)

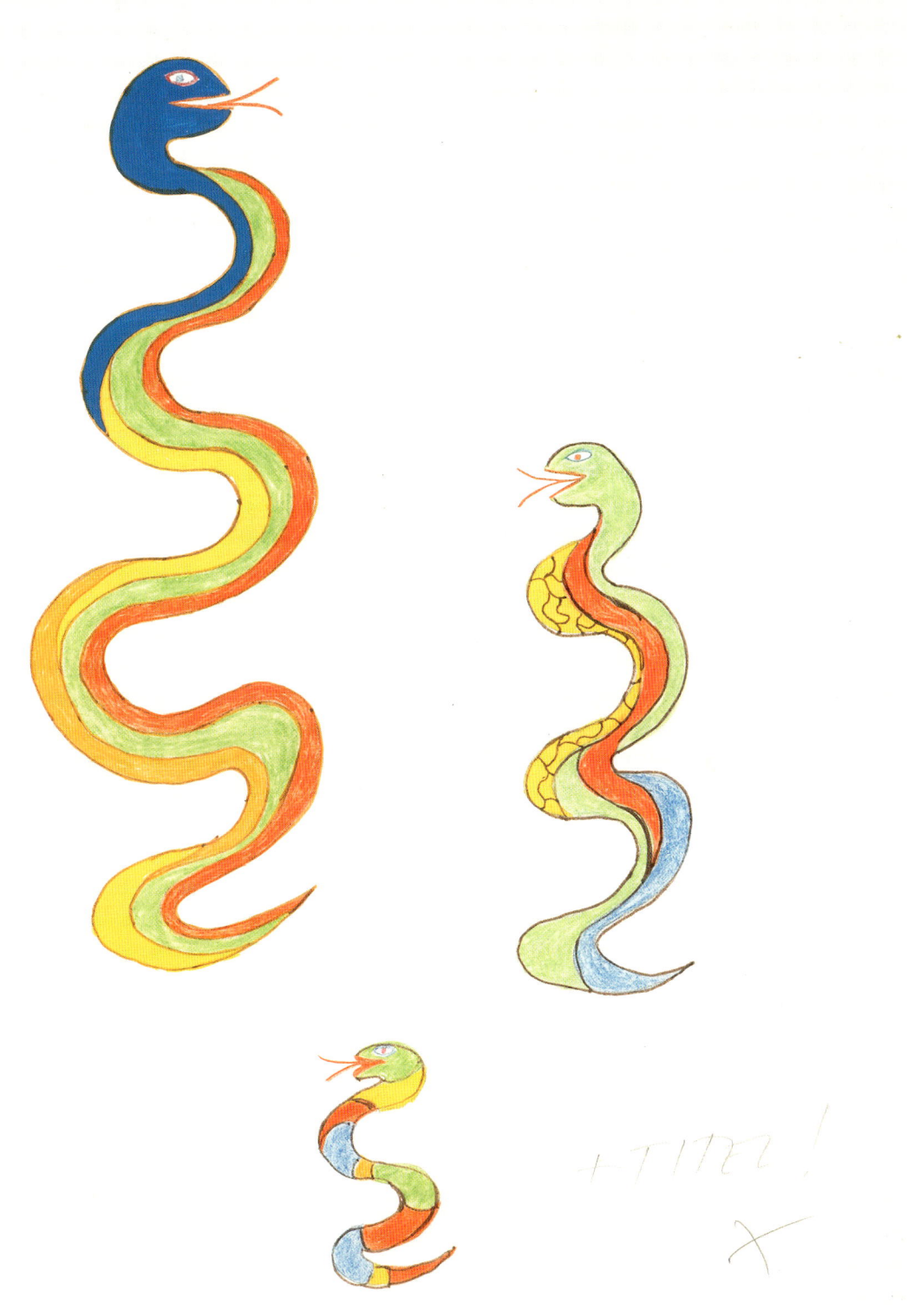

Sans Titre (Serpents spirales) [Esquisse pour Fontaine Stravinsky]
Untitled (Spiral snakes) [Sketch for Stravinsky Fountain], c. 1983
Felt-tip pen, gouache, ankd colored pencil on glossy paper
11 1/4 x 9 1/16 inches (28.6 x 23 cm)

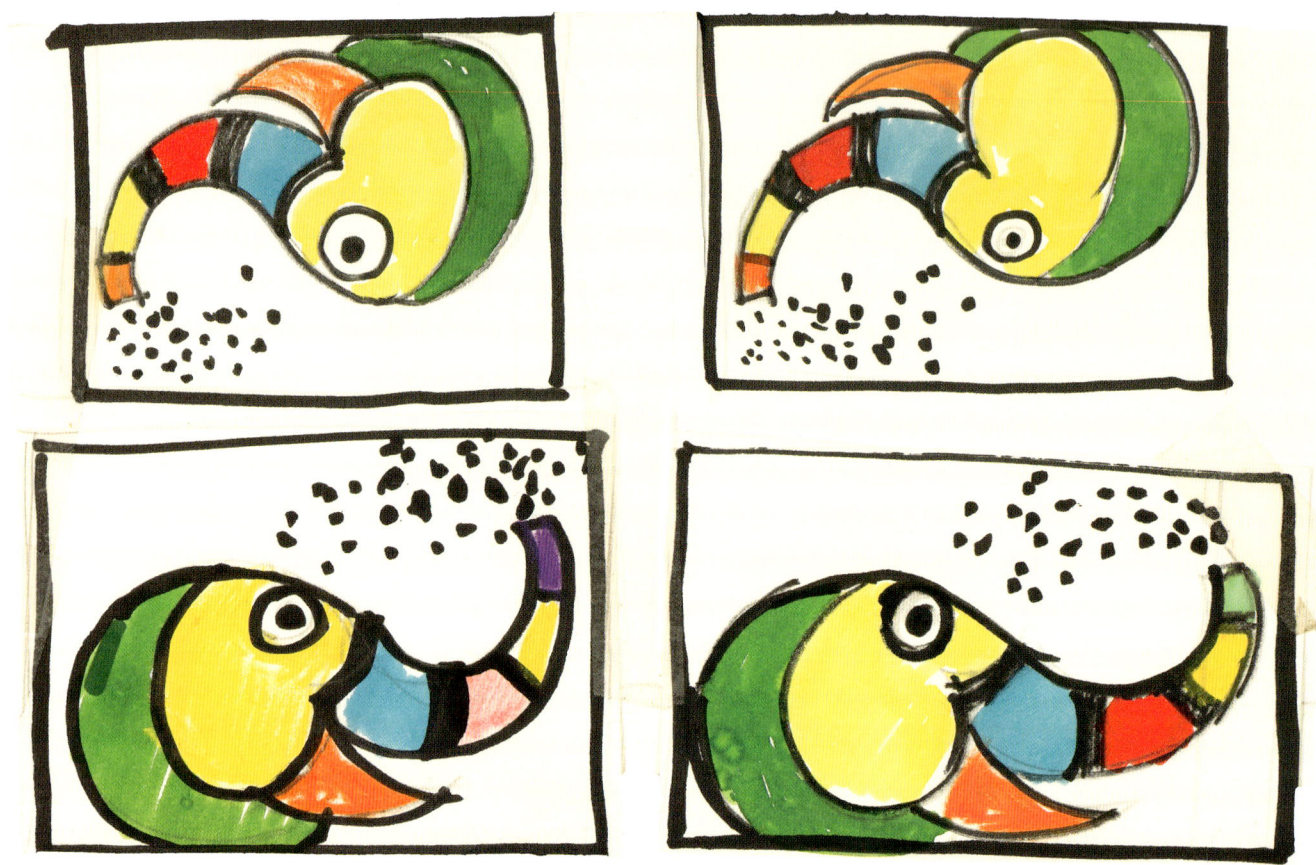

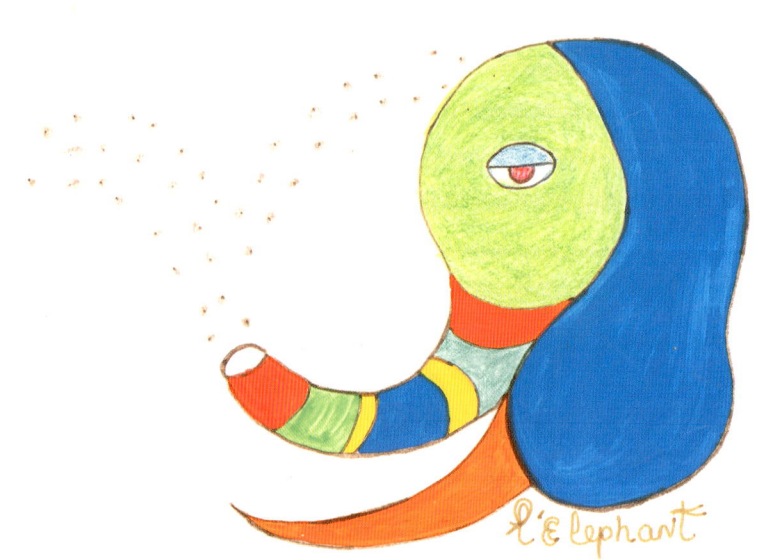

Sans Titre [Eléphants] (Untitled [Elephants]), c. 1983
Felt-tip pen and black pencil on BFK Rives paper; two images cut out and
taped to paper on which the other two images are drawn 6 ¹¹/₁₆ x 10 ¹³/₁₆ inches (17 x 27.5 cm)

L'Eléphant [Esquisse pour Fontaine Stravinsky] (Elephant [Sketch for Stravinsky Fountain]), c. 1983
Felt-tip pen, gouache, and colored pencil on glossy paper
5 ⁹/₁₆ x 9 ¹/₈ inches (14.2 x 23.1 cm)

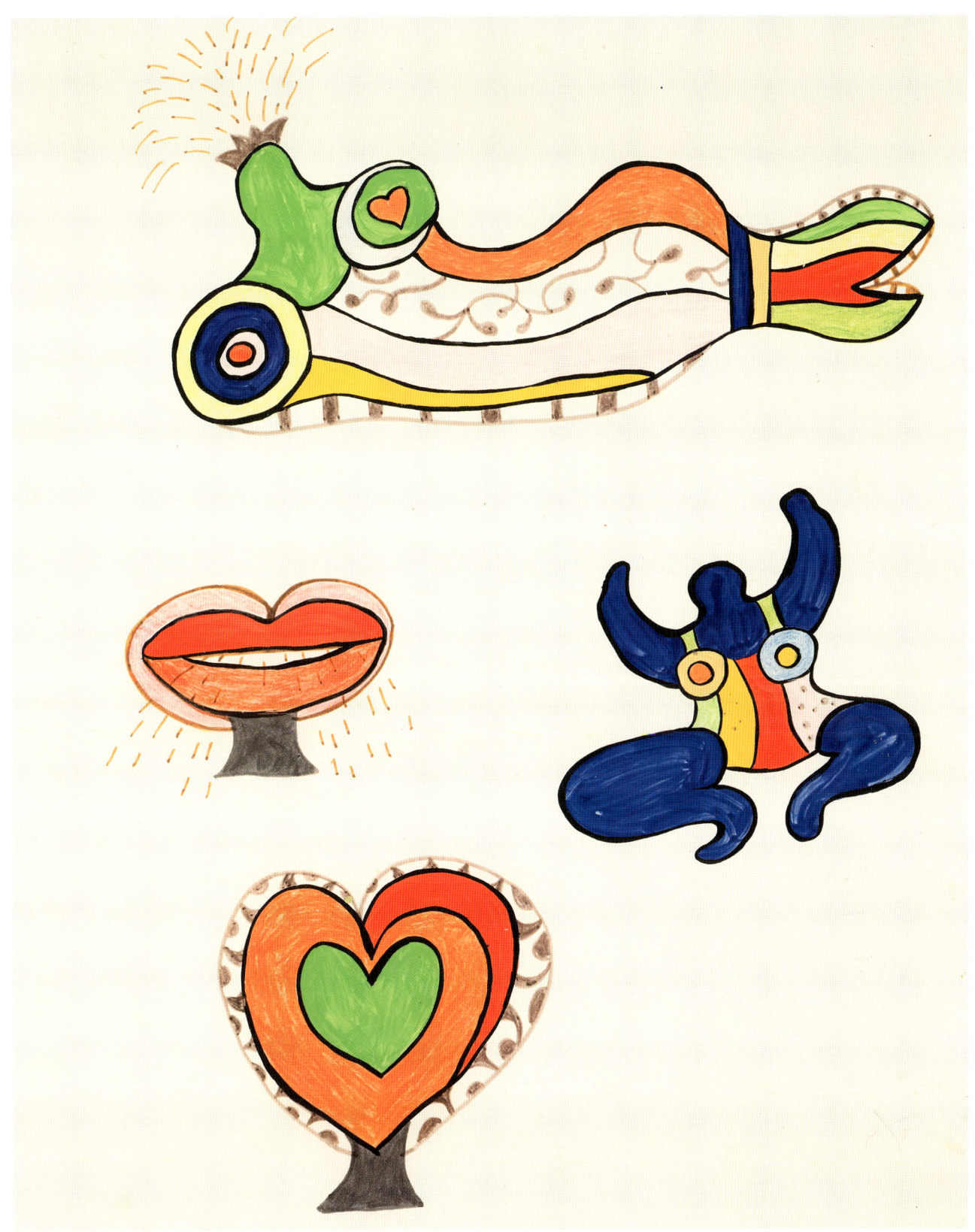

Sans Titre [Coeur, Sirene, Levres...] (Esquisse pour Fontaine Stravinsky)
(Untitled (Heart, Siren, Lips...) (Sketch for Stravinsky Fountain), c. 1983
Felt-tip pen, gouache, and colored pencil on glossy paper
11 $\frac{1}{4}$ x 9 $\frac{1}{16}$ inches (28.5 x 23 cm)

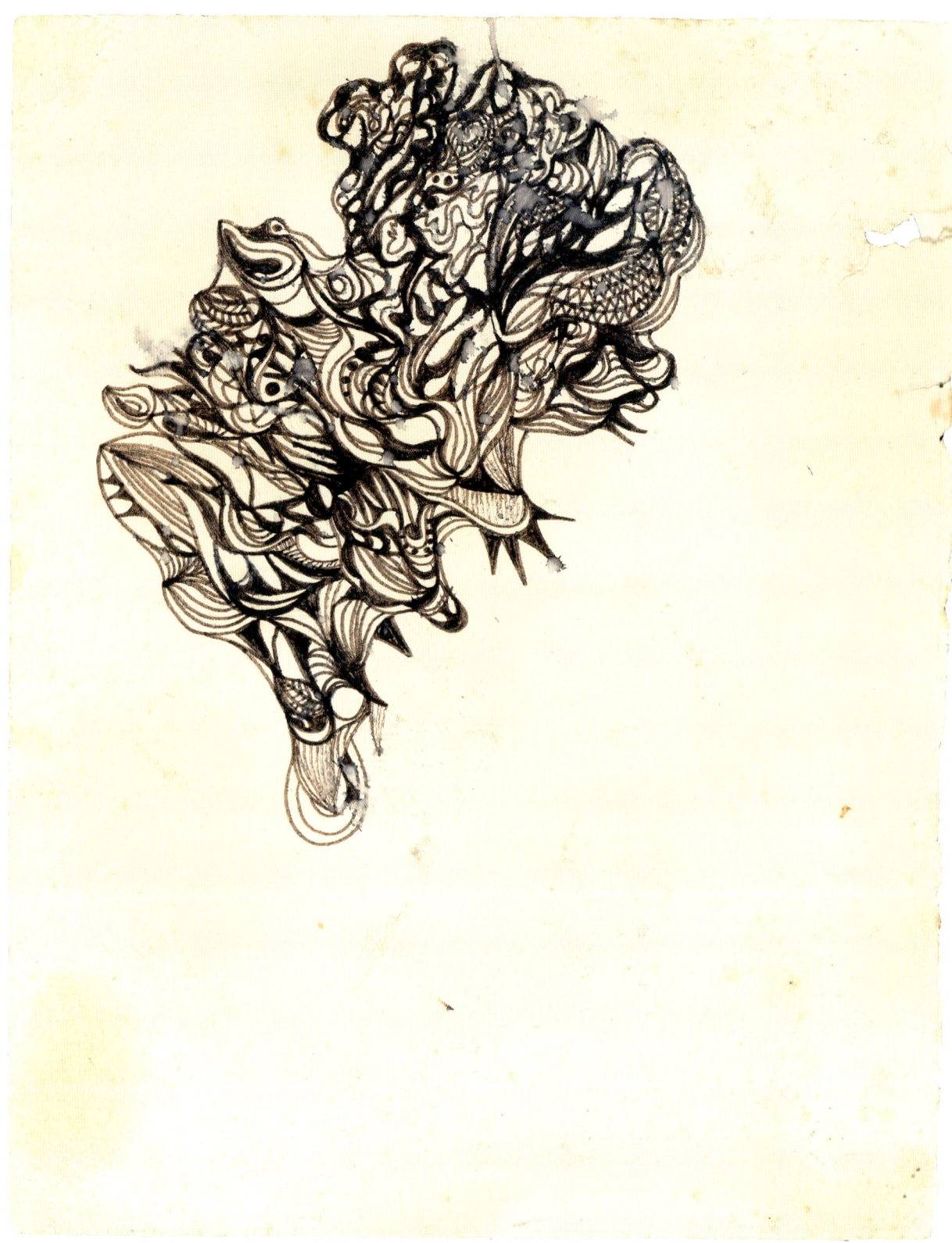

Design, n.d.
Pencil on paper
12 $^3/_8$ x 9 $^3/_4$ inches (31.4 x 24.7 cm)

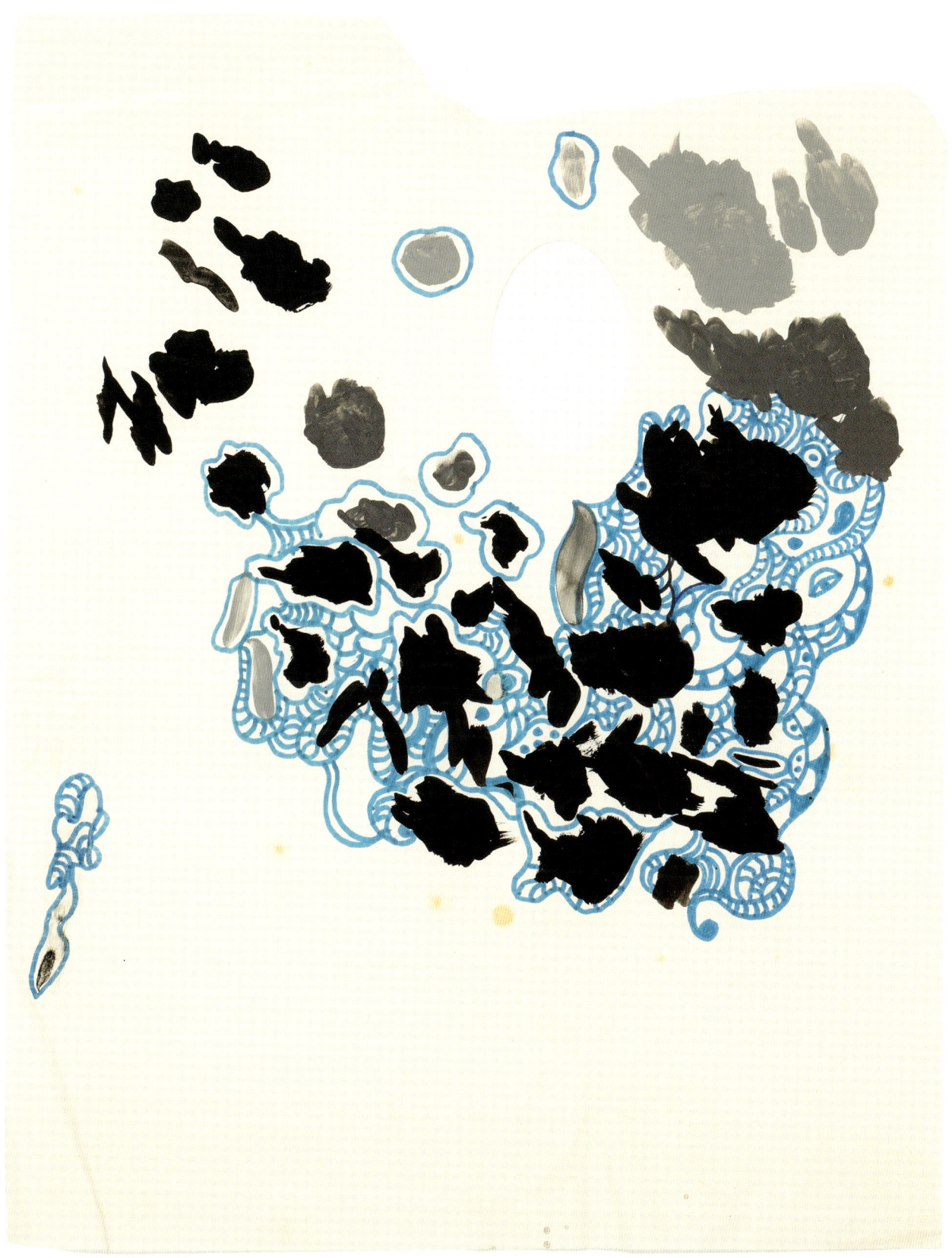

Design, n.d.
Blue marker and gray and black watercolor on glossy paper
13 ³/₄ x 10 ⁵/₈ inches (35 x 27 cm)

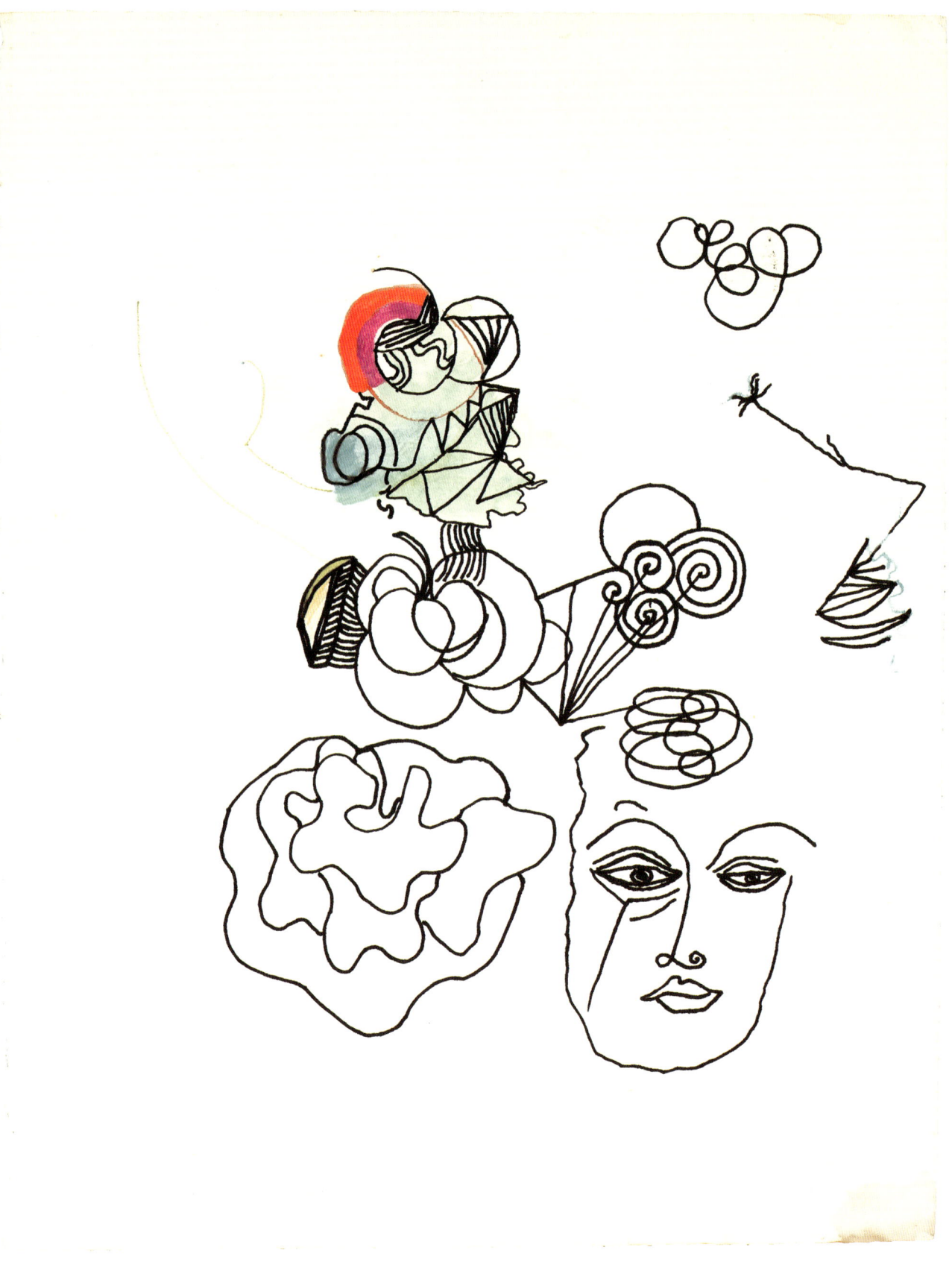

Design (*Face, Scribbles*), n.d.
Black marker and watercolor on paper
12 3/8 x 9 5/8 inches (31.5 x 24.5 cm)

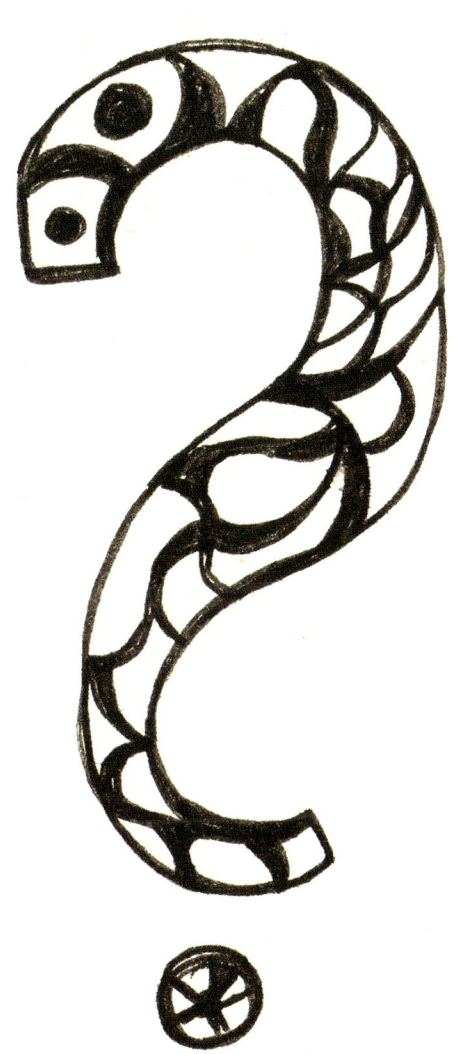

Question (Design for ceramic tile), c. 1985
Black ink on paper
5 $\frac{1}{8}$ x 3 $\frac{7}{8}$ inches (13 x 9.8 cm)

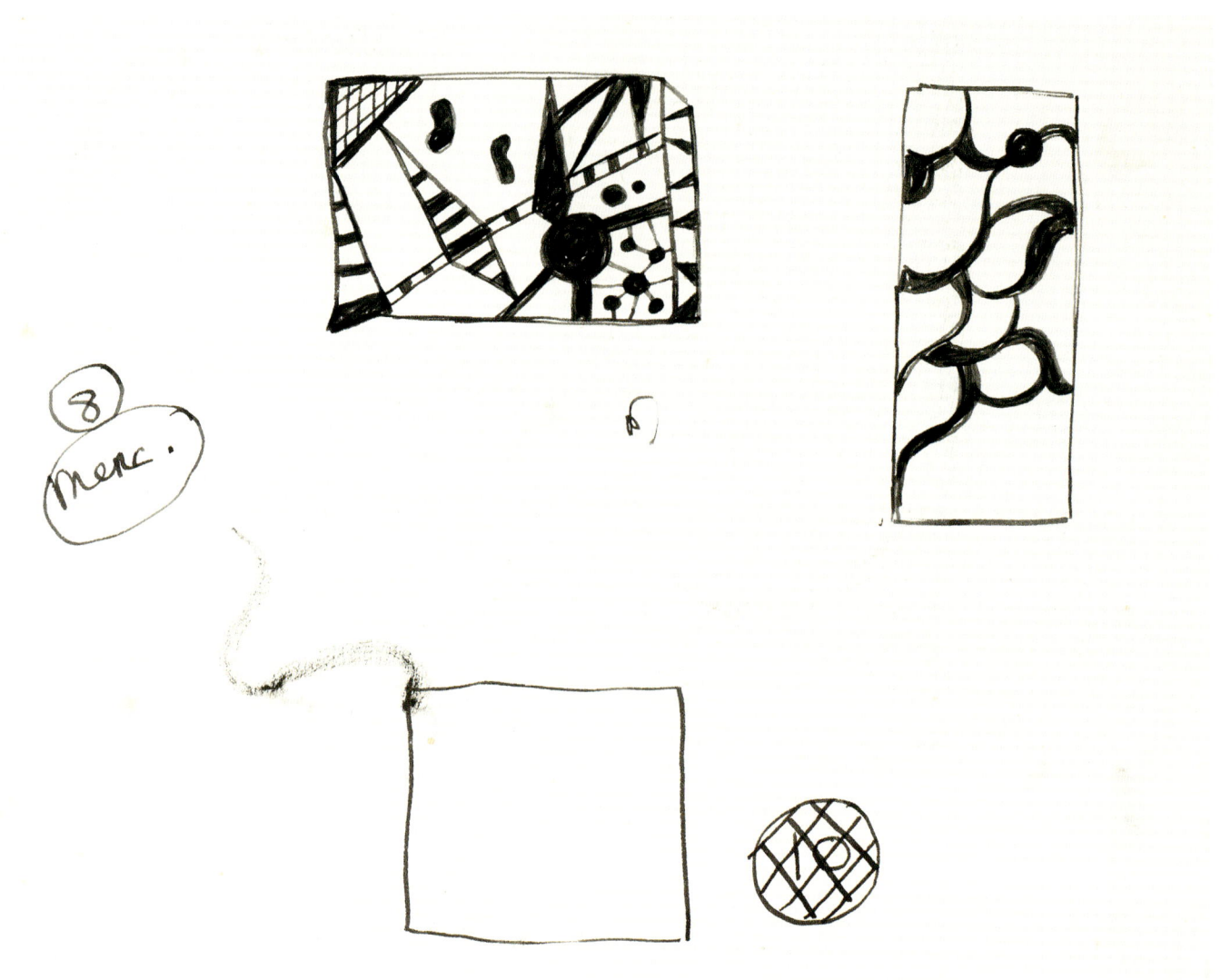

Design (Boxes), n.d.
Black ink on paper
9 x 11 $^{15}/_{16}$ inches (22.9 x 30.4 cm)

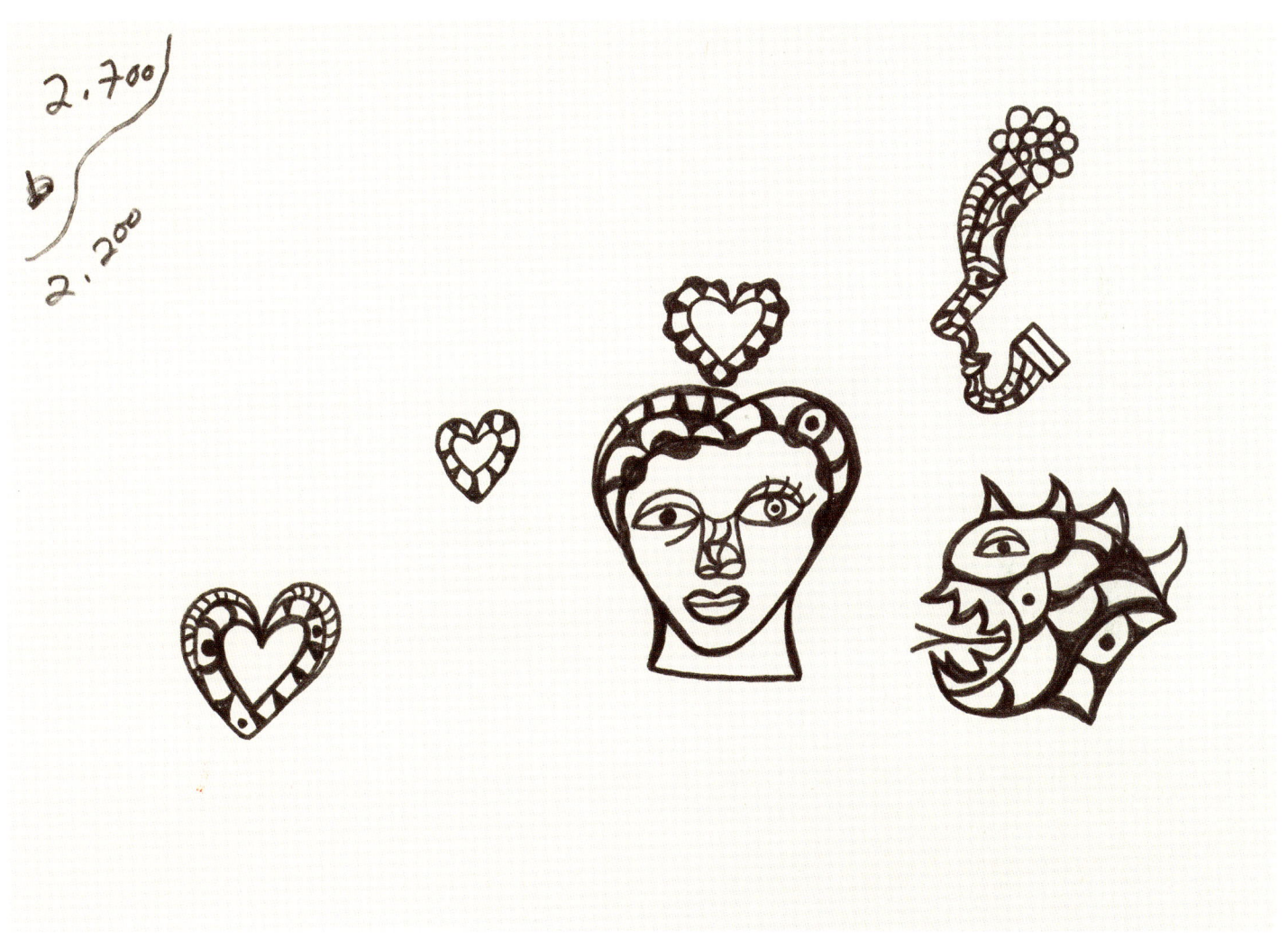

Faces, Hearts, Dragon, n.d.
Black marker on paper
8 1/4 x 11 11/16 inches (21 x 29.7 cm)

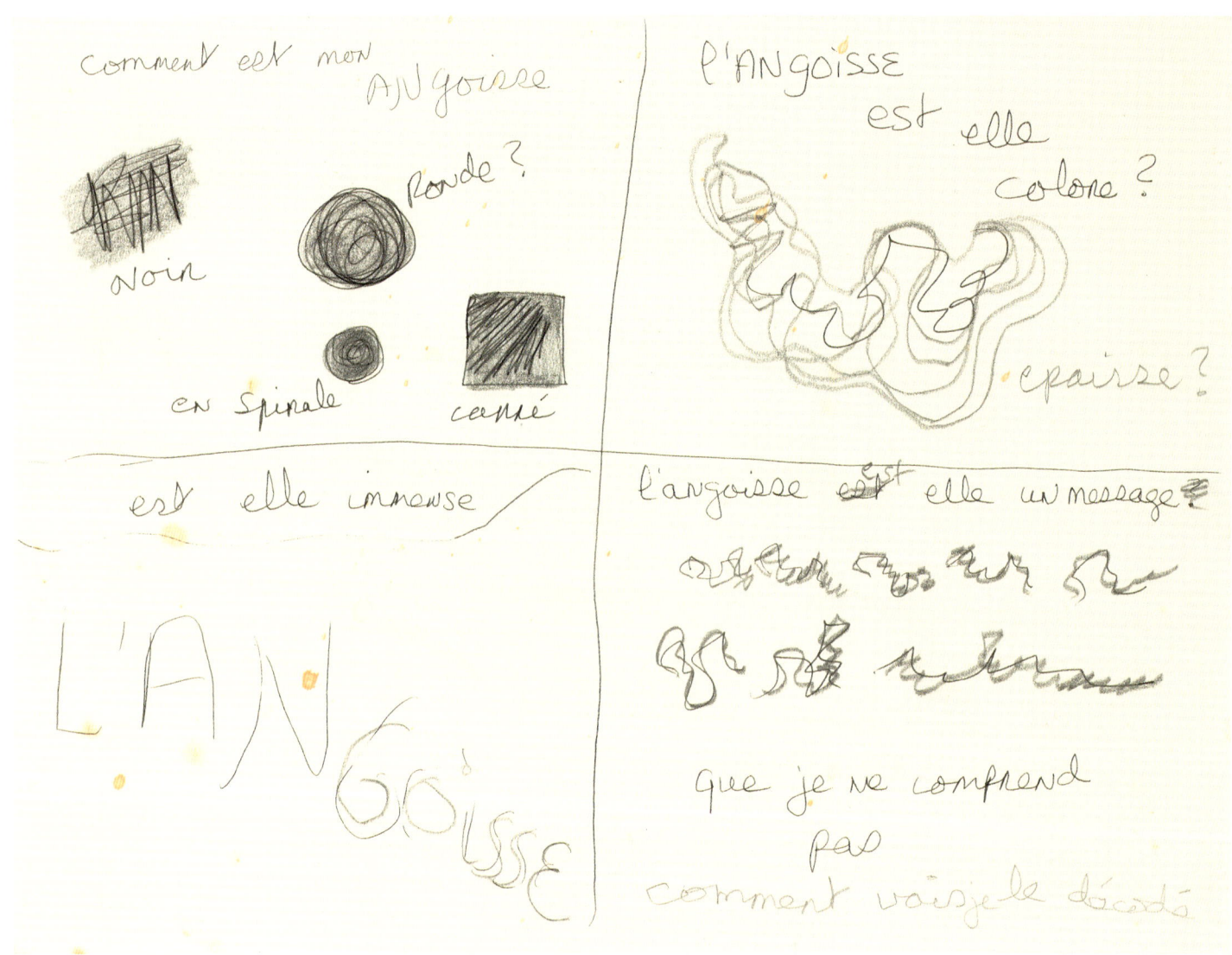

comment est mon ANgoisse

Noir

Ronde ?

en Spirale

carré

L'ANGOISSE

est elle colore ?

epaisse ?

est elle immense

l'angoisse est elle un message

que je ne comprend pas

comment vais je le décodé

L'Angoisse (Anxiety), n.d.
Black fine-line pen and pencil on sketchpad cardboard
9 7/16 x 12 5/8 inches (24 x 32 cm)

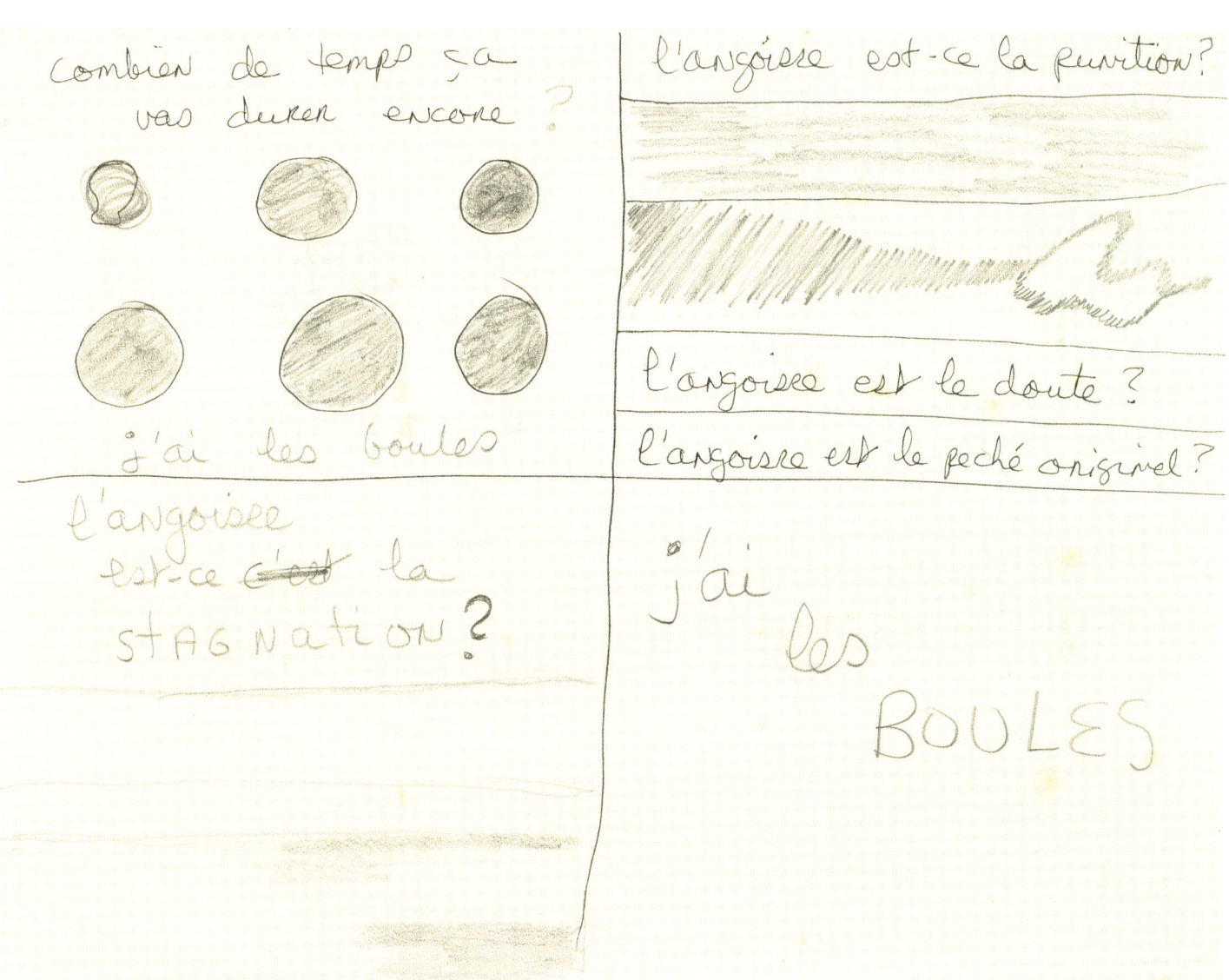

combien de temps ça
vas durer encore ?

j'ai les boules

l'angoisse
est-ce c'est la
STAGNATION ?

l'angoisse est-ce la punition?

l'angoisse est le doute ?
l'angoisse est le péché originel?

j'ai
les
BOULES

L'Angoisse (Anxiety), n.d.
Black fine-line pen and pencil on sketchpad cardboard
9 7/16 x 12 5/8 inches (24 x 32 cm)

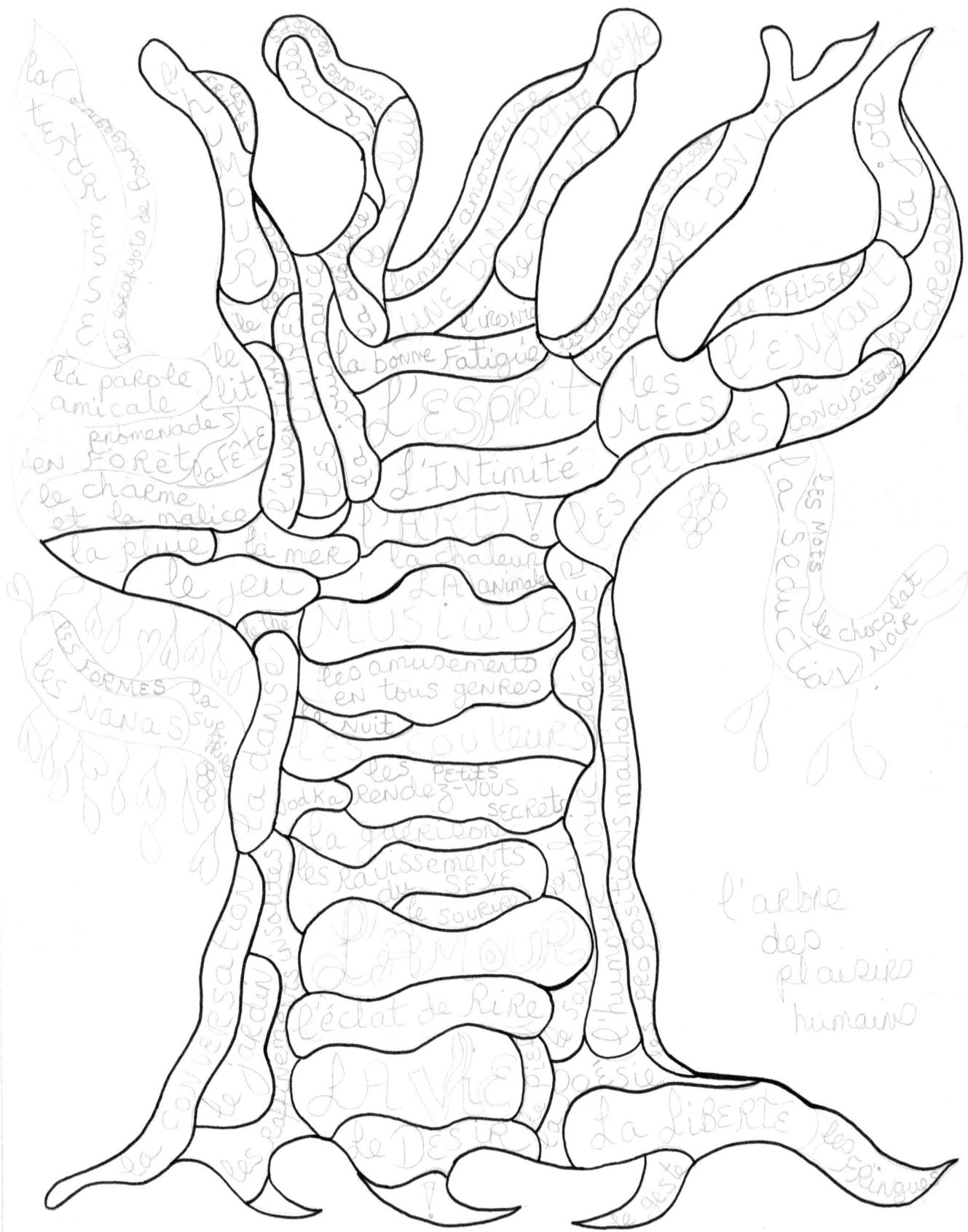

L'arbre des plaisirs humains (The Tree of Human Pleasures), n.d.
Felt-tip pen and black pencil on drawing pad page
16 ¹⁵/₁₆ x 14 inches (43.1 x 35.6 cm)

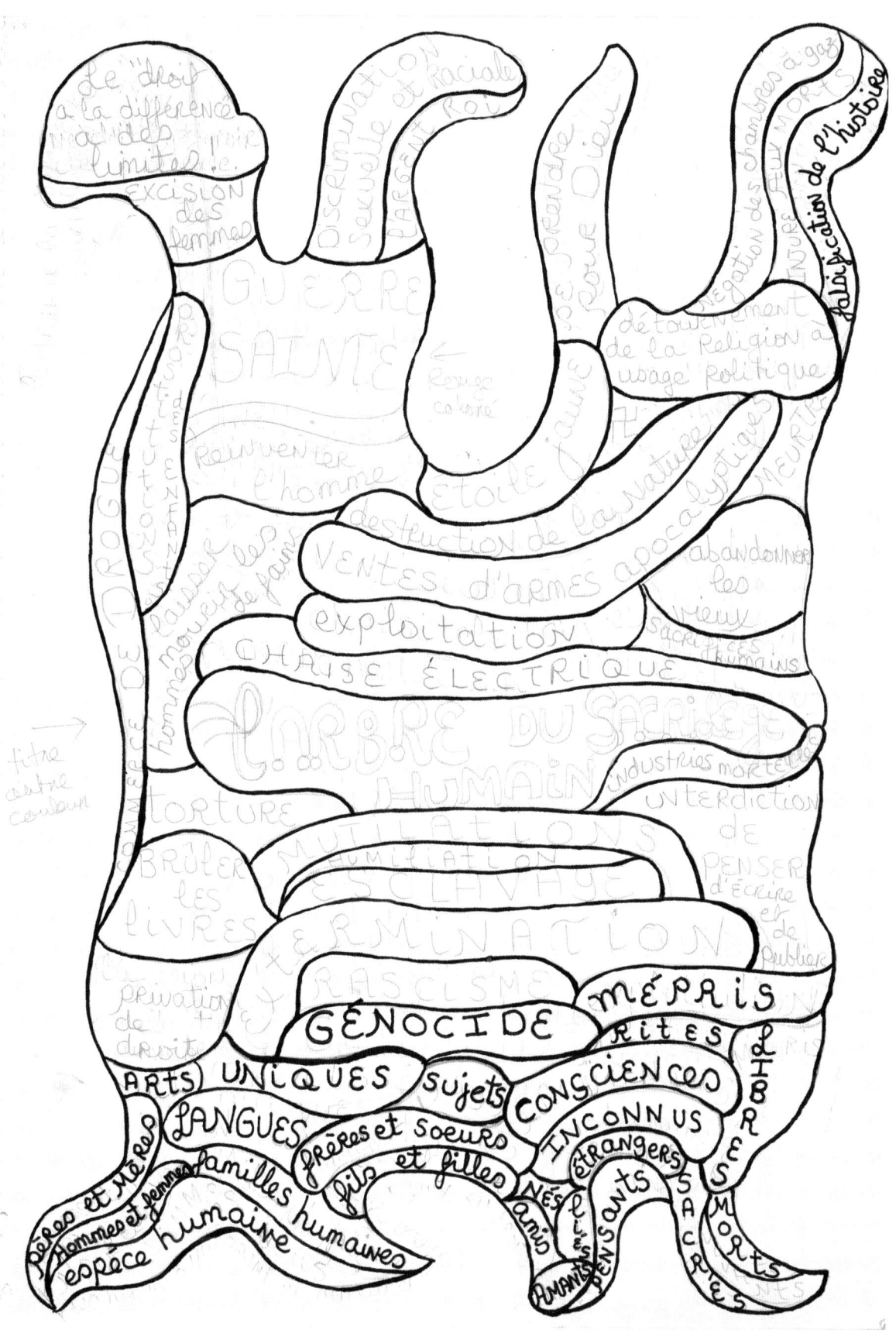

L'arbre du sacrifice humain (The Tree of Human Sacrifice), n.d.
Black pencil and felt-tip pen on paper
16 9/16 x 11 5/8 inches (42 x 29.5 cm)

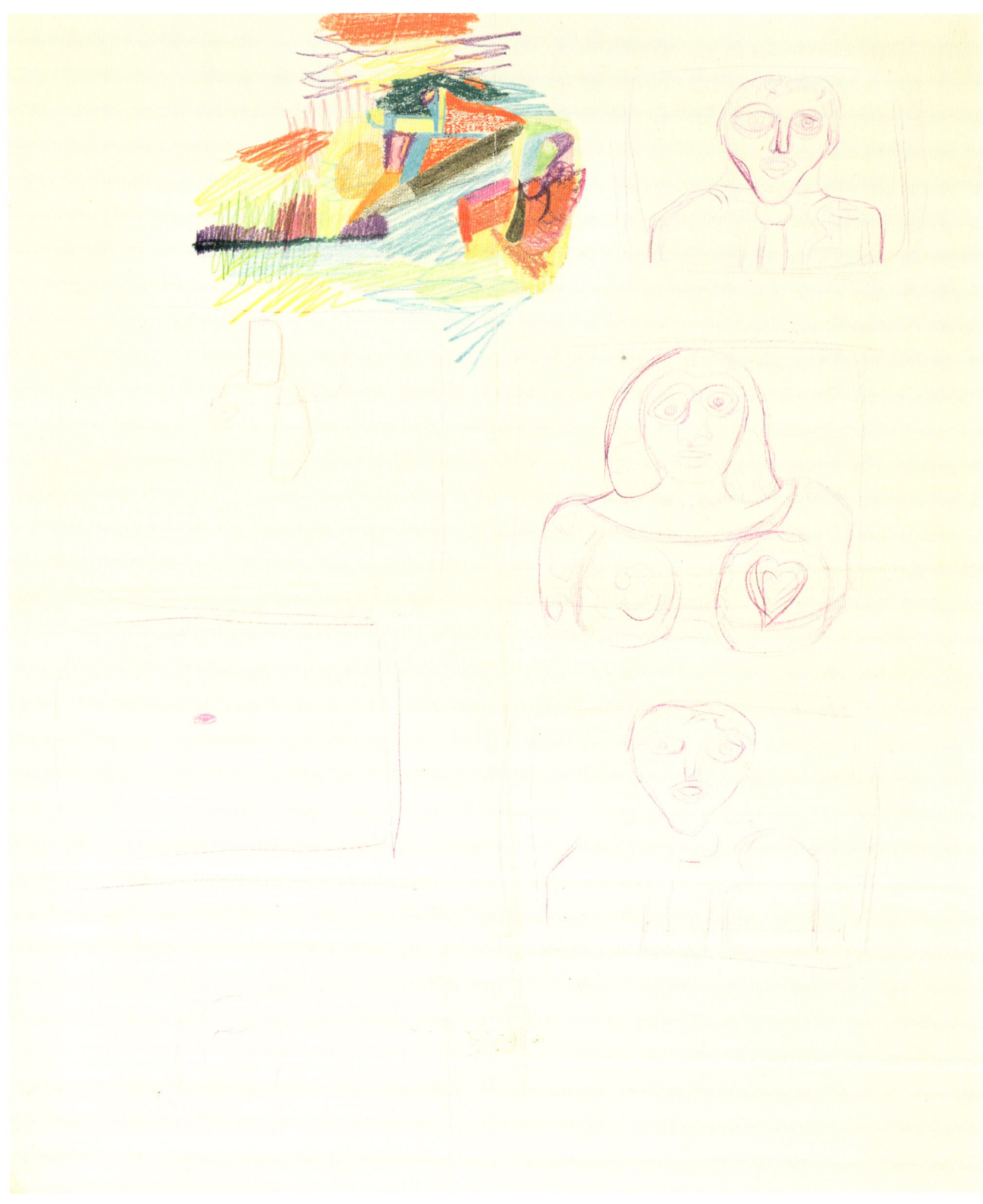

TV Brain, 1977
Colored pencils on drawing pad page
18 x 14 $^7/_8$ inches (45.7 x 37.8 cm)

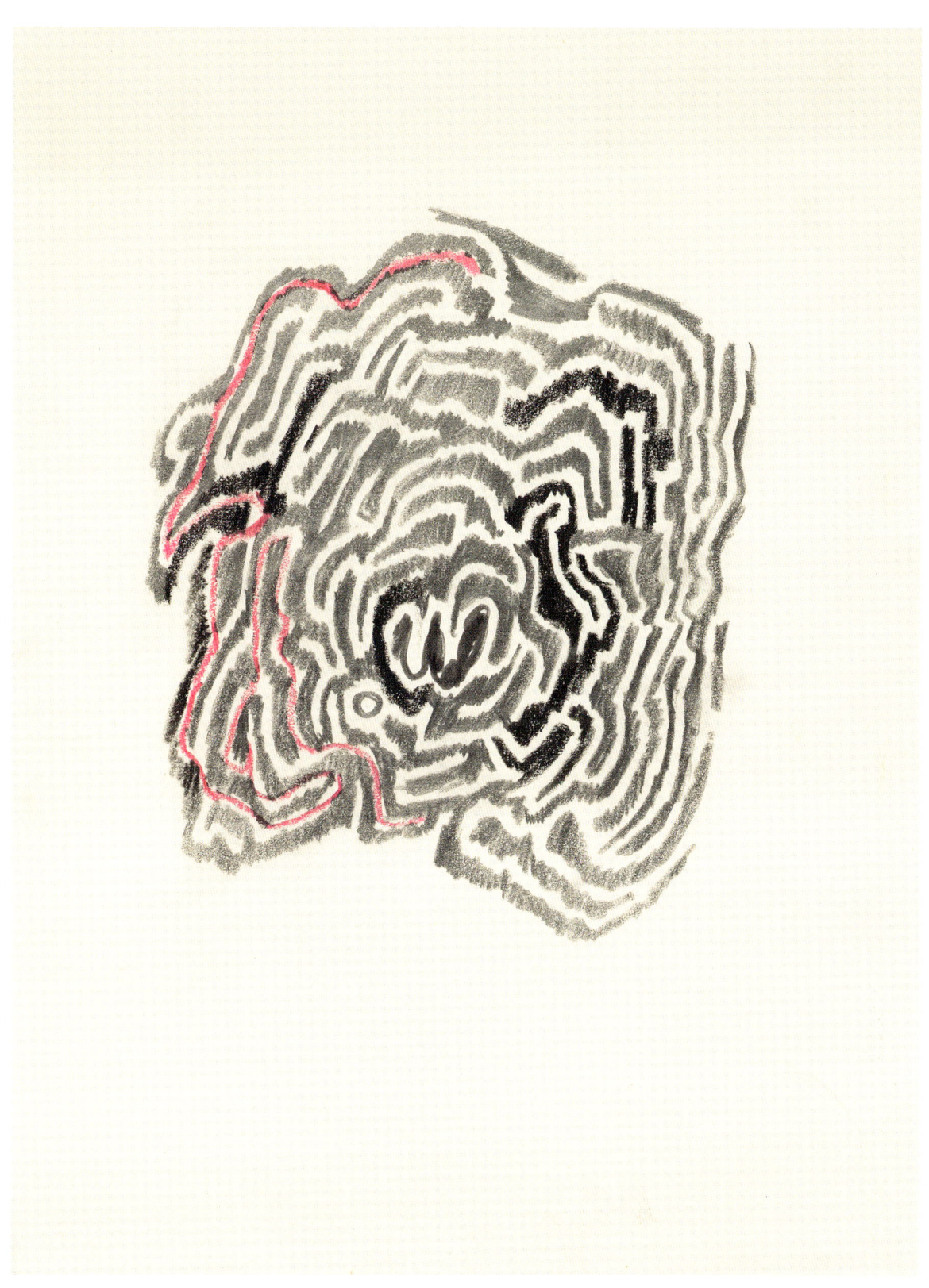

Labyrinthe (Labyrinth), n.d.
Pastel and pencil on paper (spiral bound book)
10 $^{15}/_{16}$ x 8 $^{7}/_{16}$ inches (27.8 x 21.4 cm)

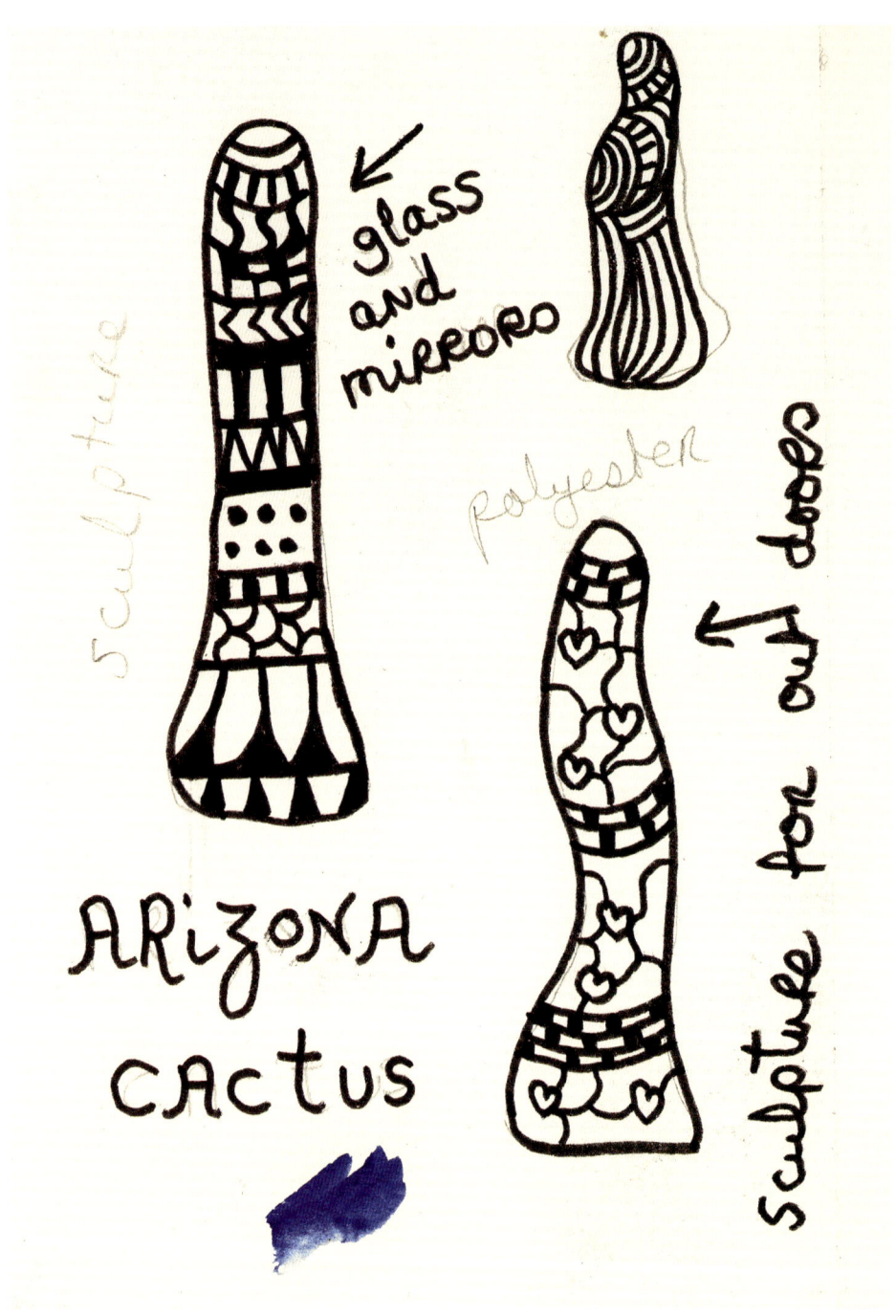

Arizona Cactus, c. 1987
Black felt-tip pen, black pencil, blue paint, and tape on paper
5 ⁷/₈ x 4 ³/₁₆ inches (15 x 10.6 cm)

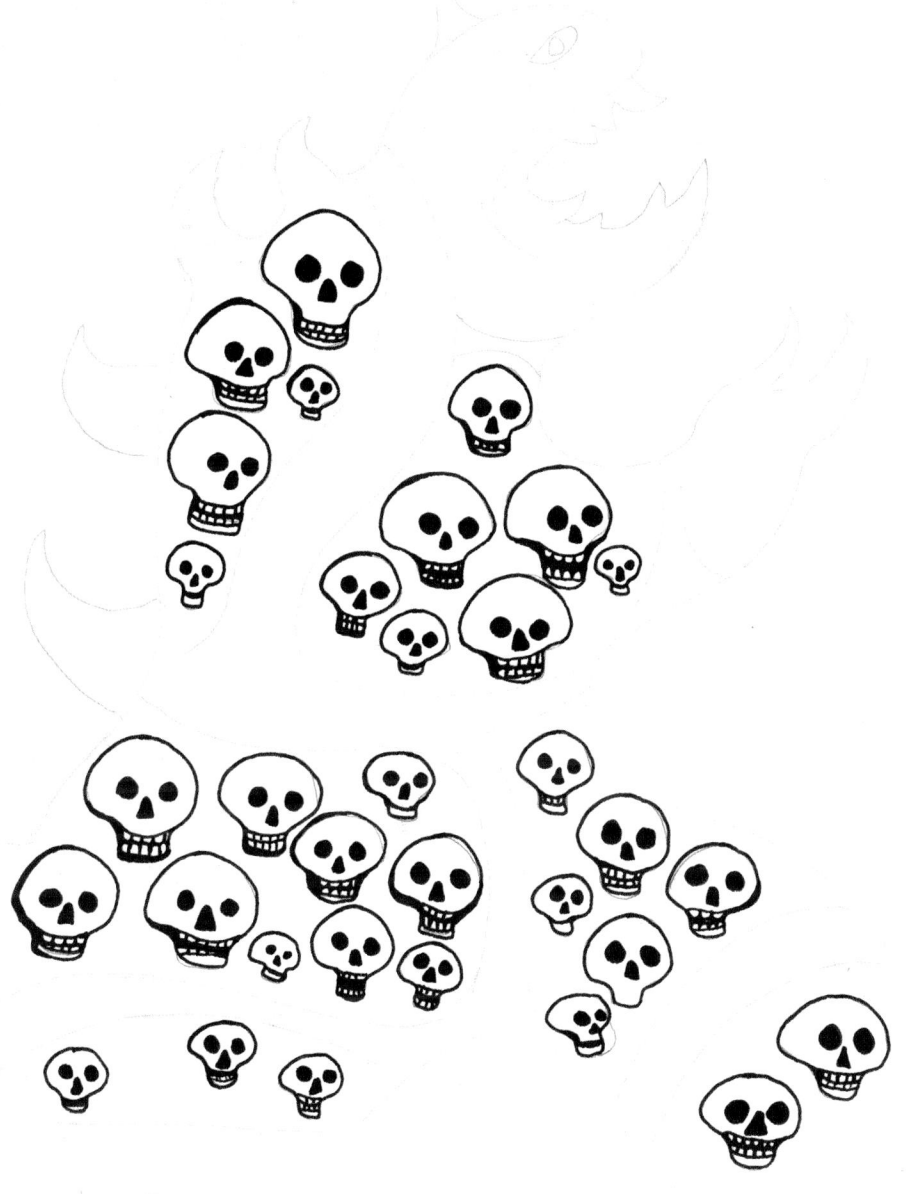

Le Sida ça se... (AIDS is...), 1986–1988
Ink and black pencil on paper
12 $^5/_8$ x 9 $^7/_{16}$ inches (32 x 24 cm)

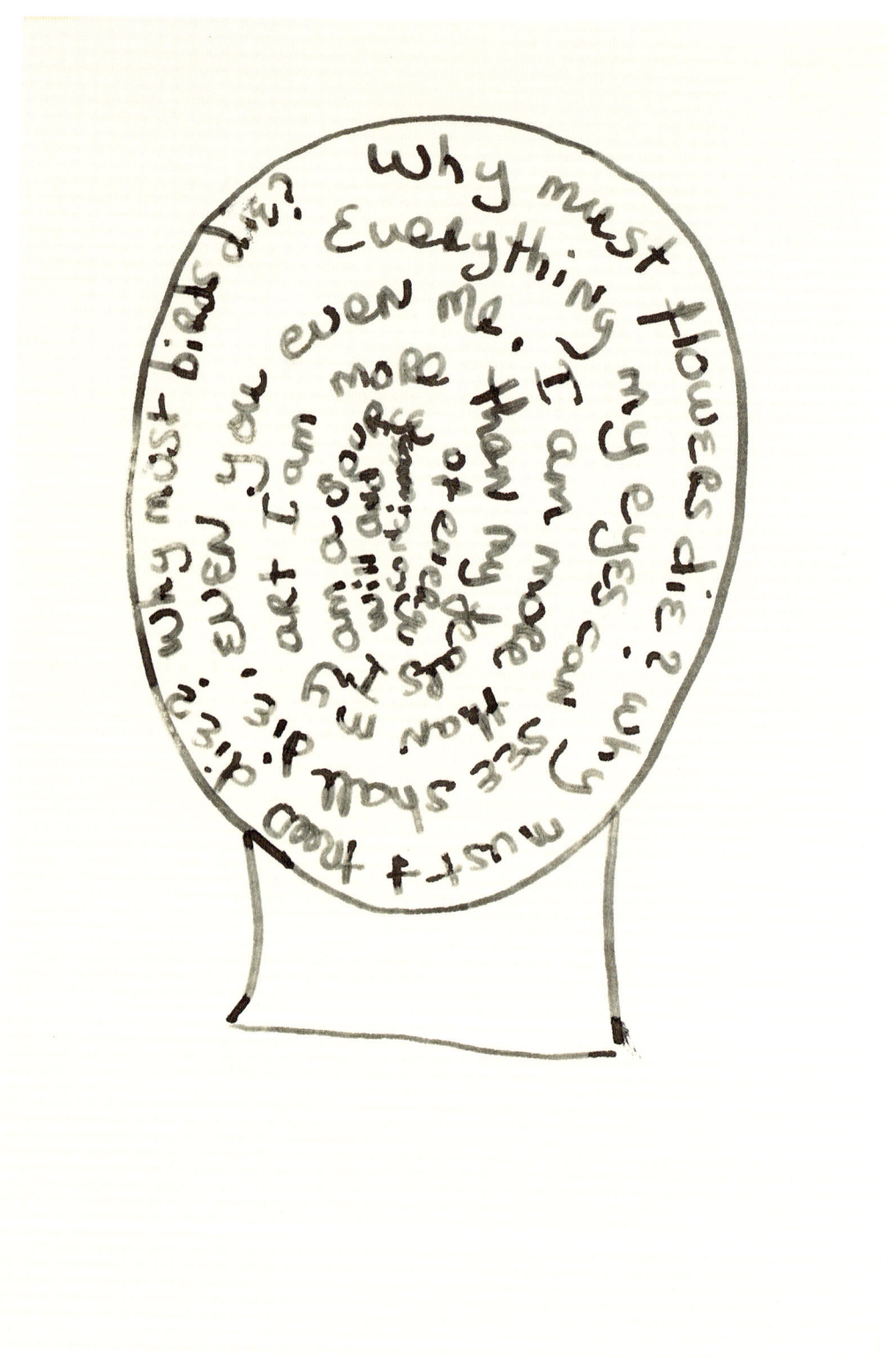

Page from Sennelier Paris Dessin sketchbook, n.d.
Black ink on white cardboard (spiral bound book)
6 5/16 x 4 5/16 inches, (16 x 11 cm)

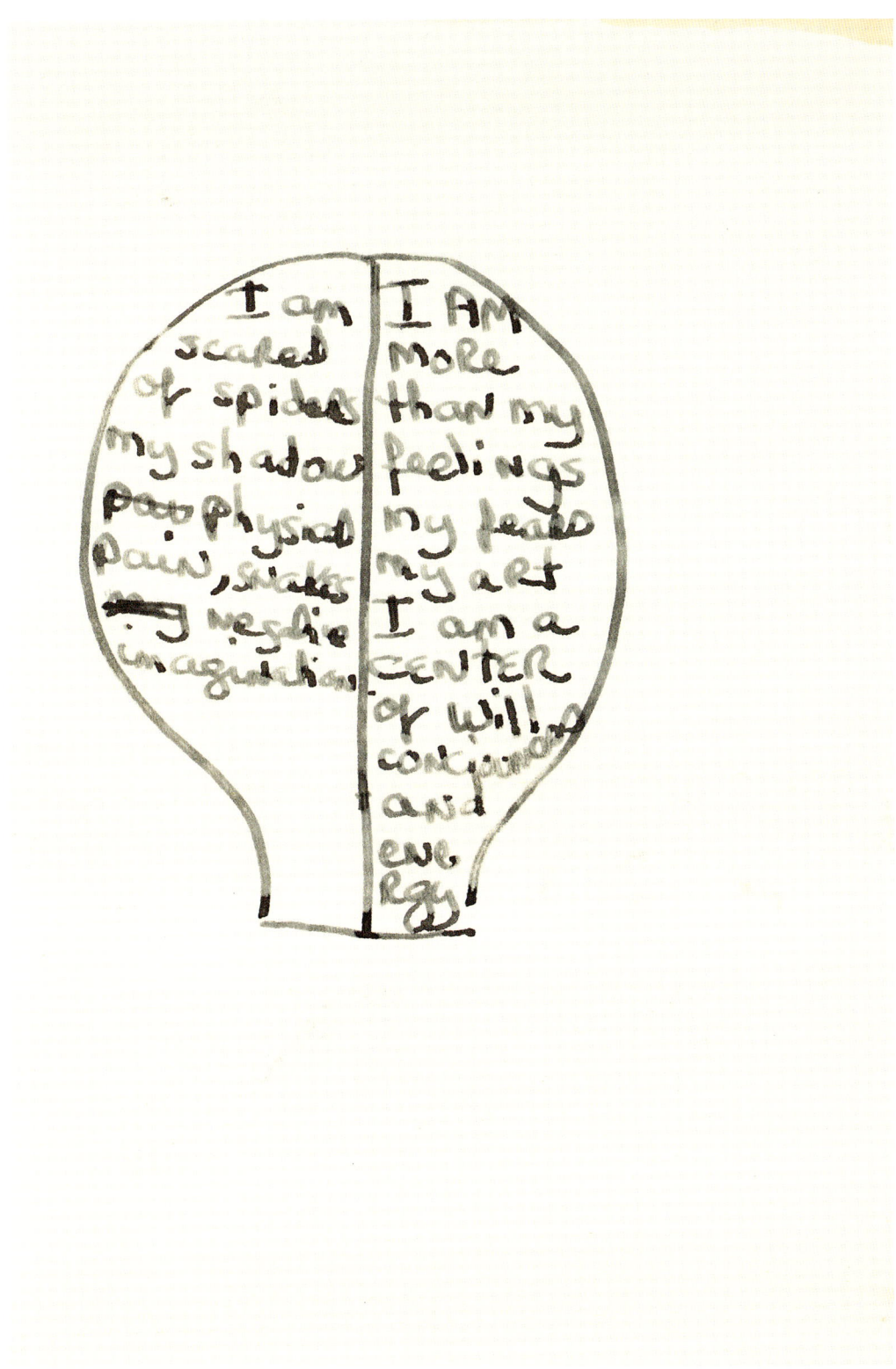

Page from Sennelier Paris Dessin sketchbook, n.d.
Black ink on white cardboard (spiral bound book)
6 5/16 x 4 5/16 inches, (16 x 11 cm)

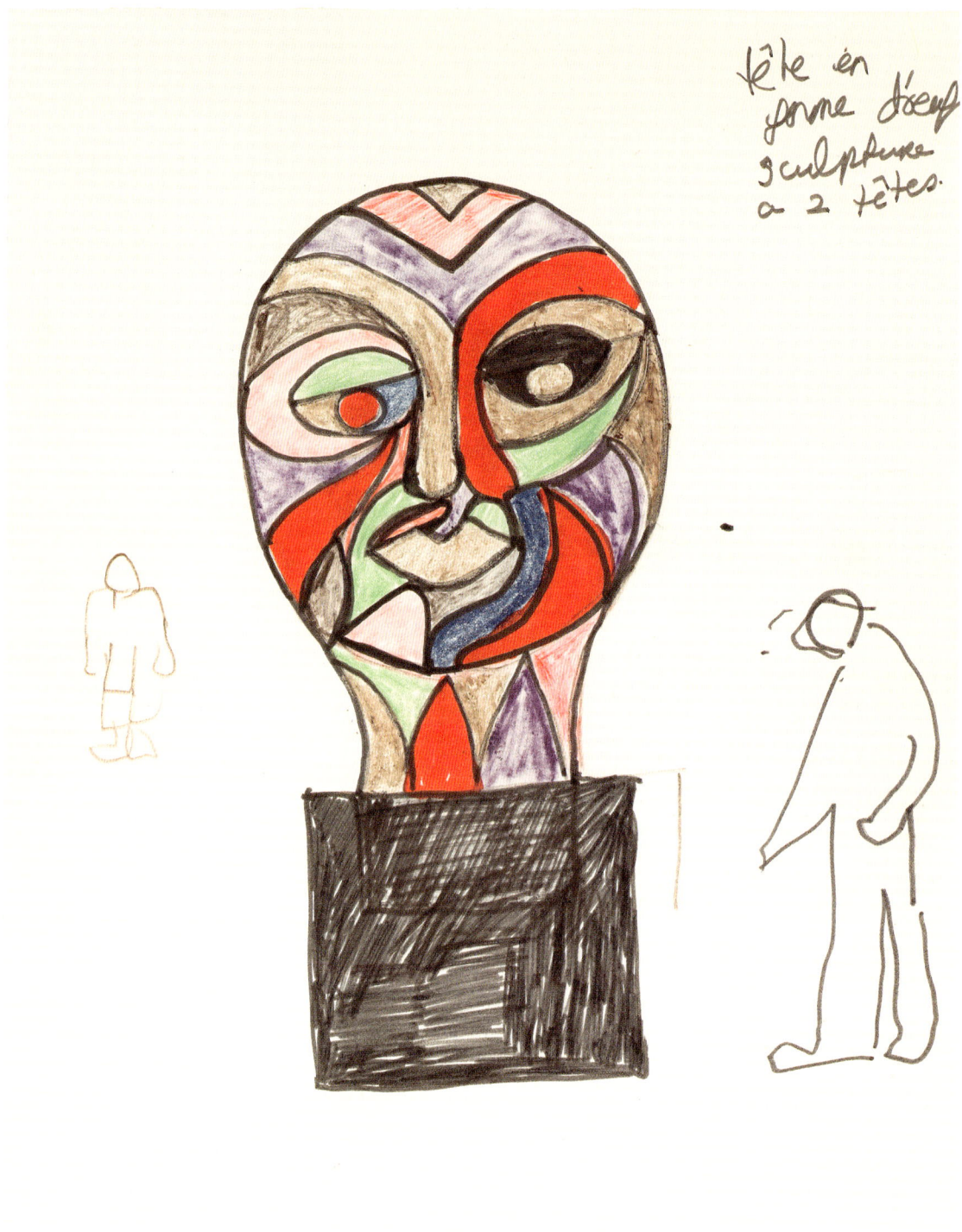

Tête en forme d'oeuf (Egg-Shaped Head), n.d.
Felt-tip pen on paper (spiral bound book)
10 $^{15}/_{16}$ x 8 $^{7}/_{16}$ inches (27.8 x 21.4 cm)

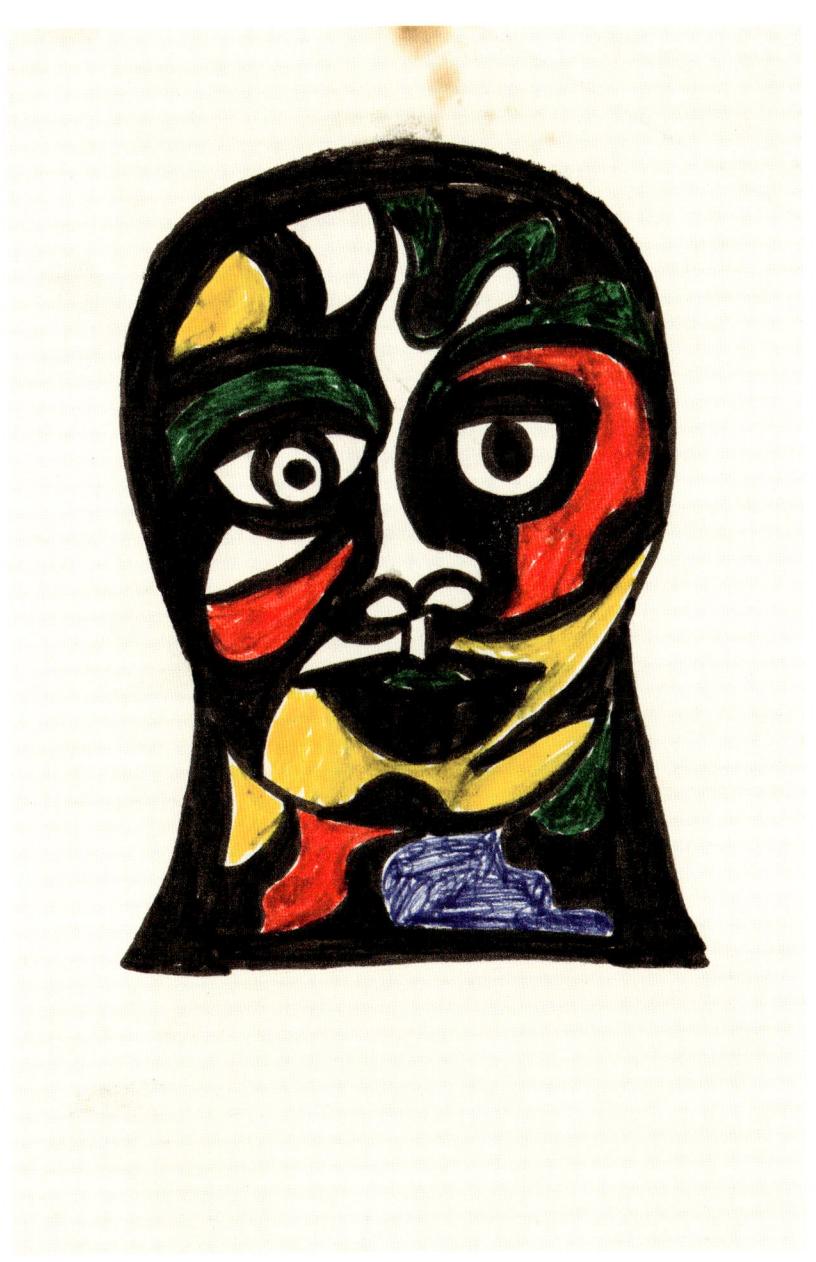

Tête (Head), n.d.
Black and colored marker on paper
5 $^{13}/_{16}$ x 3 $^{3}/_{4}$ inches (14.7 x 9.5 cm)

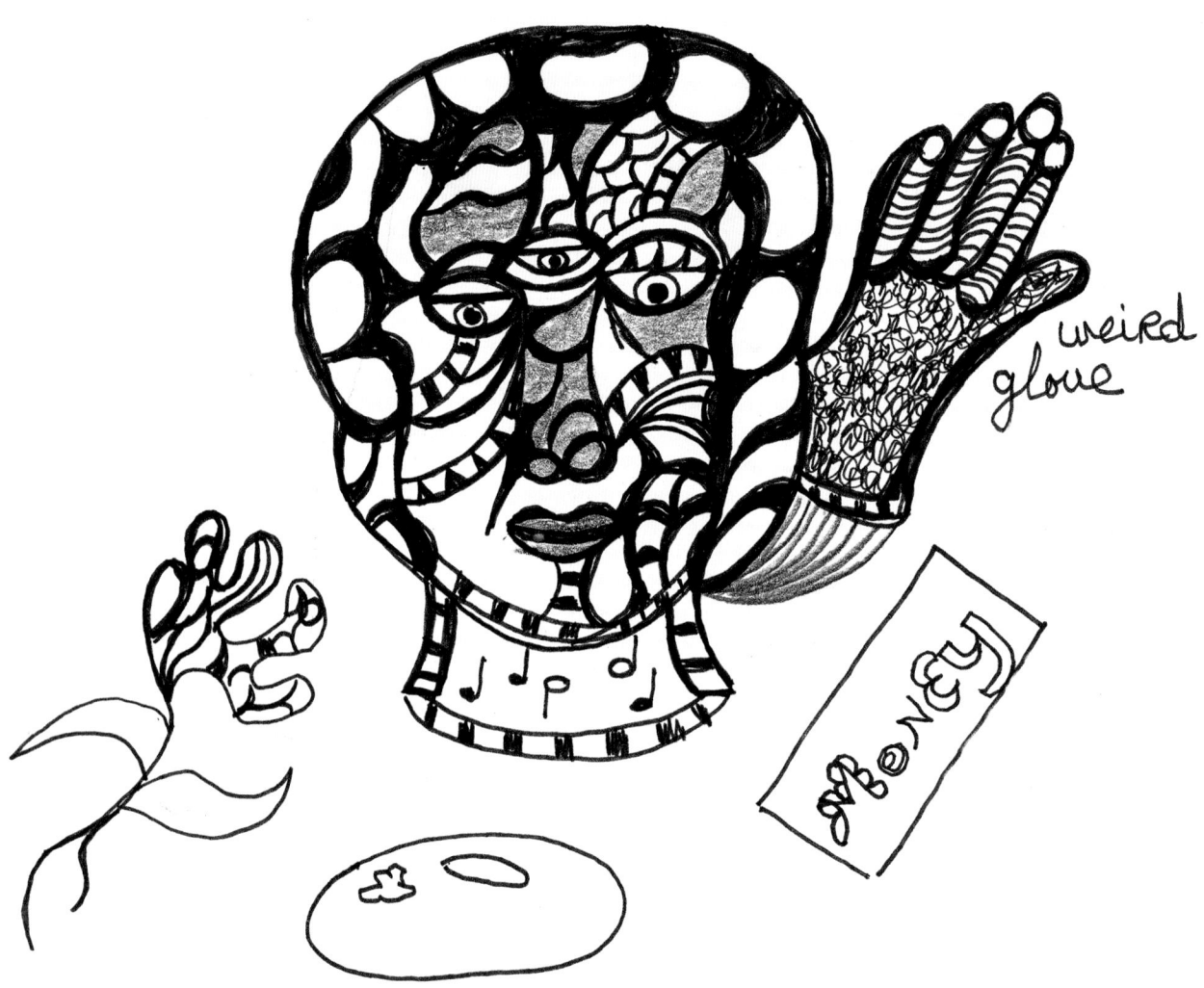

Head, Hand, Flower, Money, n.d.
Black marker on paper
11 x 8 ⁷/₁₆ inches (28 x 21.5 cm)

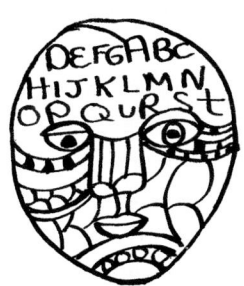

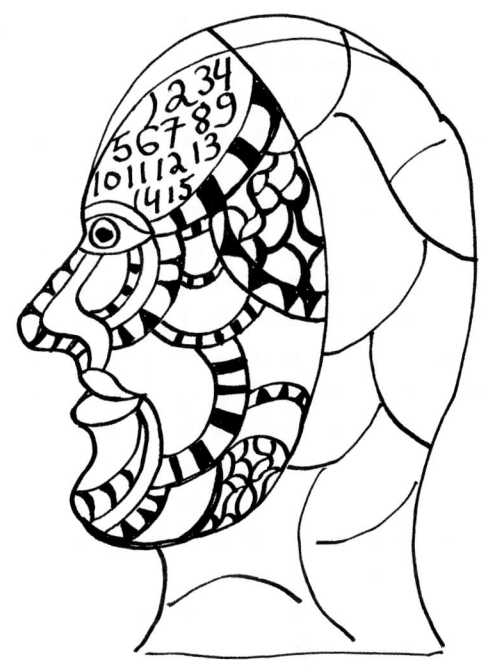

Têtes, alphabet et nombres (Heads, Alphabet and Numbers), n.d.
Black ink on paper
11 $^5/_8$ x 8 $^1/_4$ inches (29.5 x 21 cm)

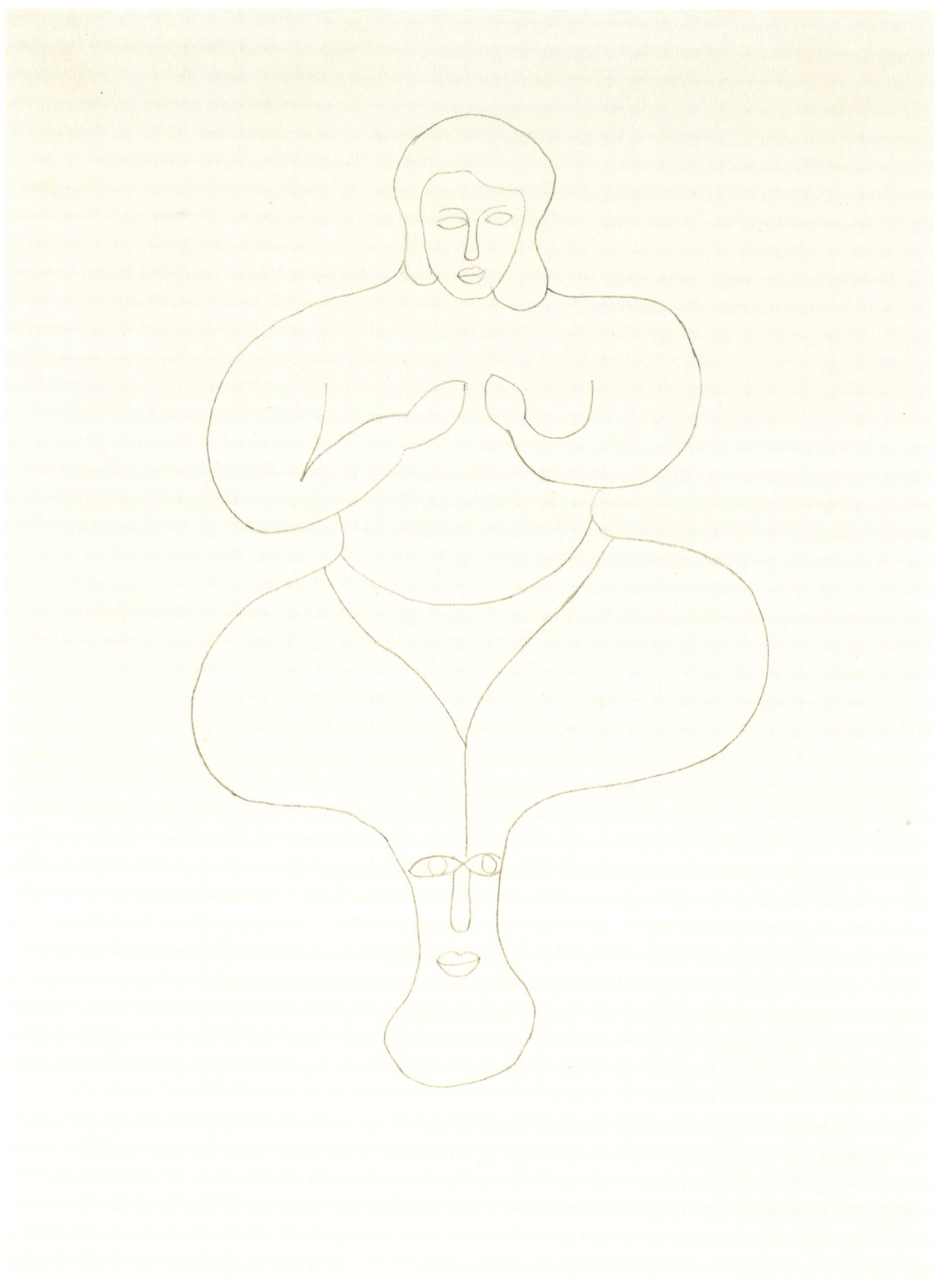

Femme (Woman), n.d.
Pencil on paper
11 ¹³/₁₆ x 9 ¹/₁₆ inches (30 x 23 cm)

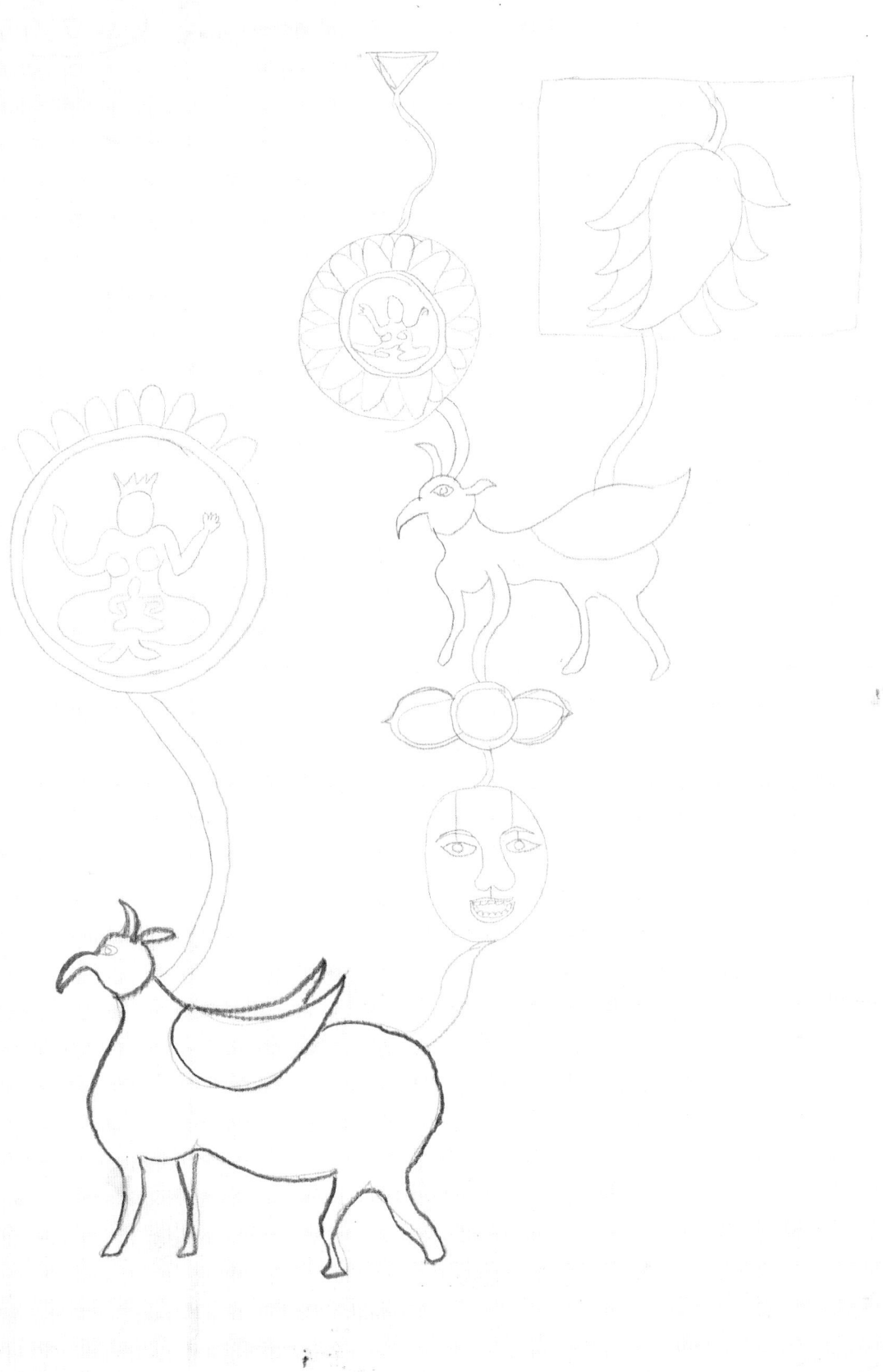

Design (*Mandala, Animals*), n.d.
Pencil and black marker on paper
12 ³/₈ x 9 ⁷/₁₆ inches (31.4 x 23.9 cm)

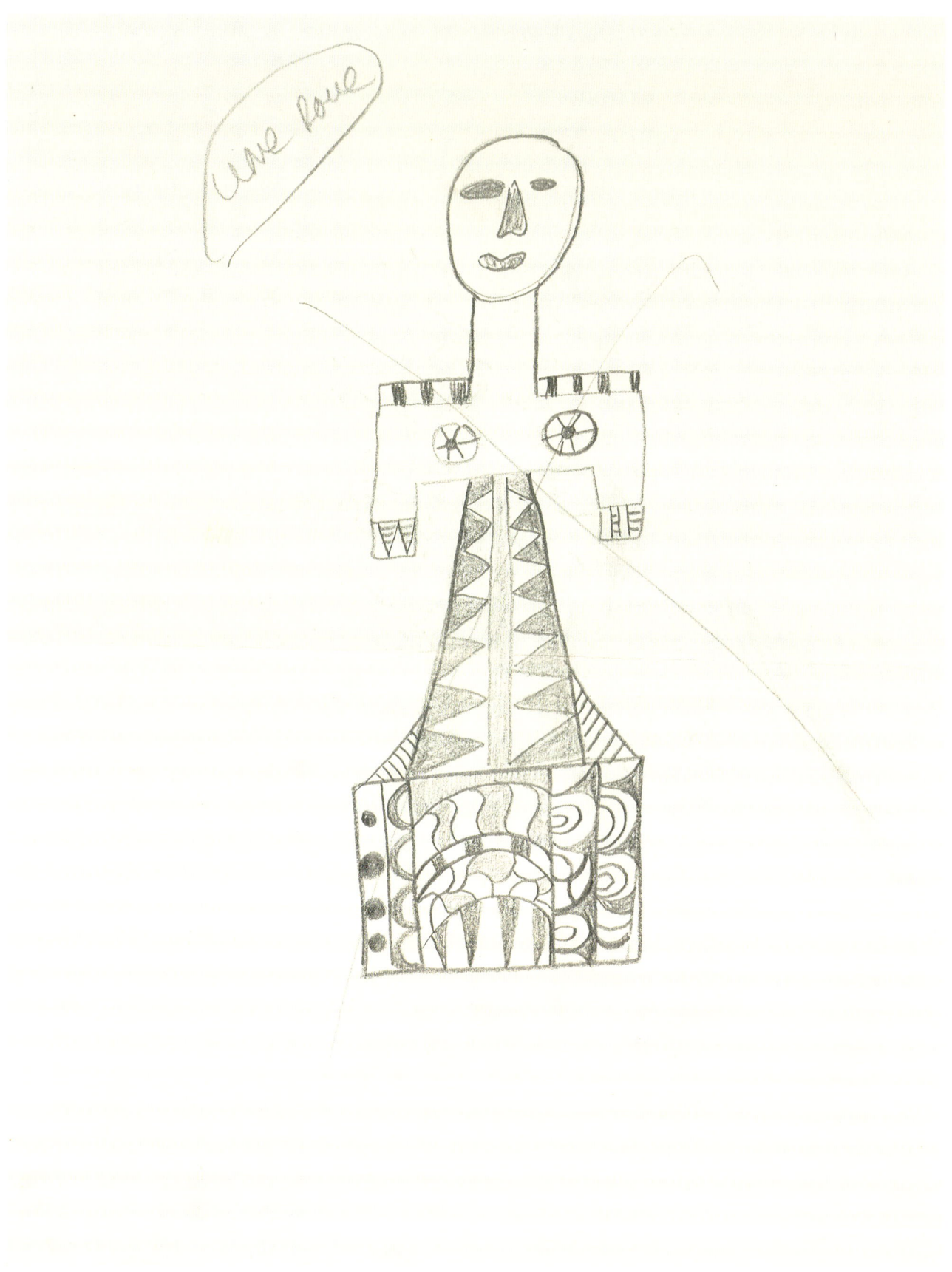

Une roue (A Wheel) / Easter Island, n.d.
Pencil on paper
14 ^{1}/$_{16}$ x 11 inches (35.7 x 28 cm)

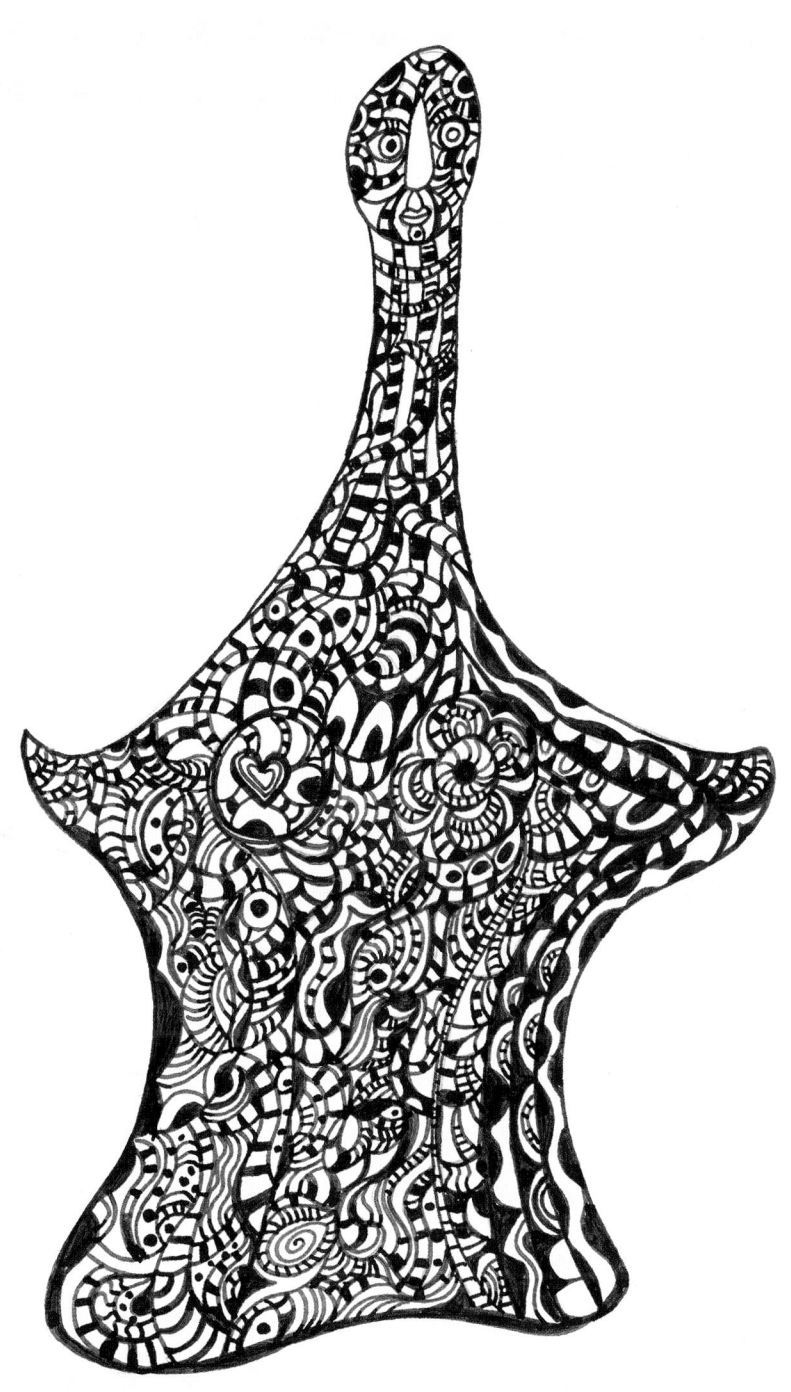

Masculin feminin I, c. 1988
Black fine-line pen and marker on paper
12 x 9 ¹⁄₁₆ inches (30.5 x 23 cm)

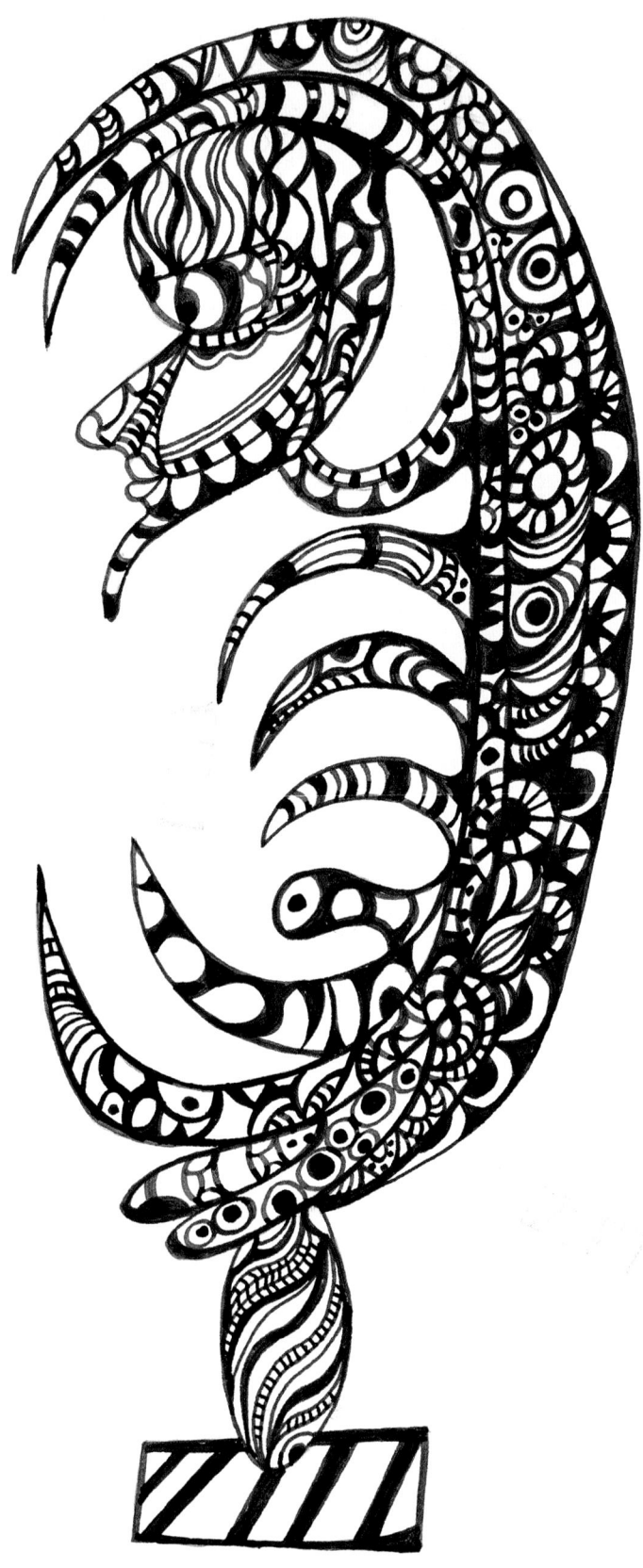

Skinny Study III, 1990s
Black pen on paper
11 $^{15}/_{16}$ x 9 inches (30.4 x 22.8 cm)

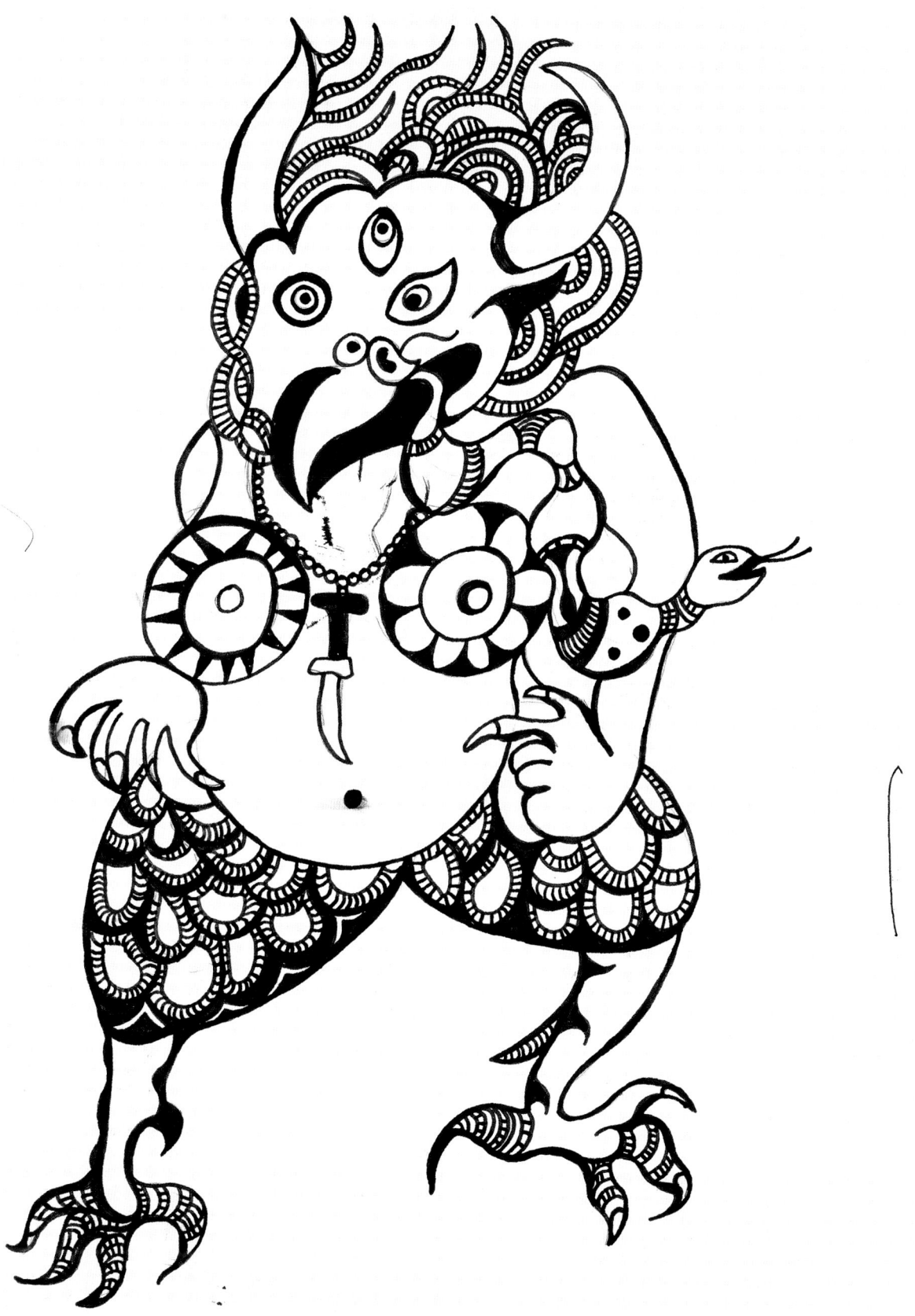

Goddess Creature, 1992
Black fine-line pen on paper
12 x 9 $^1/_{16}$ inches (30.5 x 23 cm)

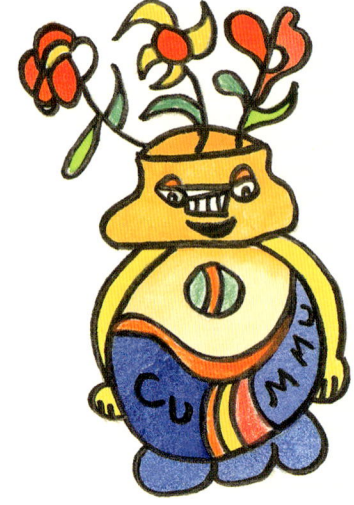

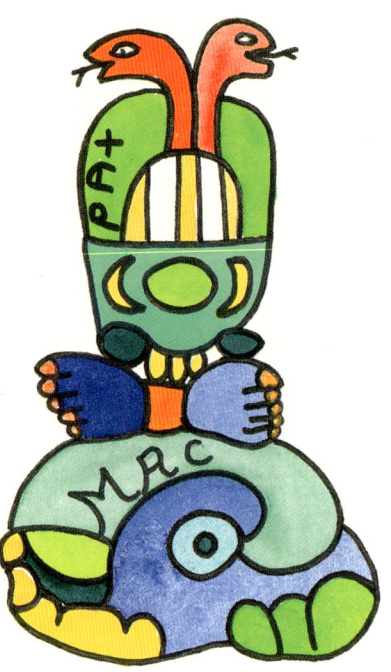

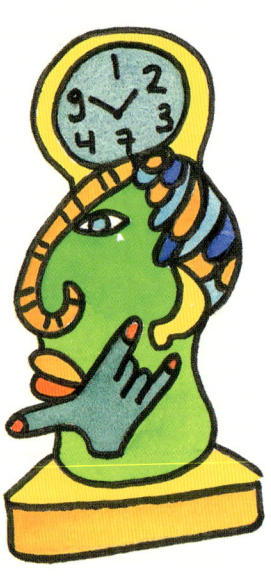

Design for Vase, Clock..., c. 1999
Marker and watercolor on lithograph paper
9 $^3/_8$ x 12 $^3/_{16}$ inches (23.8 x 31 cm)

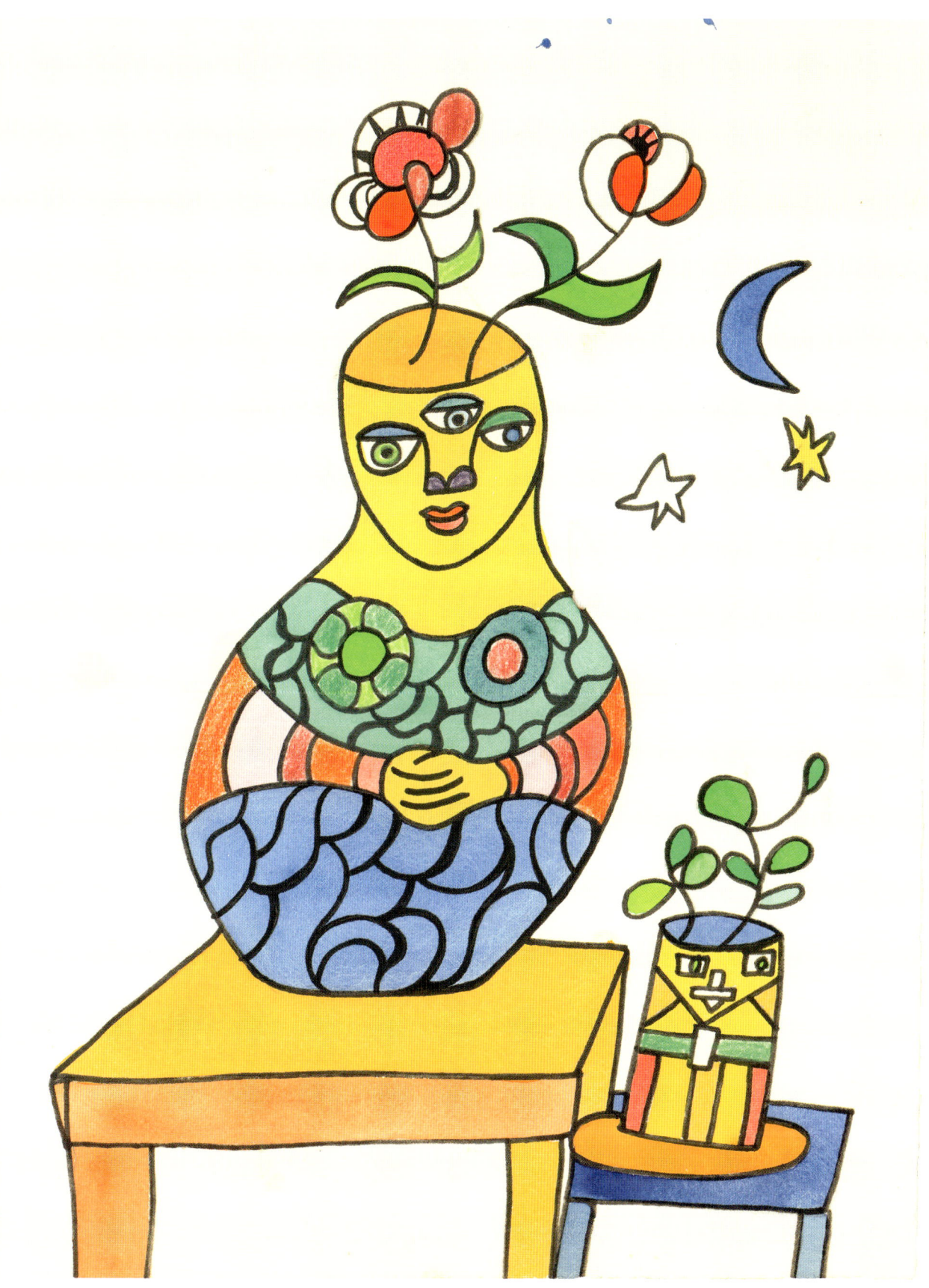

Azteca Nana Vase, 1999–2000
Aquarelle, marker, and colored crayon
11 x 8 ½ inches (28 x 21.6 cm)

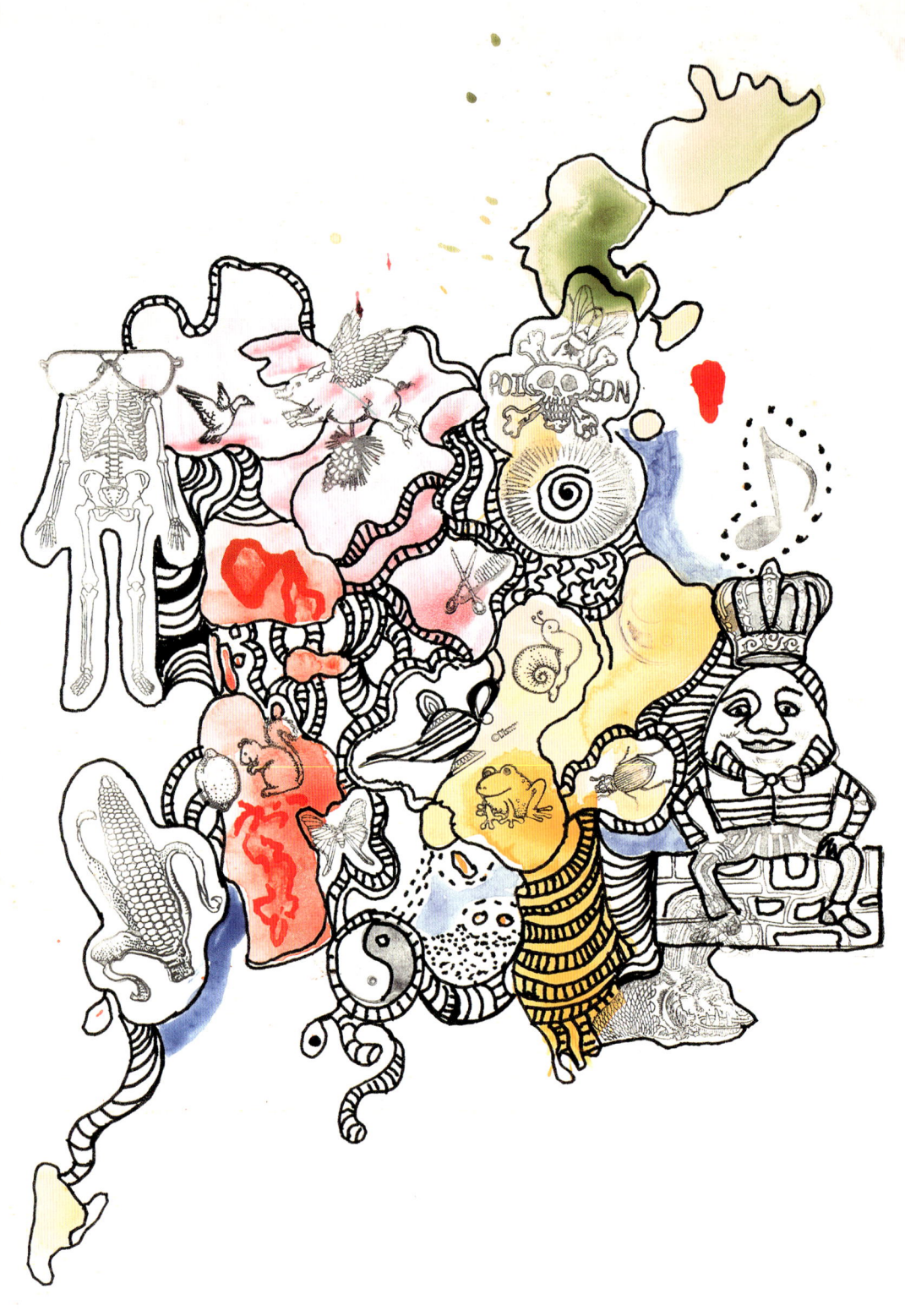

Collage, c. 1998
Watercolor, black fine-line pen, and ink stamps
12 $^5/_8$ x 9 $^7/_{16}$ inches (32 x 24 cm)

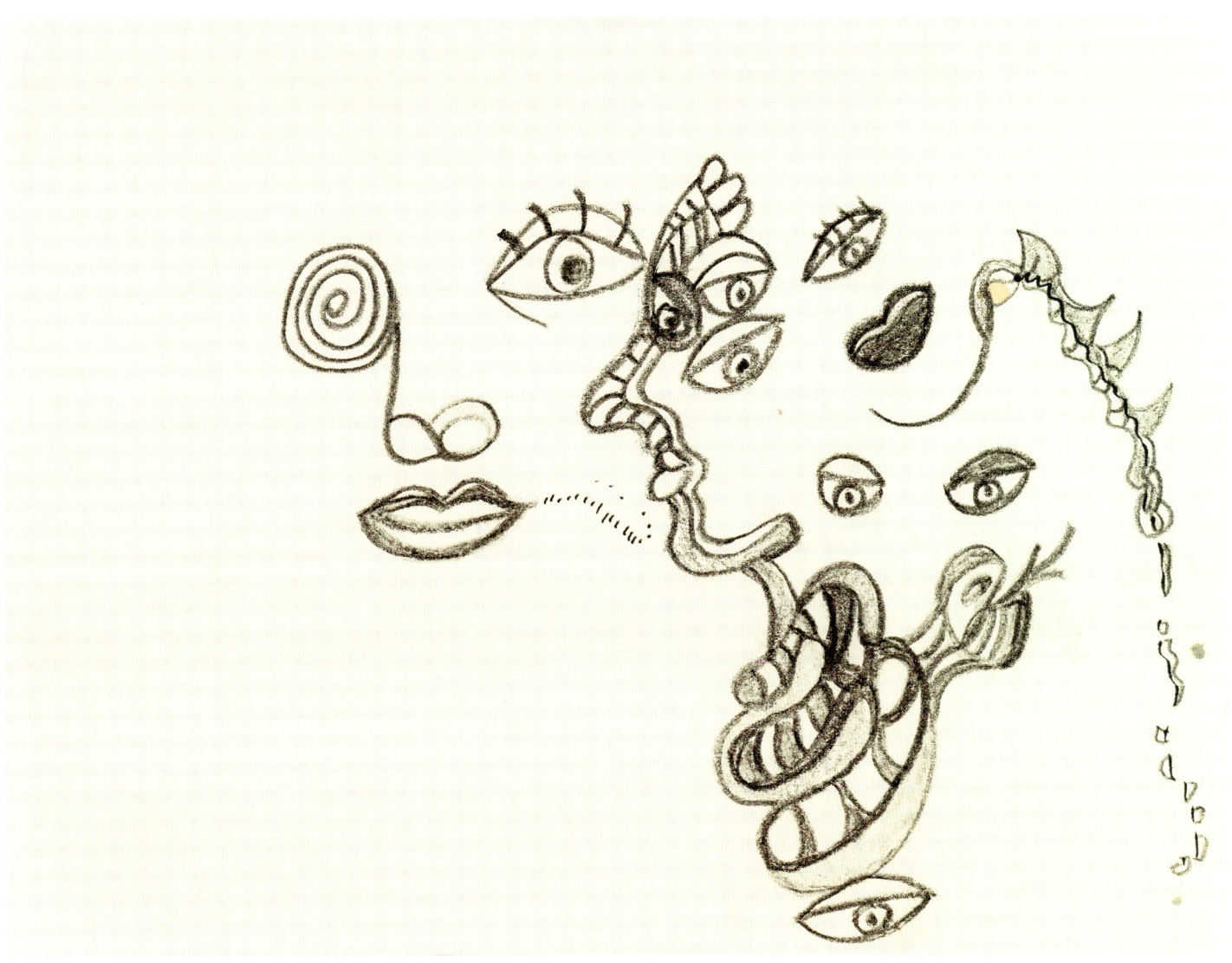

Faces, n.d.
Black pastel on paper
11 $^5/_8$ x 8 $^7/_8$ inches (29.5 x 22.5 cm)

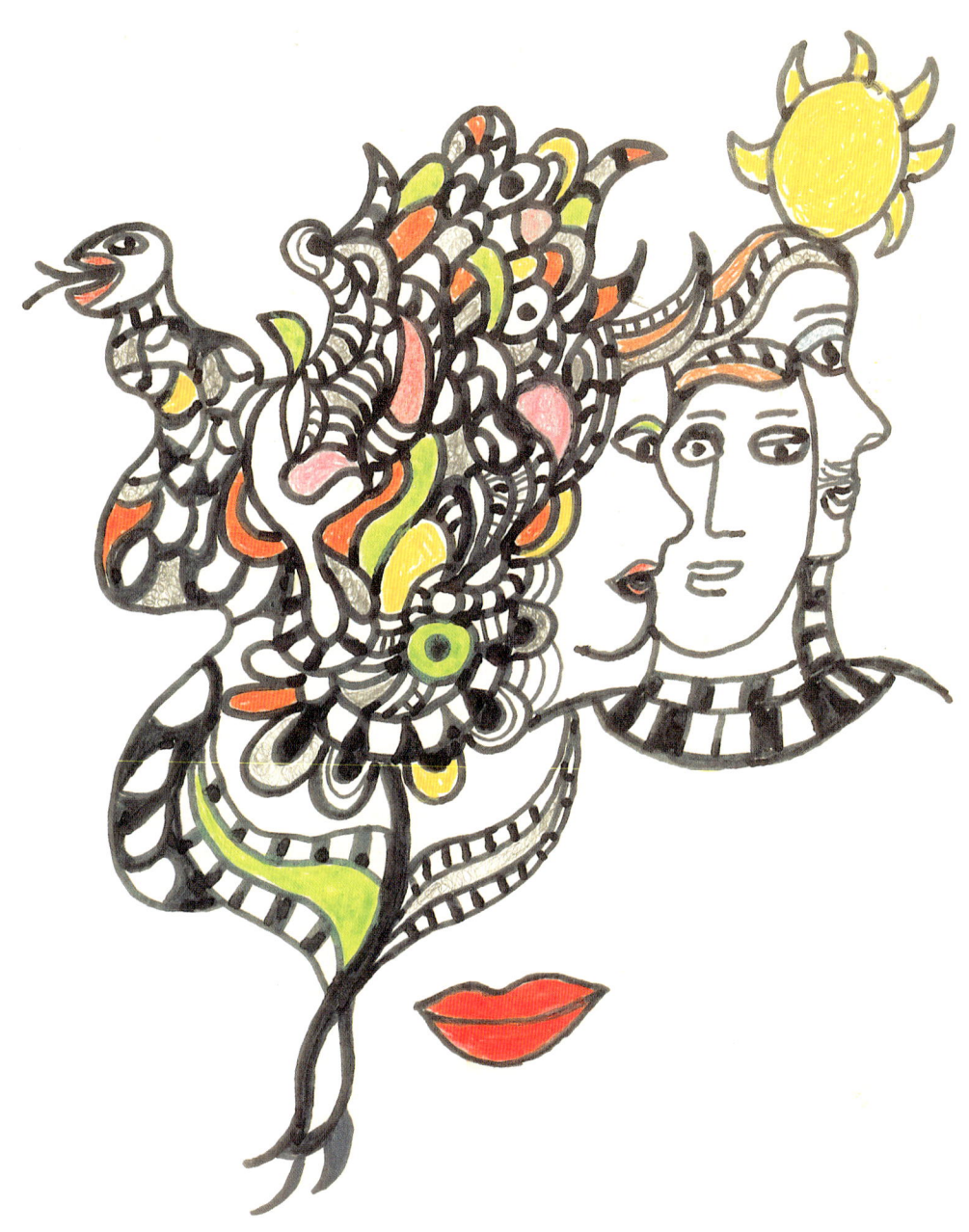

Faces, Serpent, c. 1999
Black and colored marker on clayboard
9 ¹⁵/₁₆ x 8 inches (25.3 x 20.3 cm)

Niki de Saint Phalle

Niki de Saint Phalle was born Catherine Marie-Agnès Fal de Saint Phalle on October 29, 1930 in Neuilly-sur-Seine, France. After a childhood of moving and changing schools in New York City and Connecticut, she married Harry Mathews, who would become a prominent New York author. Personal crisis led Saint Phalle to painting, and in the early 1950s she decided to become an artist. Experimental assemblages gave way to *Tirs*, or shooting paintings. These works brought her international fame and, in 1961, membership in the group of artists known as the "New Realists," which included Christo, Yves Klein, Arman, and the Swiss kinetic sculptor Jean Tinguely, among others. A close relationship with Tinguely developed into creative collaboration and, in 1971, marriage. Saint Phalle and Tinguely worked together in the construction of many sculpture projects, including *Hon* in Stockholm (1966); *Paradis Fantastique* in Montreal (1967); *Le Cyclop* in Milly-la-Forêt (1969–1994); *Golem* in Jerusalem (1972); *Tarot Garden* in Italy (1980–1998); and *Stravinsky Fountain* in Paris (1983). A multi-genre artist, Saint Phalle was also a film director, playwright, stage designer, and author. She never ceased exploring and working with different materials, including polyester, bronze, and mosaic. Other monumental projects of Niki de Saint Phalle include *Sun God* at UC San Diego (1983); *Noah's Ark* in Jerusalem (1998); *The Grotto* at the Royal Gardens of Hanover, Germany (1996–2003); and *Queen Califia's Magical Circle* in Escondido, California (1999–2003). Saint Phalle died on May 21, 2002 in La Jolla, California.

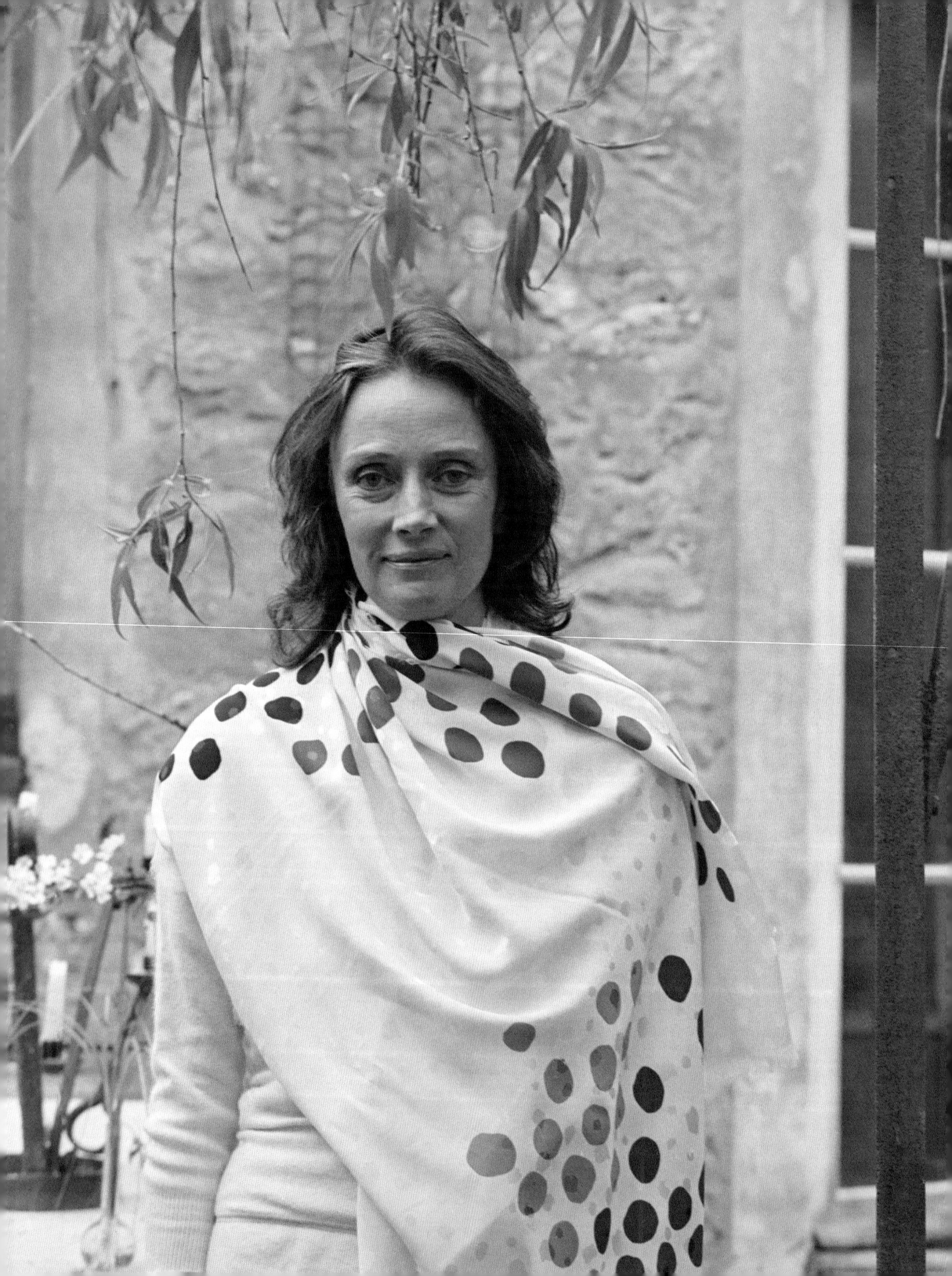

Chronology*

1930–1948
Catherine Marie-Agnès Fal de Saint Phalle is born on October 29, 1930 in France. Her father is French, her mother American. She is the second of five children in a wealthy family that loses its business and its fortune in the 1929 stock market collapse.

Early in her childhood her mother begins calling her "Niki." Going forward, she is known by that name.[1]

She spends most of her childhood and adolescence in New York City, though strong ties are maintained with the family in France through frequent visits. In an early display of her later artistic temperament, as a teenager in a convent school she paints the fig leaves on the school's classical sculptures red. She transfers to a new school shortly thereafter.

As a young woman, Niki's first career is as a fashion model. Her photographs appear in magazines like *Vogue* and *Life*.

1949
At 18, she elopes with childhood friend Harry Mathews.

1950
Saint Phalle begins making her first paintings while her husband studies music at Harvard University.

1951
Laura, the couple's first child, is born in Boston.

1952
Saint Phalle and her family move to Paris. There, she studies theater and acting while Mathews studies music. They summer in the south of France, Spain, and Italy, visiting museums and cathedrals.

---

1 Susan Stamberg, "How Niki De Saint Phalle Channeled Pain Into Joyful, Vibrant Works Of Art," *NPR*, April 8, 2021, https://www.npr.org/2021/04/08/982223967/how-niki-de-saint-phalle-channeled-pain-into-joyful-vibrant-works-of-art.

*Adapted from Niki de Saint Phalle's official biography, published by the Niki Charitable Art Foundation

Niki de Saint Phalle. Portrait © Laurent Condominas

1953

Saint Phalle is hospitalized for a nervous breakdown. She finds that painting helps her overcome this crisis. She decides to give up acting and become an artist.

After her recovery she and Mathews briefly return to Paris, where she is encouraged by other artists to continue painting in her unique, self-taught style. They then move to Mallorca.

In Spain, Saint Phalle discovers the work of Antoni Gaudí and is deeply affected by it. She is especially influenced by Gaudí's Park Güell in Barcelona. Giving her the idea to create her own sculpture garden, it also inspires her to use diverse materials and found objects as essential elements in her art.

1955

Saint Phalle and Mathews' second child, Philip, is born in Mallorca.

Mid-1950s–1959

The couple returns return to Paris. Saint Phalle meets Jean Tinguely, who will become an artistic collaborator. She is further inspired by the art of Paul Klee, Henri Matisse, Pablo Picasso, and Henri Rousseau.

Saint Phalle visits the Musée d'Art Moderne de la Ville de Paris, where she also discovers the work of Jasper Johns, Willem de Kooning, Jackson Pollock, and Robert Rauschenberg.

1960

Saint Phalle and Mathews separate. Mathews moves to a new apartment with the children and Saint Phalle sets up a studio to continue her artistic experiments. She is included in an important group exhibition at the Musée d'Art Moderne de la Ville de Paris. By the end of the year she and Jean Tinguely move in together, living in an artists' colony and sharing a studio.

In the early 1960s Saint Phalle creates her "shooting paintings" (Tirs)—complex assemblages with concealed paint containers that are shot by pistol, rifle, or cannon fire. The impact of the projectile creates spontaneous effects which finish the work.

The shooting paintings evolve to include elements of spectacle and performance. She becomes part of the Nouveau Réalisme group of artists—the only woman in a group that includes Arman, Christo, Yves Klein, Jean Tinguely, and Jacques de la Villeglé, among others.

1961

Saint Phalle has her first solo exhibition in Paris. She becomes friends with American artists staying in Paris, including Robert Rauschenberg, Jasper Johns, Larry Rivers, and his wife Clarice.

Marcel Duchamp introduces Saint Phalle and Tinguely to Salvador Dalí. They go to Spain with Dalí for a celebration in his honor. As part of the event, they create a life-size exploding bull out of plaster, paper, and fireworks. It is presented as the finale of a traditional bullfight.

Saint Phalle is included in *The Art of Assemblage* at the Museum of Modern Art in New York.

1962
Saint Phalle and Tinguely visit California, where they view Simon Rodia's Watts Towers in South Los Angeles. They travel in California, Nevada, and Mexico, participating in exhibitions and happenings.

1963
Saint Phalle and Tinguely move to an old country inn outside Paris. She begins creating figurative reliefs—confrontational depictions of women, some giving birth, as well as dragons, monsters, and brides.

1965
Inspired by the pregnancy of Larry Rivers' wife Clarice, Saint Phalle makes her first *Nanas*, archetypal female figures that are updated versions of "Every(wo)man." (The word "nana" is French for "dame" or "chick.")

The first exhibition of *Nanas* is accompanied by Saint Phalle's first artist book. This develops into another of her prolific art forms: hand-lettered graphic works in the form of invitations, posters, books, and other writings.

1966
Saint Phalle collaborates with Tinguely and Swedish artist Per Olof Ultvedt on *Hon* (Swedish for "she") for the Moderna Museet, Stockholm. The outer form of *Hon* is a building-size reclining *Nana*, with an interior environment entered between her legs. This piece garners worldwide attention and intensifies her desire to build her own sculpture garden.

1967
She works with Tinguely on *Le Paradis Fantastique*, a commission for the French Pavilion at Expo '67 in Montreal. Working on *Le Paradis Fantastique*, she is exposed to the toxic fumes of polyester resin. This and other materials used in her work cause severe damage to her lungs, resulting in recurrent health problems.

She designs *Nana* inflatables, a multiple in plastic that is produced and distributed in the United States.

1971
Saint Phalle completes her first permanent architectural project: a private commission for a summer residence in the south of France. She begins to develop other "fantastic" architectural projects requiring intensive planning and organization.

She travels to India and Egypt, broadening the repertoire of cultural experiences and visual associations used in her work.

She marries Jean Tinguely on July 13.

Saint Phalle receives a public commission to create *Golem*, an architectural project for children in Jerusalem's Rabinovitch Park, which is completed the following year.

1972
She receives a second private architectural commission in Belgium.

She begins a productive association with art fabricator Haligon for her large-scale sculptures and editioned works.

She makes her first jewelry design for GEM Montebello Laboratory, Milan.

1974
Saint Phalle creates three large-scale *Nanas* for a permanent site near the town hall in Hanover, Germany. The citizens nickname them Sophie, Charlotte, and Caroline, in honor of three historically distinguished women of Hanover.

Saint Phalle is hospitalized with a serious lung ailment. While recuperating in the Swiss mountains, she meets Marella Caracciolo Agnelli, an old friend from her time in New York in the 1950s. Saint Phalle shares her dream of building a sculpture garden based on the Tarot. Marella's brothers, Carlo and Nicola Caracciolo, offer a parcel of land in Garavicchio in Tuscany, Italy, as a site. The massive undertaking of the garden will consume her thoughts and energies for nearly twenty years.

1975
Saint Phalle's sculptural tableau *Last Night I Had a Dream* is installed on the façade of the Palais des Beaux-Arts in Brussels for an arts festival. She returns to Switzerland and further develops ideas for her Tarot Garden.

1978
Saint Phalle makes the first models for the figures that will be represented in the Tarot Garden, and foundations for the garden are laid.

1979

Struggling with lung-related health issues, Saint Phalle is inspired to use air and light as elements in her sculpture. She begins the *Skinnys*, a series of totem-like pieces that resemble drawings in space, often embellished with colored lights or other elements.

"When my lungs were severely damaged by working in polyester, air came into my life," she later said. "I had to learn how to breathe again, breathe deeply. The *Skinnys* reflected that change."[2]

1980

Construction begins on *The High Priestess*, the first architectural sculpture for the Tarot Garden, representing female creativity and strength. Saint Phalle will spend the major part of the next ten years on site at the garden, receiving assistance from many friends and supporters.

The Ulm Museum organizes the first retrospective of Saint Phalle's graphic work. She receives a major retrospective at the Musée National d'Art Moderne, Centre Georges Pompidou, Paris, which travels around Europe. She also exhibits in Japan.

Saint Phalle creates the first of her snake chairs, vases, and lamps.

1982

Saint Phalle moves into *The Empress*, a building in the Tarot Garden in the shape of a sphinx. It serves as her home and studio.

Saint Phalle creates a perfume bearing her name, presented in a sculptural vial. Created for the Jaqueline Cochran Company, it helps finance the Tarot Garden.

Saint Phalle and Tinguely collaborate on a fountain next to the Centre Georges Pompidou in Paris, created as an homage to the groundbreaking modern composer Igor Stravinsky.

1983

Saint Phalle designs prints for a project to support the Temporary Contemporary in Los Angeles. This work, in the form of a pictographic letter, expresses her early awareness and concern for those afflicted by AIDS. She continues to be involved in AIDS prevention and education efforts.

The Stuart Foundation commissions a sculpture, *Sun God*, for the campus of the University of California at San Diego.

Saint Phalle suffers the first of her recurring and debilitating attacks of rheumatoid arthritis.

---

2 Niki de Saint Phalle, in *Insider/Outsider World Inspired Art*, Exhibition Catalogue (San Diego: Mingei International Museum, 1998).

1984–1987
Saint Phalle spends most of her time at the Tarot Garden. There, she completes several large structures, including the *Magician*, the *High Priestess*, and the *Empress*. She begins a series of flower vases in the shape of various animals.

In collaboration with Dr. Silvio Barandun, she writes and illustrates the book *AIDS: You Can't Catch It Holding Hands*. This informative text, presented in a positive and compassionate format, is published in seven languages.

She has major retrospectives in Germany and America.

1987
At Jean Tinguely's request, Saint Phalle begins to decorate the face of *Cyclop*, his monumental sculpture in Milly-la-Forêt, with "a sparkling cloak of mirror mosaic." It will not be finished until 1991.

1988
French President François Mitterrand commissions Tinguely and Saint Phalle to design a fountain for the town of Château Chinon. He unveils it in front of the town hall on March 10.

Saint Phalle revives a sculptural theme from the mid-1970s by making *L'Oiseau amoureux* (Bird in Love), a gigantic kite, for a worldwide traveling kite exhibition.

1991
Saint Phalle makes a large-scale model for *Le Temple Idéal*, a place of worship for all religions. This architectural sculpture was originally conceived in the early 1970s as a response to the religious intolerance she observed while working in Jerusalem.

She receives a commission from the city of Nîmes, France, to build *Le Temple Idéal*, but politics prevent the project from being realized.

In August, Jean Tinguely dies in Bern, Switzerland. In his honor, Saint Phalle makes her first kinetic sculptures, the *Meta-Tinguelys*.

1993
For health reasons, Saint Phalle moves to La Jolla, California, where she lives for next eight years. She establishes a studio for working with mirrors, glass, and stones, which she is increasingly using in her sculptures instead of paint.

1995

Saint Phalle and Swiss architect Mario Botta begin a major sculpture/architecture project, *Noah's Ark*, in Jerusalem. It is inaugurated in 2000.

2000

Saint Phalle works on the *Black Heroes* series, an homage to prominent African Americans. The series includes athletes and musicians such as Michael Jordan, Miles Davis, Josephine Baker, and Louis Armstrong.[3]

She begins work on *Queen Califia's Magical Circle* in Escondido, California. Much of its imagery is drawn from her interpretations of early California history, myth, and legend, Native American and Meso-American cultures, and the study of indigenous plants and wildlife.

Saint Phalle receives the 12th Praemium Imperial Prize in Japan, one of the most prestigious awards in the art world.

2001

Saint Phalle is given a commission to redesign and ornament three rooms in the historic 17th-century Grotto in Hanover's Royal Herrenhausen Garden. The Grotto was originally decorated with shells, crystals, and minerals, which were removed in the 18th century.

2002

Niki de Saint Phalle dies on May 21, at the age of 71, in La Jolla, California.

2003

With work overseen by her granddaughter, Bloum Cardenas, and her longtime assistants, Saint Phalle's remaining projects are completed. *The Grotto* opens in March, with mosaic decorations of glass, mirrors, and pebbles, as well as a host of painted and sculpted figures. *Queen Califia's Magical Circle* is dedicated and opens to the public on October 26. It is her first American garden and the last major project realized by the artist.

The Niki Charitable Art Foundation, a non-profit organization, is established to promote and protect Saint Phalle's artistic legacy.

---

3 K. Curtis Lyle, "Niki de Saint Phalle's Black Heroes series at Botanical Garden closes Oct. 31," *The St. Louis American*, October 23, 2008, https://www.stlamerican.com/entertainment/living-it/niki-de-saint-phalles-black-heroes-series-at-botanical-garden-closes-oct-31/.

Acknowledgments

First and foremost, my deepest appreciation and admiration goes to the incomparable art and life of Niki de Saint Phalle. It is an honor to be involved in contributing to her legacy.

As always, I am profoundly grateful to Bloum Cardenas for her indispensable role in bringing this publication to fruition, and I continue to cherish our wonderful collaboration.

A heartfelt thank you also goes to Jana Nier Mooneyhan and the entire team at the Niki de Saint Phalle Charitable Art Foundation for their unwavering dedication and hard work in making this book a reality. Special thanks as well to David Stevenson and Marcelo Zitelli for their steadfast support of Niki de Saint Phalle's legacy.

My thanks as well to Jeanne Greenberg Rohatyn, Anya Melyantsev, Fabienne Stephan, and the entire team at Salon 94 for their continued support and inspiration.

My sincere gratitude extends to the exceptional team at Princeton University Press, including Michelle Komie, Christie Henry, Terri O'Prey, Jacqueline Poirier, Colleen Suljic, Laurie Schlesinger, Cathy Felgar, Jodi Price, Kathryn Stevens, Annie Miller, Ruthie Rosenstock, Alexandria Leonard, Billy Skurka, and Mark Bellis. I remain profoundly thankful to PUP for their enduring professionalism, encouragement, and passion for our shared projects over the years.

A very special note of thanks to Hannah Alderfer for her outstanding design work, to Susan Delson for her editorial expertise, and to Fiona Graham for her invaluable organization of this publication. Additionally, my gratitude goes to Lachlan Brooks for her meticulous copyediting.

I extend my heartfelt thanks to Taliesin Thomas for her assistance across numerous projects and to Steven Rodríguez for his ongoing and valued support.

Above all, my boundless gratitude belongs to my incredible wife, Abbey, and my wonderful children—Justin, Ethan, Ellie, and Jonah—for their unwavering love and encouragement.

Finally, as always, I send endless love and thanks to my mother, Judith.

Larry Warsh
New York City
2025

Contributors

LARRY WARSH has been active in the art world for more than thirty years as a publisher and artist-collaborator. An early collector of Keith Haring and Jean-Michel Basquiat, Warsh was a lead organizer for the exhibition *Basquiat: The Unknown Notebooks*, which debuted at the Brooklyn Museum, New York, in 2015, and later traveled to several American museums. He also served as a curatorial consultant on *Keith Haring / Jean-Michel Basquiat: Crossing Lines* for the National Gallery of Victoria. The founder of Museums Magazine, Warsh has been involved in many publishing projects and is the editor of several other titles published by Princeton University Press, including *Basquiat-isms* (2019), *Haring-isms* (2020), *Futura-isms* (2021), *Abloh-isms* (2021), *Arsham-isms* (2021), *Warhol-isms* (2022), *Hirst-isms* (2022), *Pharrell-isms* (2023), *Judy Chicago-isms* (2023), *Holzer-isms* (2024), *Neshat-isms* (2024), *Jean-Michel Basquiat: The Notebooks* (2017), and *Keith Haring: 31 Subway Drawings* (2012), among others. Warsh has served on the board of the Getty Museum Photographs Council, and was a founding member of the Basquiat Authentication Committee until its dissolution in 2012.

KYLA MCDONALD is an art historian and curator based in Berlin. Her research encompasses inquiries into overlooked narratives in art history, with specific reference to underrepresented genders, intergenerational dialogue, and the practice of queer, feminist, and de-colonial methodologies. Her doctoral thesis (2024) explored the notion of "rediscovery," producing a timely study on the rise of exhibitions focused on the previously overlooked artists Hilma af Klint, Lee Lozano, and Betye Saar. McDonald has held curatorial roles at Bonner Kunstverein, Glasgow Sculpture Studios, Tate Modern, and Tate Liverpool. She has curated two retrospective exhibitions of Niki de Saint Phalle—first at Tate Liverpool in 2008, and at Beaux-Arts Mons, Belgium in 2018.

NO MORE RULERS (NMR) is on a mission to rethink the way we define art and creative expression. Based in New York, NMR is a publishing company dedicated to empowering the creative community and questioning the status quo. Our artist publications erase the boundaries between high and low, popular culture and fine art, and between traditional categories like design, music, and fashion. By partnering with global institutions and focusing on topics ranging from contemporary culture to artistic process to creativity, we're creating a world where art can truly be for everyone.

NO MORE RULERS